C0-EFL-254

Computer Systems for Foodservice Operations

Computer Systems for Foodservice Operations

Michael L. Kasavana

A CBI Book
Published by Van Nostrand Reinhold Company

A CBI Book
(CBI is an imprint of Van Nostrand Reinhold Company Inc.)
Copyright © 1984 by Van Nostrand Reinhold Company Inc.

Library of Congress Catalog Card Number 83-3925

ISBN 0-8436-2274-1

All rights reserved. No part of this work covered by the coyright
hereon may be reproduced or used in any form or by any means—graphic,
electronic, or mechanical, including photocopying, recording, taping,
or information storage and retrieval systems—without written permission of the publisher.

Printed in the United States of America

Designed by Ann Schroeder
Production coordinated by Bookwrights, Inc.

Published by Van Nostrand Reinhold Company Inc.
135 West 50th Street
New York, New York 10020

Van Nostrand Reinhold Company Limited
Molly Millars Lane
Wokingham, Berkshire RG11 2PY, England

Van Nostrand Reinhold
480 La Trobe Street
Melbourne, Victoria 3000, Australia

Macmillan of Canada
Division of Gage Publishing Limited
164 Commander Boulevard
Agincourt, Ontario M1S 3C7, Canada

16 15 14 13 12 11 10 9 8 7 6 5 4 3 2 1

Library of Congress Cataloging in Publication Data

Kasavana, Michael L., 1947–
   Computer systems for foodservice operations.

  Includes index.
  1. Food service—Data processing. I. Title.
TX911.3.E9K37 1984   647'.95'02854   83-3925
ISBN 0-8436-2274-1

This book is dedicated to my life, my love, and my lady . . . Holly Lynn.

Contents

Preface ix
Acknowledgments xi
  1   Foodservice Information Systems 1
  2   Data Processing Concepts 21
  3   Computer Operating Systems 35
  4   Cash Register Concepts 59
  5   Electronic Cash Register Configurations 73
  6   Automated Precheck Systems 99
  7   Precost Systems 117
  8   Menu Engineering 149
  9   Back Office Systems 189
10   Beverage Control Systems 211
Glossary 243
Index 255

Preface

This book is unique in its approach to the foodservice area. It is written for both the industrial and educational sectors of foodservice management, with a special focus on automation. The foodservice system is viewed as a complex business composed of many operations, production considerations, and managerial involvements. Computer technology is introduced early in the text and is carried throughout all chapters. This book is truly the first of its kind. Point-of-sale (POS) systems, control systems, and accounting-based systems are all presented from a user's perspective. Compiling this information is not an easy task for an industry as diverse and segmented as the foodservice industry.

Commercial restaurants, institutional foodservice, food distribution companies, and other industry-related elements will all find chapters applicable to their special needs. The two chapters on cash register technology, systematization, and networking are intended to be a broad scope survey of feasible, alternative register designs. The delineation of electronic cash register (ECR) configuration is provided as a case in point.

Computer systems can change the way business is planned, conducted, and analyzed—but perhaps more than anything else, the computer offers unique advantages in the area of controls. Precheck systems, with open-check tracking and sophisticated methods of cashier reconciliation, begin monitoring the guest cycle from the time an item is requested. Unless an item is entered into the precheck system, it will not be prepared or available for service. Precost systems, which are helpful in assessing the feasibility of a menu plan before its service, also offer many advantages not available elsewhere.

The fact that all food ingredients are stored in the system's data base enables simulation ("what if" questions) as well as forecasted and actual cost analyses of menu mixes. The chapter on menu engineering presents a revolutionary approach to foodservice management and answers many questions concerning pricing, promotion, replacement, and retention of current and future menu items. The premise of menu engineering is that each successive menu will be more profitable (have a higher contribution margin) than its predecessor. This mode and its computer requirements are illustrated through a case problem within the chapter.

Back-office accounting-oriented systems, aimed at general ledger, payroll, and inventory concerns are presented in Chapter Nine. The scope of advanced systems technology has led to sohisticated tracking and tracing schemes to assist with the accounting function.

Computer-based beverage control systems are discussed in some detail in the following chapter. It is anticipated that all segments of the foodservice cycle will have some degree of automation by 1990, and the bar area is no exception. Similarly, the restaurant-vendor order entry interface is also perceived as a development likely to impact on the foodservice business. Will salespeople need to call on operators to serve as order takers, or will telecommunications be sufficient to transmit purchase order requirements automatically? The availability of order entry techniques will streamline the purchase function and will help personnel concentrate more on expanded guest service.

The selection and implementation of a computerized system is a complex process requiring a significant amount of analysis. Understanding the user's needs, surveying the market place, and preparing RFPs (request for proposals) must be done to insure procurement of a feasible system design. Implementation, training, and the maintenance of a continuous operating system are also important elements in the computer system decision process.

Acknowledgments

Without the expertise, assistance, support, and advice of Mr. Donald I. Smith, this book would never have been completed. He is a man capable of motivating his staff, directing their pursuits, and acknowledging their accomplishments. For all these qualities I am truly grateful.

Similarly, the efforts of my colleague, Dr. Ray Schmidgall, were also vital to the completion of this manuscript. Ray is a sounding board and possesses a wealth of knowledge of many areas addressed in this book.

Mr. Michael Speer of Laventhol and Horwath Consultants deserves special mention for his willingness to withstand my insults while making his expertise available to me.

Also helpful was one of the best experts in hospitality systems, Mr. John Cahill of the Sheraton Corporation. John was an invaluable source of information.

Also deserving of mention are Mr. Paul Gordon, Mr. Art Surowiec, and Mr. Gary Kortz of Gordon Foodservice, and Mr. Gordon Meister of NCR.

Additionally, Cybex and Aerial, Inc., were extremely instrumental to this project since they left me alone long enough to write the following chapters within a reasonable time.

I am deeply indebted to my parents, who have always provided the necessary support and encouragement I have ever needed throughout my life.

My lovely wife, Holly Lynn, is also to be acknowledged because without her none of this would matter.

Ms. Gail Whiting is given special recognition for her assistance in the preparation of this manuscript. This is the fourth book on which she and I have collaborated, and each has been easier to write than the one before. Gail is a professional person who has kept me in line and on track. She is at the top of her field.

1

Foodservice Information Systems

Chapter Objectives

1. To introduce the concept of a foodservice information system (FIS)
2. To enumerate the specific application areas for an FIS based on unique industry characteristics
3. To identify important operational characteristics and design concerns in the development of an FIS
4. To define the nature and scope of the foodservice cycle and its subcomponents

Perhaps no other industry is so diverse, or important, as the foodservice industry. Worldwide it is one of the largest volume industries, and nationally it is considered to be a major indicator of life-style patterns. Foodservice operations can range from a six-foot take-out counter to a 4,000-person capacity banquet facility.

No matter what the size of the establishment, the goals of foodservice remain the same: to provide a quality product, with efficient service, at a marketable price. With this premise in mind, many operators have devised sound operational techniques to insure the delivery of wholesome food and beverage items in a relatively short time. Such common practices as pre-preparation, portion size controls, and standardized recipes are outcomes of an industry historically run by intelligent, aggressive, and creative entrepreneurs.

Only recently, however, has management come to acknowledge the applicability of computer-based technology to the labor-intensive hospitality workplace. This technology can be used to help achieve outstanding operational controls and levels of production. Automated equipment is available in a variety of designs (including cash registers, beverage dispensers, and processor units) to assist in monitoring both the guest check and financial cycles of the business.

FOODSERVICE CHARACTERISTICS

Nearly all aspects of the hospitality industry require large volumes of paperwork and communication interfaces to insure proper coordination of service and controls. Foodservice is no exception. Although foodservice shares many common hospitality industry characteristics, it also possesses some unique factors. Foodservice is differentiated from most other business enterprises based on: 1) the nature of the service provided; 2) the qualities of goods offered; 3) the level of inventory turnover experienced; 4) the number of points-of-sale maintained; 5) the unique accounting and information systems employed; 6) variable product mixes (breakfast, lunch, and dinner) and price modes (menu, coupon, discounts, happy hour, and entertainment prices) and 7) the communication networks generated within a service environment. Figure 1-1 contains a brief sketch of the foodservice cycle.

Foodservice operations provide goods and services that possess no lasting or recoverable value. A meal consumed and not paid for can never be reclaimed; the revenues it represents are simply gone forever. Restaurants are perceived as providing "experiences," and their goods and services are assumed to be an integral part of the total dining occasion. From a financial viewpoint, goods and services combine to cost management nearly sixty-five

FIGURE 1-1 Introduction to the Foodservice Cycle

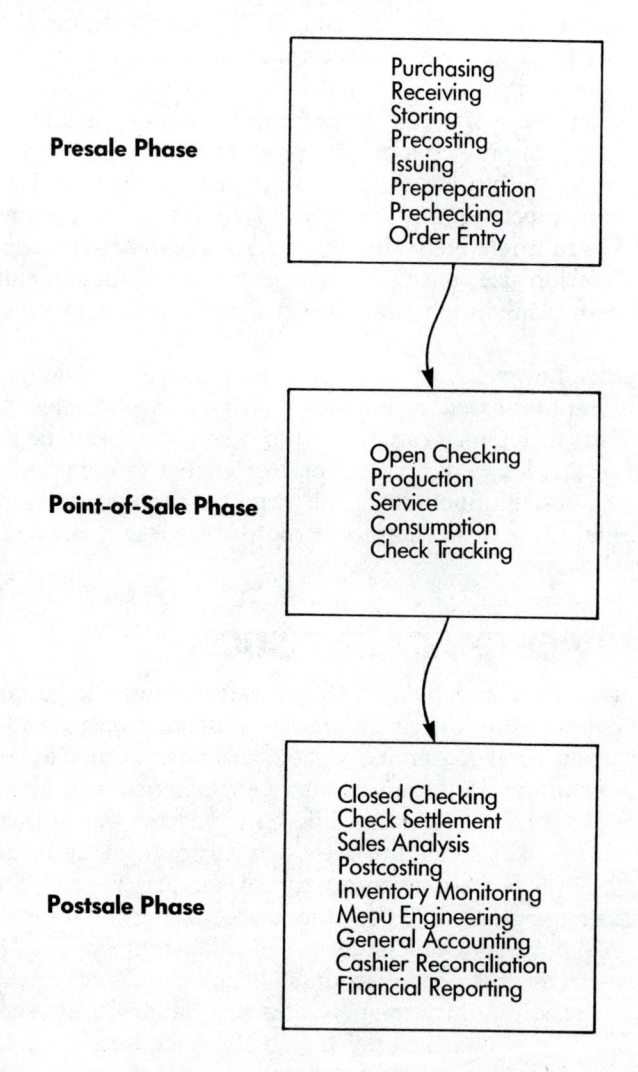

Presale Phase
- Purchasing
- Receiving
- Storing
- Precosting
- Issuing
- Prepreparation
- Prechecking
- Order Entry

Point-of-Sale Phase
- Open Checking
- Production
- Service
- Consumption
- Check Tracking

Postsale Phase
- Closed Checking
- Check Settlement
- Sales Analysis
- Postcosting
- Inventory Monitoring
- Menu Engineering
- General Accounting
- Cashier Reconciliation
- Financial Reporting

cents of every dollar collected as revenue. This disproportional expenditure ratio is not common to other industries.

The restaurant business, which is highly labor and commodity intensive, tends to be very inflation sensitive. As inflation begins to erode a restaurant's bottom line, new methods for tracking and monitoring goods and services will be investigated. Automated technology in the form of computer systems is oriented to this end. By helping management develop recession-proof menus and enhance production capabilities, the foodservice industry should continue to provide its unique goods and services at a reasonable rate of return.

Restaurants experience a high inventory turnover, one that often ties up a large amount of capital. The process of ordering, receiving, storing, issuing, producing, and servicing of food products can be quite complex. Most operators do not attempt to manually trace a raw ingredient through the production maze and to the point of purchase. Not many other industries place orders on a daily basis, maintain a *perpetual inventory*, or deal in multiple units of the same product. The perishability of food items governs their shelf life. The amount of available cold, frozen, or dry storage space dictates the volume of goods that can be purchased, by type.

As sales occur, operators chart and calculate their effect on inventory *reorder points*. Restaurants often make use of a *par stock*, or one of numerous alternatives, to determine order quantities. Once received, purchase units are usually broken down into issue units for physical inventory. These units are, in turn, reduced to recipe units for use in the production process. In general, table-service restaurants report a food inventory turnover of twice per month and a beverage inventory turnover of once per month. Obviously, fast-food restaurants, heavily liquor-oriented establishments, and other specialty markets will not approximate these industry averages.

Restaurants will operate at least one point-of sale (POS) station for each revenue center. There are more POS locations in the foodservice industry than in most others because of the nature of the goods and services and the rapid exchange of transactions. An eatery that has a lounge and small dining room, for example, will have two physical POS stations. Both areas house a cash register and employ a cashier. This arrangement is not necessarily used for a retail store that features many departments or for a medical facility composed of specialized modules. Most industries have been able to develop central settlement stations to handle multiple operations. This is not the tendency in foodservice.

Probably no other business has such a large volume of small (less than $25) transactions as the restaurant industry or has as many employees who handle cash. In fact, it is not uncommon to find some form of *server banking*, which eliminates the need for a cashier entirely, in a majority of enterprises. All of these factors reflect the dependence of foodservice operators on their accounting and information systems. Internal controls and a uniform system of accounts are designed to provide operational safeguards to and effective measurements of financial success. All in all, a foodservice operation is a dynamic workplace requiring comprehensive accounting controls and information-handling procedures to insure optimal levels of service, production, and profitability.

THE FIS CONCEPT

The initial conceptualization of a management information system predates the development and implementation of automated and computer-assisted systems. The advent of the digital computer did, however, alter the context and extend the capabilities of a data processing system within the business environment. Management information systems, in general, have evolved out of the application of language and mathematics to symbolic logic (the use of codes in place of a complete set of operational instructions). As knowledge increased and specialized areas of business became isolated, dedicated industry-oriented systems technology began to grow. One such industry application is the *foodservice information system (FIS)* area.

Until recently, the only automated FIS applications were in the cashier work station. Cash register devices evolved from purely mechanical units, to electronic tools, to computer-based terminals. Their orientation shifted from primarily transaction focused to report directed. As the sophistication of restaurateurs moved from a steady fixation on menu and meal planning toward bottom-line profits, computer capabilities also shifted to this end. For this reason, the discussion of computers in foodservice is usually divided into two broad classifications: service oriented and management oriented. Knowledge pertaining to the life of a guest check is basically a service question, although the proper allocation and implementation of resources are managerial concerns. Both of these perspectives are important to a complete understanding of an FIS design.

Information System Characteristics

Although management information system design may vary from industry to industry, or within any industry, basic underlying principles can be identified. Five common information system characteristics are:

1. The information system provides a means by which to achieve organizational objectives.
2. An information system treats information as an important resource and takes responsibility for its proper handling and flow.
3. The comprehensive product of an information system will enable improved integration of operations, communications, and coordination.
4. The information system will interface people and equipment in relationships designed to free personnel to fulfill jobs requiring a human capability *(human engineering)*.
5. An information system will store large volumes of transactional data to support planning, decision making, and analytical activities.

Task Criteria

Given that an information system will possess the basic characteristics discussed here, a task being considered for inclusion must be analyzed according to the following four criteria:

1. *Repetitive nature of task*–How often does the task need to be performed? Is it a routine procedure dependent on objective, not subjective evaluation? (e.g., order entry, inventory measurement, and employee timekeeping).
2. *Urgency of output*–Are results of the task and/or results of preceding tasks needed quickly? How much speed is desired in obtaining the output? (e.g., guest-check preparation, daily report of operations, and out-of-stock information.
3. *Availability of input data*–How easily can support data be identified and captured? Is there sufficient input to generate desired output? (e.g., development of a guest check from *preset* and *price look-up keys*).
4. *Effect of output*–What effect will the output have on managerial effectiveness? Will it improve customer service? Will it aid decision making? (e.g., open-check tracking, cashier reconciliation, and financial reporting).

After a review of these factors, a tentative decision concerning the addition of a task to the FIS network can be made. Final consideration must be given to adjusting manual procedures currently used to meet the requirements of this new design. The manual operations should, of course, be scrupulously analyzed with regard to feasibility, necessity, achievement, and freedom from bias.

If an operation is performed in a long, drawn-out fashion, requiring numerous intermediate processing procedures, adding it to the FIS may not be feasible or practical. A manual procedure of several steps may contain unnecessary operations (many rehandlings of the same data) and can be simplified in the FIS process. The value gained from performing a given task must also be resolved so that unnecessary procedures are not continued. The manner in which a data operation is presently performed may be a result of the capabilities or preferences of the person doing the job. The implementation of an automated application may require the creation of a new procedure. Normally, the flow of an FIS procedure is different from the manual one it replaces, since more symbolic logic leads to fewer complications.

Hence, the application of the FIS process, or the inclusion of presently performed manual tasks in an automated system, requires close attention and analysis. The preparation of a task for inclusion in the system may be of major benefit to the eatery. Frequently this evaluation benefit is overlooked or underestimated. The task-oriented characteristics stated above can also be applied to large-scale processes or operations.

COMPUTERS IN FOODSERVICE

The introduction of a computer system into the foodservice environment can significantly change the way business is conducted and charted. Both cash register (front-of-the-house)- and accounting (back-of-the-house)-oriented packages are available, which, if used together, can produce a complete information system. Restaurant networks can be installed on a modular basis, application by application, or can be interfaced into an integrated system. Common cash register applications include *prechecking*, *menu explosion*, and *cashier reconciliation*. Typical accounting areas are general ledger, inventory, payroll, and financial statement preparation. Although many of the available program components within a system can be installed somewhat independent of one another, cost savings usually result from multiple applications. In other words, once the system equipment and program costs of one module are borne, additional modules are relatively inexpensive. This savings occurs because subsequent software enhancements usually can run on previously purchased hardware and because many departments in a foodservice operation will share the same data base files.

Foodservice Hardware

Computer *hardware* is visible, movable, and easier to distinguish than is computer *software*. Table 1-1 offers a basic guide to foodservice hardware options. The arrangement of hardware in a computer system is referred to as a *configuration*. The configuration of any computer system must include a *central processing unit (CPU)*, a *memory unit*, and *input and output (I/O) devices*. The CPU is the "brains" of the system and is responsible for controlling all system components. The processor also performs all the arithmetical (mathematical) computations and logical (sorting and ranking) functions available through computerization. Large CPU devices are classified as mainframes, or macrocomputers, and smaller units can be labeled as minicomputers or microcomputers. A computer receives a macro, mini, or micro classification based on the size, speed, and capability of its CPU component.

Information is retained in a computer system by its memory unit. Foodservice systems depend on *disk drives* and *disk packs* to provide most of their necessary storage space. The disk drive (similar to a stereo turntable) rotates a disk pack unit at high speeds and deposits information to be stored at various locations on the pack's surfaces. Some disk pack units resemble a stack of five long-playing record albums. The disk drive has a disk head mechanism analogous to a stereo needle arm. This mechanism places data

TABLE 1-1 Quick Guide to Foodservice Hardware

Input Options	Processing Options	Output Options

1. Keyboard Devices
   a. Cash Register (POS)
   b. Key Pad
   c. Cathode Ray Tube (CRT)
   d. Teletype (TTY)
2. Optical Readers
   a. Preprinted Forms
   b. Character Recognition (OCR)
   c. Mark Sense Devices
   d. Universal Product Codes (UPC)
3. Transmission Media
   a. FM Signal (wireless)
   b. Closed Circuit TV
   c. Lightwave Cabling
   d. Electronic Wand
   e. Magnetic (Tape/Disk)
	1. Local Devices
	   a. Stand-Alone Register
	   b. Master-Slave System
	   c. Processor-Based Network
	2. Remote Equipment
	   a. Microcomputer
	   b. Minicomputer
	   c. Macrocomputer
	3. Peripheral Devices
	   a. Remote Order Entry
	   b. Telecommunications
	   c. Intelligent Terminals
		1. Hard Copy
		   a. Teletype (TTY)
		   b. Line Printing Terminal (LPT)
		   c. Receipt Printer
		   d. Journal Printer
		   e. Guest-Check Printer
		2. Soft Copy
		   a. Cathode Ray Tube (CRT)
		   b. Register Display (LED, LCD)
		   c. Remote Display (LED, LCD)
		3. Transmission Media
		   a. Magnetic (Tape/Disk)
		   b. FM Signal (wireless)

into *sectors* (addressable locations) on the pack. Information is stored in random order (versus sequential filing), not according to how or when it was entered into the system. Information also can be retrieved in a similar, random fashion because the computer will remember which data it placed where. This feature is especially valuable for the foodservice industry, where most events do not occur in a predictable, chronological order.

The information processed by the CPU and stored in the memory unit enters the system through an *input device*. The two most common foodservice input devices are the point-of-sale (POS) terminal and the cathode ray tube (CRT). The POS terminal is really a cash register device that must be connected to a remote CPU to function. The CRT is composed of a television-like video screen and a typewriter keyboard. As information is entered into either unit, it can be reviewed and/or edited before its communication to the CPU device. The output of processed information can be obtained in printed (*hard copy*) or displayed (*soft copy*) format, or both through an *output device*. A transaction total, for example, can be both displayed at the POS terminal as well as printed on its receipt printer. Note that any piece of hardware located outside the CPU is termed a *peripheral device* and must be interfaced to the processor to operate.

Foodservice Software

Computer systems contain two types of software. *System software* is designed by the manufacturer and is part of a component called *firmware*.

Application software is designed specifically for the user. Firmware is the term used to describe the computer's operating system. Because the operating system is really software that is permanently etched into a piece of hardware, it is called firmware. A variety of operating systems are currently on the market, and an experienced manufacturer is likely to offer more than one type. What really differentiates one computing system from its apparent equivalent is how their operating systems compare. Just as two automobiles can be compared and one eventually selected, so, too, can operating systems be evaluated. Since firmware components are not all similar with respect to operating speed, logic, and overall capabilities, a comparative analysis is a feasible approach to system selection.

If someone told you that they would reward you with a large sum of money if you could deliver a package, within six hours to a person three thousand miles away, you might be interested. For example, how would you plan to make this delivery to Louis Uben, 1234 Aerial Street, in the city of Cybex? Given the distance, you would probably consider an airplane trip to a city close to Cybex. Let's assume that the city of Holly is close to Cybex. You leave your present location by car, fly to Holly, and arrive within five hours. You then would most likely flag down a taxi and tell the driver to go to the twelve hundred block of Aerial Street in the town of Cybex. You finally arrive at building number 1234, a towering apartment complex. You look up Louis Uben in the building's directory and find his suite to be 429. You take an elevator to the fourth floor, go to apartment 429, and ring the bell. A woman answers and you ask to speak to Louis. Now only 3 minutes remain on the time clock. Louis comes to the door and you ask him to sign for the package. You have successfully accomplished your mission!

Some persons might have walked, biked, or taken a train to the airport, but you drove. Some might have sought alternatives to air travel, but you knew none could get you there on time. After the plane landed, you hired a taxi, even though a rental car or public transportation could have been used. When you reached the tower, you realized that some research work had to be done to find Uben's apartment number. All of these actions, decisions, and behaviors are a result of your operating system.

Just as two persons might have located Mr. Uben on time but through different channels, so, too, would two computer operating systems seek out last year's sales data. One system might use a series of software routines to aid in the search, whereas the other might simply rely on its hardware media to carry out the retrieval. In any case, just as people have various means and speeds by which they operate, so do different computer systems. The firmware that is the most powerful and works at the highest speed will be the most expensive. Care must be taken to assure that the proper operating system is selected for the foodservice operation under study.

Application software is very different from system software in that it is dedicated to a specific function. Figure 1-2 offers a simplified guide to food-

FOODSERVICE INFORMATION SYSTEMS 11

FIGURE 1-2 Quick Guide to Foodservice Software

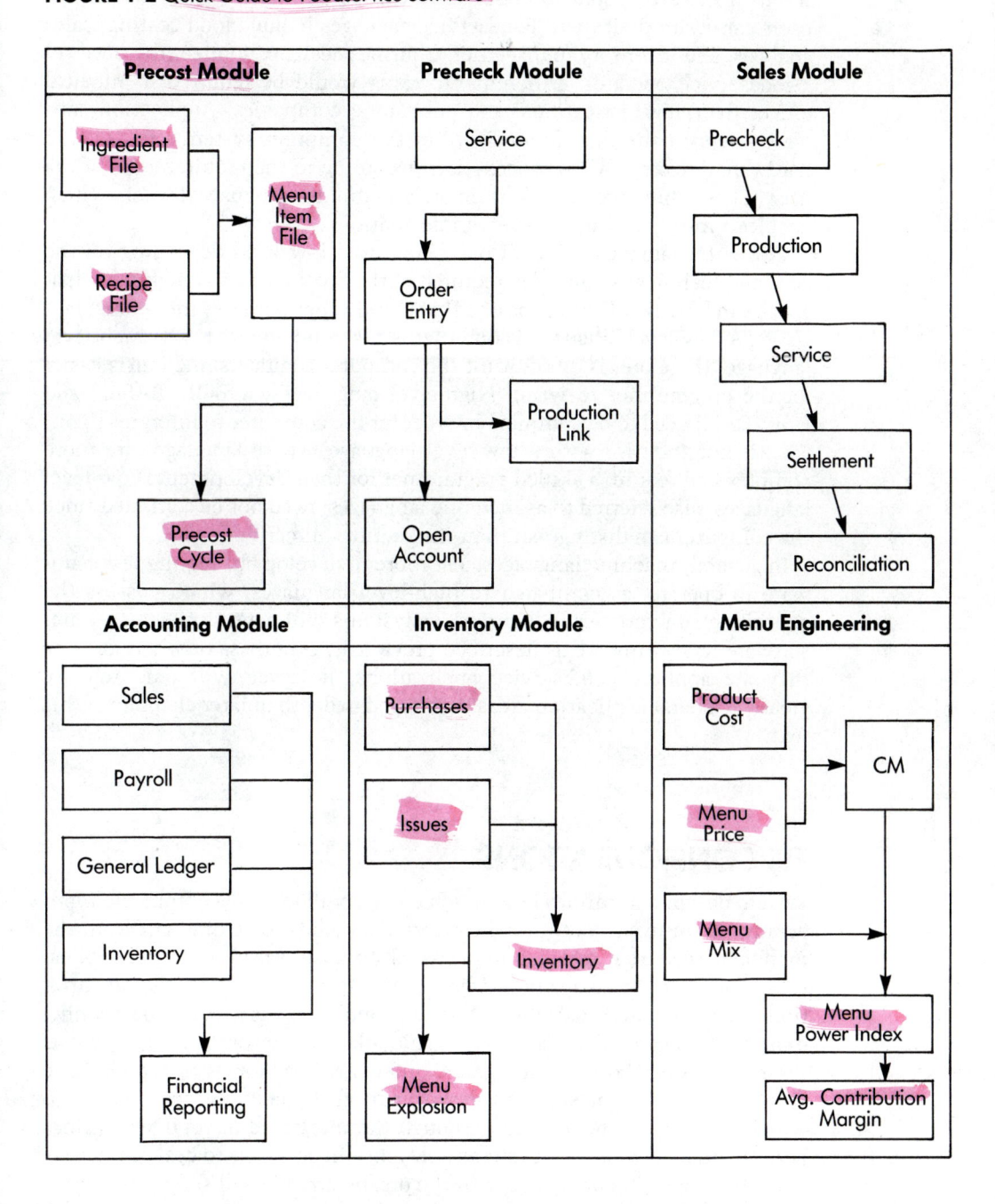

Precost Module	Precheck Module	Sales Module
Ingredient File, Recipe File → Menu Item File → Precost Cycle	Service → Order Entry → Production Link; Order Entry → Open Account	Precheck → Production → Service → Settlement → Reconciliation

Accounting Module	Inventory Module	Menu Engineering
Sales, Payroll, General Ledger, Inventory → Financial Reporting	Purchases, Issues → Inventory → Menu Explosion	Product Cost, Menu Price → CM; Menu Mix → Menu Power Index → Avg. Contribution Margin

service software. Application software can be purchased, ready to run, or users can write their own. Foodservice packages include food costing, sales analysis, and inventory management routines designed to meet the needs of a foodservice operator. Different programs would be required in medical offices, banking institutions, and publishing companies. Application software refers to the instructions within the computer system that tell the hardware devices how to process data according to the requirements of the user. These directives are written in a computer language (code), which enables a more rapid processing of information.

Computer languages range from a high to a low level depending on the skill and technical knowledge required of the programmer. A high-level language can be defined simply as one that closely approximates the spoken language. A low-level language is one that is machine oriented. The high-level language, therefore, is difficult for the computer to understand but is easier for the programmer to write. High-level languages (COBOL, BASIC, and FORTRAN) need to be compiled in order for the computer to interpret them. This is not the case with a low-level language. These languages are more complex and require a skilled programmer for their development. Low-level languages, also referred to as machine languages, need not be compiled since the computer can distinguish their instructions directly.

In general, machine languages cost more to develop but require less hardware to operate, as compared to high-level languages, which possess the opposite characteristics. All computer systems will have similar hardware, software, and firmware as described previously, regardless of where or how they are applied. Food service applications, however, will tend to vary greatly. General application areas are treated in depth in later chapters of this text.

FIS CONFIGURATIONS

System design determines how much change will take place from the input data to the resultant output. The design also tends to be different from the manual procedure it replaces and is usually a customized computer application. The overall management information system can serve the organization as an *integrated configuration* (i.e., monolithic), as a *distributed configuration* of independent systems (i.e., modular), or as some *combination* of these two. Since both the integrated and distributed forms of the FIS have strengths and weaknesses, no determination is generally accepted as to which one is more beneficial. Although the integrated or total system has become more fashionable, systems analysts will continue to design a configuration to be most consistent with the organization it will serve.

The Integrated Configuration

Initially, most businesses used an application-by-application approach to satisfy their data processing needs. Within the past decade or so, firms became interested in a complete system that could serve many organizational functions. Administrative emphasis shifted the computer away from well-structured tasks and reductions in clerical operations to improvements in the abstract areas of strategic planning and decision making. The development of advanced-generation computing hardware and the increased acceptance of the computer as a managerial tool are credited with enabling system users to gain potential economic and competitive advantages over nonusers. The "total system" approach revolves around the consolidation of all data processing and information generation functions. This approach may impose significant changes, or demands, on the way business is conducted. The integrated configuration features a large, singular *data base* and therefore requires a centralization of information to work well.

Critics of this total system approach object that meeting all the informational requirements of a business is technically impossible and economically not feasible. Other critics feel that unless management makes a total commitment to this system, chaos will result, since the system depends on all levels of the organization for support. Another criticism centers on the fact that although all the internal departments may be represented in the total system, the system fails to include the important external variables that may be nonroutine yet affect the restaurant. Also, the integrated system forces functional areas to become more dependent on one another than is normally the case, and this dependence may result in disastrous outcomes for the firm. Figure 1-3 depicts a basic integrated configuration. Note that all data processing operations branch to one central data base.

The Distributed Configuration

Unlike the integrated configuration, the distributed FIS is a series of systems, not one large system. Frequently, the total system concept is achieved by the implementation of *modular* systems that are eventually linked together to create a large singular structure. The design and development of individual systems enable management to comprehend that functional area better and to provide internal data and evaluation to each department. The distributed FIS network is interfaced for communications, but the subsystems are relatively independent. No dependencies are artificially created like those that may be experienced with the integrated design.

Normally, it is possible to identify three basic conditions that differentiate subsystems found in distributed systems: 1) subsystems that will need to interact with other subsystems (e.g., sales information and menu explo-

FIGURE 1-3 Sample Integrated FIS Configuration

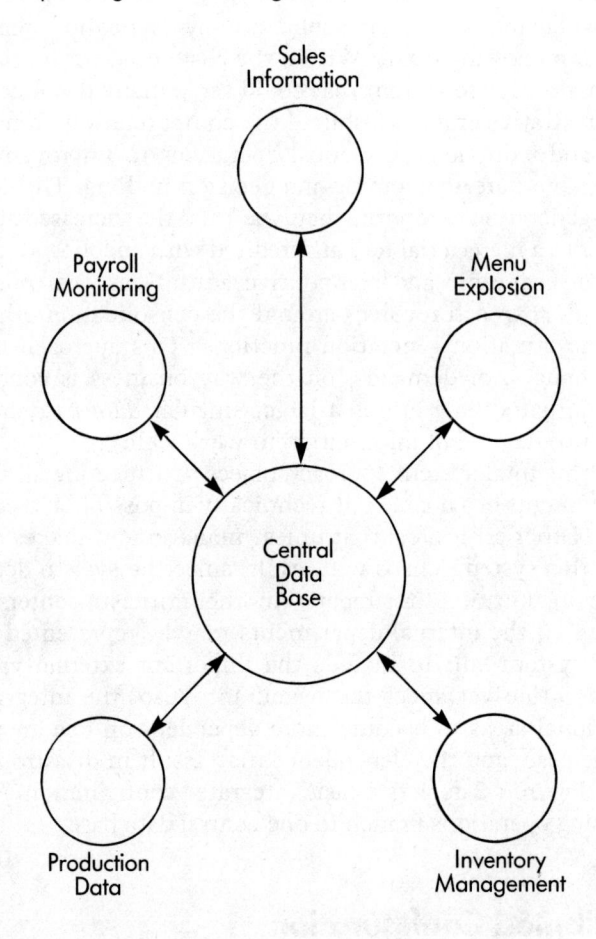

sion); 2) subsystems that will need to share files and data processing facilities (e.g., sales information and payroll monitoring); and 3) subsystems that will require very little interaction, remain isolated, and for the most part remain self-sufficient (e.g., inventory management).

Systems analysts have argued that because some firms have such diverse operating departments, it does not make sense for all departmental data to flow into one common data base. Perhaps the real advantage of the distributed system is that the data and output of the FIS are located close to their end users (where they are most needed).

Unlike the centralization and interdependencies highlighted in the integrated configuration, the distributed design tends to be a series of modules

FIGURE 1-4 Sample Distributed FIS Configuration

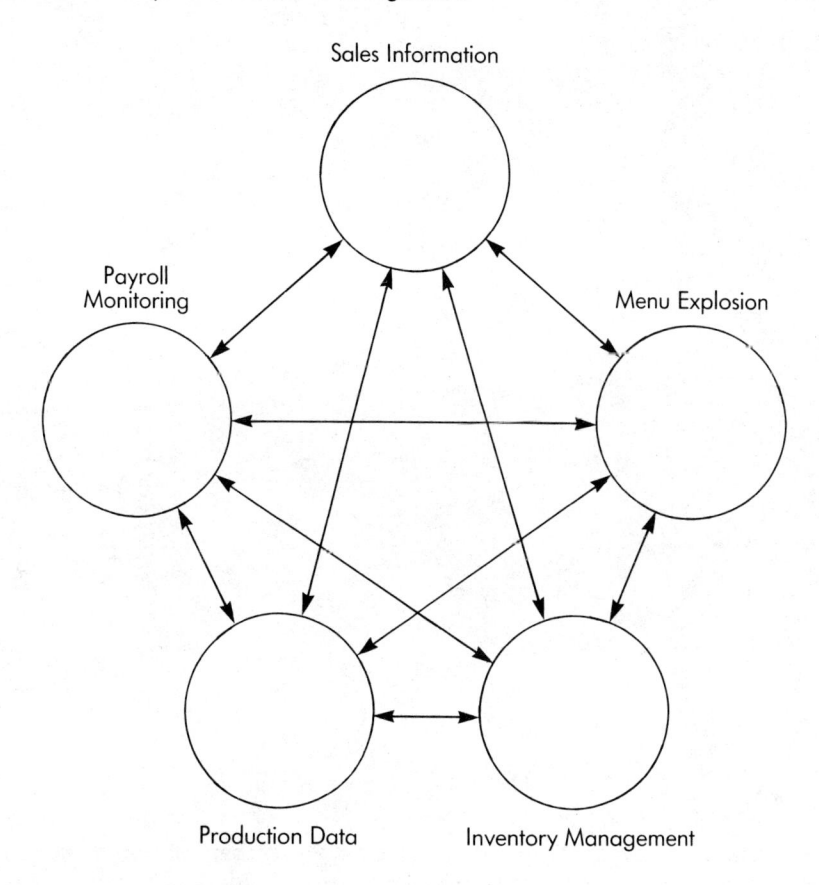

Sales Information

Payroll Monitoring

Menu Explosion

Production Data

Inventory Management

informally linked and independent of one another. See Figure 1-4 for a simplified diagram of a distributed configuration.

Combined Networks

Most organizations that use an FIS probably will have both distributed and integrated system characteristics to some degree. Although it is possible to discuss and theoretically identify monolithic and modular system networks, frequently the FIS configuration found within the operation is difficult to segment. In the case of multiple unit management, for example, each restaurant may have its own in-house integrated data base system. When a host computer polls each store in the chain, a new central storage of information is developed. In this situation, an integrated single system becomes an input mode for a chain-wide telecommunications data collection process. This

FIGURE 1-5 Sample Combined Polling Configuration

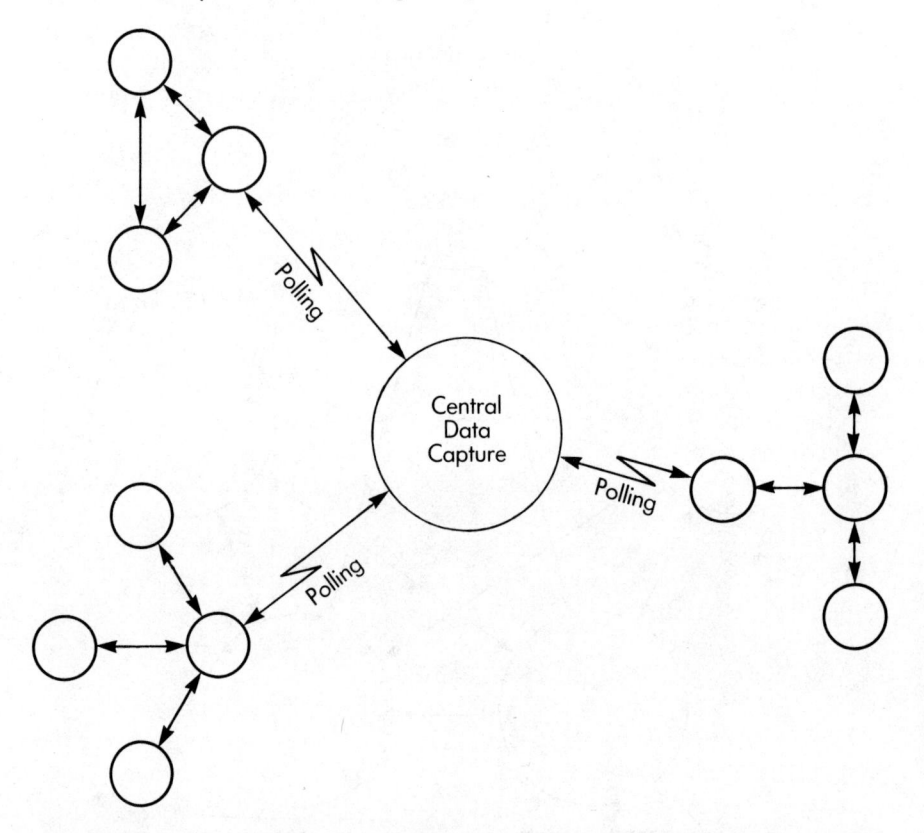

arrangement is different from an integrated system that communicates to a series of in-house distributed component networks for data capture. Figure 1-5 contains a diagram of a sample combined configuration.

During the preliminary development of formalized information systems, systems designers began marketing the FIS concepts by touting their potential capabilities to restaurants. Some of these premises were unrealistic and therefore have not been realized to date. This embarrassment has led to much criticism of the FIS in general and has dissuaded some users from its pursuit. The claim that the FIS can define the information needs of the firm has attracted the attention of restaurant organizations eager to improve their decision making. The FIS is also supposed to: 1) provide rapid answers at a low cost, 2) be the central communications link of the operation, 3) reduce clerical work and errors, and 4) improve the overall coordination and consistency of the operation. Since the FIS is supposed to guarantee better management, it is also expected to provide a means of improved allocation of a company's resources.

FIS PERFORMANCE EVALUATION

Due to the lack of a universally accepted definition, the performance of a foodservice information system has been difficult to evaluate. Although specific businesses have developed their own criteria, five basic evaluative approaches can be enumerated:

1. *Cost justification*–also referred to as cost effectiveness. What does the FIS cost and what benefits are derived from it? If the benefits outweigh the costs, then the system is believed to be performing well. This cost-benefit criterion loses much of its applicability when management tries to assign dollar values to intangible, informational output (e.g., improved customer services).
2. *Speed and accuracy*–a measurement of the FIS throughput mechanism in terms of speed and accuracy as compared to the procedures it replaces. Since the computer's major advantage lies in its speed and attention to detail, this may not be the most realistic evaluation criterion (e.g., comparison of preparation of financial statements).
3. *Reliability*–the belief that only a system that is reliable is worth having. The reliability of a system will affect its performance, but a reliable system that is underemployed may not score well on an overall critique (e.g., a high percentage of up-time).
4. *Satisfaction of demand*–the ability of the system to satisfy the user's requests for information, a common yardstick for FIS evaluation. The biggest problem with this type of standard is that the user's requests may in no way meet the user's needs. The system does not evaluate the legitimacy of the user's demands, it merely transmits information from its files. The system may not be performing well even though it is producing information (e.g., production of volumes of irrelevant information).
5. *Operational simplicity*–the ease of system operation both in terms of hardware and software, also a common evaluation criterion. Again, attention is usually given to the system's ability to meet user's requests, no matter how irrelevant the requests may be (e.g., preset, price look-up and function keys).

The FIS deals with the transmission of messages and not with evaluating the meaningfulness of their content. For this reason, an FIS evaluation should be made on the basis of all five criteria, not just one, as has often been the case.

Both management and systems engineers can be held responsible for some of the failures that have taken place: the inadequate follow-up by both parties; the designer's lack of understanding of the foodservice industry; management's improper training and use of systems; and the interference of a computer orientation with overall business objectives. All of these factors combine to show the total weakness of the earliest FIS systems.

Progress in the foodservice information systems marketplace has been exceptional, and the future looks even brighter. The increased acceptance of computer-based systems and the new awareness of technical computer operations by foodservice management personnel combine to create a more favorable environment for improved configurations.

SUMMARY

The concept of a foodservice information system is not a new one. The recent advent of computers has, however, altered and extended the capabilities of FIS configurations. The information system is normally modeled on the organization it is designed to serve and is constructed to allow departments to pursue their individual areas of interest.

Although no definition of an FIS is universally accepted, a broad definition usually includes the provision of timely information, data transformation, assistance in management functions, and reporting formats. The author offers the following definition: The FIS is a collection of interrelated, interdependent subsystems dependent on a data base that supports: 1) the managerial decision-making process, 2) monitoring and control operations, and 3) responsiveness to the dynamic needs of the firm. The ambiguity of broad definitions has led to problems in evaluation. Unless the FIS functions and responsibilities are specified for a particular application, it is almost impossible to construct performance objectives and to evaluate the benefits of a system.

Common system characteristics include: organizational goals, responsibilities for information-handling, integration and coordination of the firm, human engineering, and a collection of transactional/historical data. The FIS is designed to serve the organization and to help it meet its objectives through efficient use of its most important resource—information.

The delineation of tasks for FIS application depends on repetition, urgency, availability, and the effectiveness of the output. Additional characteristics include such factors as feasibility, necessity, achievement, and freedom from bias. All things considered, the FIS should include only tasks that will enhance managerial effectiveness and further the goals of the organization.

System design determines how much change will occur between the input data and the resultant output. The design might be distributed, integrated, or some combination of these two. The distributed, or modular, FIS is a series of small systems rather than the one large system found in the integrated design. But almost all configurations have some integrated and distributed system characteristics, and, in reality, it is difficult to decipher where one system design begins and/or ends.

Early FIS promises have led to criticism and dissatisfaction with loosely designed configurations and have dissuaded some organizations from pursuing their application. However, a rapid upsurge in FIS applications is anticipated due to advancements in both systems science and computer technology.

KEY CONCEPTS

The end of each chapter contains a list of concepts introduced, or reintroduced, in that chapter. The reader should also consult the glossary at the back of the book for more complete or additional definitions.

The following concepts were introduced in this chapter. Their meanings should be completely understood.

1. *Application Software*-user-purchased or developed for specific function in a particular environment.
2. *Cashier Reconciliation*-management's ability to audit a cash terminal and its operator; the verification of transactional balances and procedures.
3. *Central Processing Unit (CPU)*-the "brains" of a computer system; responsible for controlling all systems functions and component parts.
4. *Configuration*-the layout and design of equipment in a system or network.
5. *Cost Justification*-financial analyses aimed at determining whether the benefits of a system outweigh its costs.
6. *Data Base*-large central storage of data and information available to a computer system.
7. *Disk Drive*-electronic device used to rotate a disk pack at high speed to create magnetic fields.
8. *Disk Pack*-random access storage medium that is rotated by a disk drive.
9. *Distributed Configuration*-a series of independent systems tied together for redundancy.
10. *Firmware*-a term used to describe the operating system of a computer; software that is physically part of hardware.
11. *Foodservice Information System*-an orderly arrangement of foodservice data procedures and decision-making criteria designed to increase managerial effectiveness through proper information processing.
12. *Hard Copy*-a printed page output from an automated system.
13. *Hardware*-a piece of computer equipment.
14. *Human Engineering*-the automation of routine tasks thereby freeing personnel to apply their capabilities elsewhere.

15. *Input and Output (I/O) Devices*-communication units attached to a computer system. Data is entered through the input device; information is produced through the output device.
16. *Input Device*-data entry communication unit enabling user to interact with a computer system.
17. *Integrated Configuration*-a centralized data base intricately interfaced and available to all users.
18. *Memory Unit*-also referred to as secondary memory; consists of addressable storage locations designed to retain data and information.
19. *Menu Explosion*-the breaking of menu items into their component ingredients for costing and inventory analysis.
20. *Modular*-the segmentation of a complete system into subcomponent parts or application areas.
21. *Output Device*-system component designed to report information to a system user.
22. *Par Stock*-an inventory ordering scheme in which management identifies a feasible reorder point and a maximum stock level for each item.
23. *Peripheral Device*-any hardware element in a computer system located outside the central processing unit.
24. *Perpetual Inventory*-a running count of stock on hand based on sales transactions; must be proven through physical inventory updating.
25. *Physical Inventory*-an actual count of stock on hand.
26. *Prechecking*-a foodservice system technique requiring written requisitioning prior to the allocation of any food or beverage item from a production station.
27. *Preset*-a cash register keyboard design that dedicates a specific key to the price and inventory of only one menu item.
28. *Price Look-Up*-a technique for extending the memory capabilities of a cash register through the assignment of file numbers to menu items; a simulation and extension of preset keys.
29. *Reorder Point*-a predesignated level of stock that initiates a purchase order for replenishment.
30. *Sectors*-addressable storage locations on a magnetic disk or diskette memory unit.
31. *Server Banking*-an operational technique in which each server is responsible for self-cashiering each transaction conducted.
32. *Soft Copy*-a computer output that is displayed on an electronic video screen (e.g., CRT).
33. *Software*-a set of instructions (or data) that direct hardware routines in a computer system.
34. *System Software*-designed by a system manufacturer as part of the basic computer system structure.

Data Processing Concepts

Chapter Objectives

1. To introduce the concept of data processing in a general context
2. To explain the basic underpinnings of information and system concepts
3. To sketch the evolution of data processing techniques from early manual procedures through to modern electronic networks
4. To introduce the objectives of the data processing function

Although the processing of *data* is not a new idea, the development of automated, electronic technology has vastly altered the concept. The foodservice industry has benefited significantly from faster and more accurate means of data measurement, collection, processing, and handling. Accompanying these changes is a new combination of sophisticated and complex suboperations required to generate desired *output* or *input* to a system, in a meaningful context. Many manual, robot-like tasks have become automated, freeing management to allocate personnel to functions requiring more decision-making capability.

This form of *human engineering* has enabled the restaurant to reorganize its *data processing* network, and has enhanced its ability to comprehend its functional operating departments. Recently, foodservice data processing expanded its scope to include computer applications and *data base* management technology. As more advanced foodservice computer systems are designed and implemented, the degree of *distributed intelligence* (the capability of computer processing at remote locations) throughout the restaurant will significantly increase.

This chapter presents some basic underpinnings of *information* and *systems* concepts and a brief background of the data processing cycle. The following chapter deals with the evolution and design of computer systems and their impact on business organizations.

INFORMATION AND SYSTEMS CONCEPTS

Regardless of the organization, management has always generated some system of information for evaluating its performance. Recent pressures, however, require that a more formal and detailed information network be used. Hence, general business systems have become more structured and better automated in an attempt to facilitate the flow and handling of relevant information. Traditional manual systems (the kinds common in the hospitality industry) have been ineffective in processing large volumes of data; and as the size and complexity of individual foodservice operations continue to increase, so, too, does the demand for more and better information.

Information

Information can be defined simply as what adds to what is known or alleged. For example, a color photograph contains more information than a black and white one. Information can serve three general purposes. First, it can increase one's *knowledge* about a situation or occurrence. Second, it can reduce *uncertainty*, as in the case of decision making. Third, information provides *feedback* for evaluation and future planning. Although the acquisition of information normally heightens awareness, people differ in their reactions to it.

Knowledge, uncertainty, and feedback. As information about variables becomes available, management learns more about the business and its *environment*. Since information reduces uncertainty, it is an essential component in the decision-making process. Historically, restaurant management has suffered from the collection of too much irrelevant information and thus has had trouble discerning valuable feedback on departmental operations. Information generated within the organization is affected by the delineation of specialized areas for analysis. The number of operating departments and the number of employees will lead to certain parameters for information generation. If the wrong data are processed incorrectly, or the correct data are processed incorrectly, then the resultant information will be in error.

Pressures for information. Many factors explain the increase in the amount of information generated within the restaurant. First, the increased growth of individual companies has been so rapid that it has rendered some operations almost imcomprehensible from an administrative view. For example, on the micro level, the construction of enormous eateries with more than several hundred seats has reduced management's ability to chart, maintain, and monitor the foodservice cycle adequately. The expansion of chain operations, the development of larger franchise networks, and the popularity of conglomerate formations have decentralized operations. They have done so to the point that a recentralization of information is a tedious, but mandatory step for regaining corporate or macrolevel monitoring and control. Given trends in the economy, tighter cost and selling margins are becoming a reality. In order for foodservice managers to meet the goals of a firm, a better understanding of costs and sales information is required.

A second important factor leading to increased pressures for information can be found in the many different forms of ownership and managerial contracting in the restaurant industry. The need for accountability has further compounded the increasing pressure for more quickly obtained and more complete knowledge. Internal reports to management and owners, as well as external reports to stockholders and the public, have become standard pressure points for most companies.

A third factor leading to additional information needs has been the recent tightening of government regulations for fiscal reporting at the local, state, and federal levels. Firms are being required to report and maintain much more information about their enterprises then they were required to formerly.

All in all, the hospitality entrepreneur has experienced an increasing concern for information and a need for an efficient data processing network to formulate the facts.

Value of information. The value of information can be a function of its availability, timeliness, comprehensiveness, and/or accuracy. Information that is free from bias and adaptable to more than one decision area is more valuable than information that is limited and prejudiced. Similarly, the degree of unexpectedness (or improbability) of a message is a key factor enhancing the amount of information it contains.

Information can flow within a firm by written document, spoken message, hand or facial signal, person-to-machine transference, machine-to-machine relay, or some combination thereof. The more sources the information must flow through, the greater the risk of deletion and/or alteration of the information content.

The Systems Concept

A regular or orderly arrangement of component parts placed in an interrelated series necessary to accomplish some operation is termed a *system*. In reality, however, most systems are comprised of linked subsystems and tend to satisfy more than one purpose. A complex system, for example, is one that can be factored into its respective subsystems for analysis. The restaurant can be viewed as a complex system having preparation, production, service, and accounting systems as some of its principal subsystems.

All systems operate in an environment. The environment is defined as everything outside the system that affects or is affected by the system. The personnel, hardware, software, and the other parts of the system constitute a system's environment. In a business context, a system is a structure that coordinates the activities and operations of the organization and fosters clarity in departmental functions with regard to the overall scheme.

The term *system* has become overused and often misused. For example, the advertising community often uses the word as a product attachment, the goal being to lend a superior scientific aura to the advertised product. The injector razor system and the recessed filter cigarette system are both examples of connections created by advertising that lead to inappropriate usage. Correct use of the term includes: the solar system, a telephone system, a stereo component system, and a component system, each of which is composed of real components, interrelated to accomplish a goal.

GENERAL SYSTEM LIFE CYCLE

A thorough analysis of the user's needs and values is necessary for determining a system's performance requirements. Accordingly, a knowledge and identification of environmental factors is crucial to an effective system design. An understanding of a restaurant's available resources and time framework is also an important consideration when constructing a system to accomplish a desired objective.

The actual system design is contingent on the specification and isolation of a purpose. Once the purpose is known, the required component parts can be secured and analyzed. An interrelating and/or interfacing of the system's parts completes the system design and enables implementation, analysis, and evaluation by management.

The life cycle of a general system can be thought of as a four-phase process ranging from problem situation and environmental analysis, through design and implementation, to refinement. A brief outline of the cycle is given in Figure 2-1, and the individual stages are discussed in some detail in the following paragraphs.

FIGURE 2-1 System Life Cycle

Phase I.   System Analysis
   a. Fact-finding
   b. Fact analysis

Phase II. System Design
   a. Clerical procedures
   b. Processing control
   c. Data base construction
   d. Forms and reports development
   e. Programming development
   f. Equipment selection

Phase III. System Implementation
   a. Personnel training
   b. System testing
   c. System conversion
   d. Maintenance
   e. Auditing

Phase IV. System Refinement
   a. System usage
   b. Updating
   c. Adjusting (deleting or extending)
   d. Maintenance of continuous system operation

System Analysis

Prior to the formal development of a system, a fact-finding and fact analysis phase should be completed. The resources of the firm, the availability of input data, and the requirement of system output should be evaluated and defined. The needs of the restaurant, for example, and the capability of individual system components must be equated to produce an optimal information arrangement.

System Design

The actual development of a system is simplified if a thorough system analysis has been performed. The identification of input data will lead to clerical specifications and the design of forms for recording information. A data base or a procedural process leading to storage may be required. Normally, the change in input required to produce a desired output will lead to the construction of a data base and a determination of the size of the base. A clear statement of the flow and computational evaluations that information must undergo will not only improve programming, but also will lead to the selection of the equipment necessary for the system design. The largest single activity in the design of a system is usually in program development. A restaurant might design an elaborate communication system between its service areas and its production area, or it may elect traditional procedures for exchanging and disseminating information via paperwork. In either case, a logical information flow and control should be designed to insure a proper input and output from the system.

System Implementation

Once a system is designed, its implementation should follow. The training and educating of personnel in the system environment is perhaps the most important factor leading to a successful system application. The best designed system can fail if employees are unable to operate it properly. The weakest link in any system will certainly constrain the overall performance of the whole package. System operators and information users must be aware of the importance of training.

A system should be tested to verify its feasibility, accuracy, and reliability. If any problems arise, the system may require some conversion. Therefore a flexible system design is preferred to one that is rigid. On-going maintenance and auditing of the system components provide continual feedback on the status of successful implementation and operation of the system.

System Refinement

During system usage, it may be justifiable either to abandon or expand particular system segments. The use of inappropriate or redundant input or output, for example, may necessitate a programming or design change. Should the system refinement fail to enhance the system operation, then a thorough review and evaluation of the original anlaysis and design is warranted. A major dysfunction within the system may necessitate an innovative design or simply going back to the beginning. Basically, maintaining the continuous operation of the system is an essential phase of the system's cycle.

Machines in Systems

Over the past decades, systems have become increasingly automated. Machinery has proven capable of performing almost any function that is physically possible or logical. Machines can be used for collecting data, making measurements, transmitting signals, performing intricate calculations, or controlling physical conditions.

Varying degrees of automation are reflected in: 1) nonautomated systems that consist only of humans (e.g., the U.S. Congress); 2) semiautomated systems that are composed of people in a system's role (as in a computer system); and 3) fully automated systems in which human capabilities are only required for initiation, setting criteria of performance, and deciding on corrective behavior (e.g., an unmanned space ship). Hence, the only limiting aspects of machine capabilities appear to be in the way its controls are designed. Restaurant data processing systems, for example, have become semiautomated during the past few years. Formerly they were strictly nonautomated.

DATA PROCESSING

Data processing can be defined as the transformation of raw, isolated, unevaluated facts to comprehensive, integrated information. For example, a list of individual accounting transaction entries may not have much meaning per se, but a compiled summary of these sales figures may lend significant understanding. The objective of a data processing system is to take input (data) and formulate output (information) that will have a higher level of clarity and intelligibility. The basic data processing system consists primarily of a three-phase, input-*process*-output procedure. This procedure is a simplification of a manual-based cycle that must be drastically revised and redefined to incorporate the advancements made through computer-based assistance. Figure 2-2 illustrates some foodservice functions using the basic three-phase data processing mode.

Source Documents

In a restaurant environment, information is usually communicated in writing via a *source document*. A source document is the original recording of a transaction and establishes a permanent record. Historically, the restaurant

FIGURE 2-2 Foodservice Functions as Data Processing Items

Foodservice Data Processing

Simplified Overview of the DP Cycle (usually used in a manual or basic machine process):

1. Input
    A. Recording (capturing of data)–a guest check is the primary source document for initial input to the foodservice order entry cycle.
    B. Classifying (coding of data)–classification by type of menu item, production station, or meal period is designed to simplify analysis and tracking of transactions.

2. Process
    A. Sorting (arranging of data)–open-check tracking and cashier reconciliation are two sorting techniques that restaurants use to ease their data-handling workload.
    B. Calculating (computation and/or manipulation of data)–the posting and subsequent auditing procedures found in the foodservice industry serve to keep outstanding accounts up-to-date and provide management with operational statistics.

3. Output
    A. Reporting (summarization of data into specified formats)–inventory use and revenue and cost center reports are outputs of data-handling procedures designed to monitor and control operations.
    B. Storage (retention of file data)–the necessity of providing up-to-date figures and recording historical data for future performance comparisons leads to the maintenance of a set of files concerning business and account histories.

---

industry has been flooded with volumes of source documents. Only recently have technological advances significantly reduced their use. With the application of machines and computerized equipment, the industry appears to be on its way toward a paperless, electronic environment.

Source documents assist the front-of-the-house staff in charting the guest cycle both in the dining room and in remote production areas. They also aid the back office in its control of the entire operation. For example, the restaurant check is the basic document used to track the guest's item purchases, their corresponding prices, server, and table data. Without source documents, efficient foodservice accounting and information systems would not exist. Management could not survive.

Source documents provide both input data and output information where needed throughout the enterprise. The implementation of restaurant management information systems will most likely alter, eliminate, or reduce the need for some of the documents currently used in many foodservice operations, at least in their traditional formats and use.

Originally all foodservice data operations were manual procedures that relied heavily on repetition and extensive clerical back-up. The earliest system concentrated on hand calculations, and all postings and reports were handwritten. As typewriters, cash registers, and time-clock-type devices became available, they were quickly adopted. Later, keypunching, sorting, and collating machines significantly updated the processing function. Today, the data processing operation has advanced to computer automation involving such hardware as optical scanners, remote order entry terminals, central processing units, and memory units.

Data Processing Objectives

The objectives of the general data processing cycle can be summarized as:

1. To *transform* raw, isolated, unevaluated facts into comprehensive, integrated information (input-process-output)
2. To *satisfy* the on-going user's requests and to report output in a meaningful context to management (from input to output: *throughput*)
3. To *reduce* the handling and rehandling of data (streamlining of information procedures)
4. To *minimize* the time of the data processing cycle (*turnaround time*)
5. To *reduce* or eliminate any unnecessary source documents (except as required by law)

FIS AND DATA PROCESSING

The *foodservice information system* concept is simply a different way of viewing the on-going business of the restaurant. Instead of analyzing only the number of covers sold or determining staffing and pricing criteria, the FIS focuses on the movement of communications and paperwork throughout the facility. The FIS deals with an analysis of both the flow and usefulness of the restaurant's most important internal resource, its information. Knowledge usually is provided through revenue, financial, statistical, and productivity reports. This information gives management an increased awareness and insight into how the business is operating. Since wiser decisions might be outgrowths of better information, it appears safe to assume that management will be better able to evaluate decision alternatives, given a sound informational base. Another benefit of informational analysis is feedback. Because management can receive accurate and timely reports, memos, and analytical evaluations of the restaurant, management becomes aware of its operations and their productivity. Feedback enables management to take corrective actions before the business moves too far off target.

FIS OBJECTIVES

Not all foodservice information systems operate with the same efficiencies, procedures, and effectiveness. Irrespective of the FIS design, the system should be capable of achieving these data processing objectives and their relative functions:

1. Eliminate or reduce the number of unnecessary source documents (data collection function)
2. Eliminate or reduce the number of unnecessary, often redundant, data transfer and recording procedures (data-handling function)
3. Enable management to monitor and administrate the guest cycle more efficiently (data processing function)
4. Provide management with timely and comprehensive reports (informational output function)
5. Provide a high level of operational and internal control over business resources (control function)
6. Enable management to make more intelligent, better decisions (effectiveness function)
7. Provide cost savings to the restaurant (efficiency function)
8. Enable the restaurant to provide improved and expanded guest services (proficiency function)

What is a Computer?

The *computer* is a managerial tool capable of processing large quantities of data very rapidly and accurately. It can perform arithmetic (addition, subtraction, multiplication, and division) and logical (e.g., ranking, sorting, and assembling) operations. It dispenses results in a variety of formats. Computers can repeat programmed instructions infinitely without error, hold large quantities of information in storage, and simulate decision modeling situations. The two broad categories of computing machines are digital and analog.

Digital versus Analog Machinery

The *digital computer* operates similar to a hand calculator and is based on discrete steps. Digital computers are capable of storing programs and have a high level of precision and efficiency. The *analog computer* is akin to a slide rule. The number scales are not precise, and it is fairly difficult to identify specific output. Hence, the digital computer has made a significant contribution to the business community, whereas the analog machine has been reserved for scientific applications. Data processing (dp) can be accomplished manually (dp), with machine assistance (mdp), or electronically (edp). It is thus important to understand the specific requirements of any particular application. The next chapter focuses attention on the basic characteristics of computing systems.

SUMMARY

Management has always constructed some system of information for evaluating its performance. This information serves three general purposes: 1) to increase knowledge, 2) to reduce uncertainty, and 3) to provide feedback. The demands for more information by business firms are normally a result of growth, accountability, and government regulations. Management has experienced an increasing concern for information and has developed a need for an efficient data processing system to formulate the facts.

A system is an orderly arrangement of component parts placed in an interrelated series necessary to accomplish some operation. All systems operate in an environment and must be designed to meet the users' needs. A system life cycle consists of: 1) system analysis, 2) system design, 3) system implementation, and 4) system refinement.

An important objective of a data processing system is to reduce the handling of data. In the past, data had to be handled several times. Now each transaction may need to be recorded only once in a machine-usable form and stored and retrieved whenever desired. Through advanced technology, data can be processed many times, without rehandling and with increased speed and accuracy. Improvements in collecting, calculating, storing, and disseminating information have surpassed even the most optimistic expectations of restaurateurs. These advances promise even more spectacular future developments.

KEY CONCEPTS

The following concepts were introduced in this chapter. Their meanings should be completely understood.

1. *Analog Computer*-a machine useful for scientific research; presents approximate answers to complicated problem sets; akin to the slide rule.
2. *Computer*-a machine capable of processing large volumes of scattered data into meaningful information; a managerial tool capable of assisting in the monitoring and projecting of business.

DATA PROCESSING CONCEPTS

3. *Data*-raw, isolated, unevaluated facts; input elements in a data processing system; compiled data results in information.
4. *Data Base*-a collection of data elements and files useful to more than one department of a firm.
5. *Data Processing*-the transformation of raw data elements into comprehensible information; the data processing cycle includes input, process, and output phases.
6. *Digital Computer*-a machine useful for business application; presents deterministic solutions to well-structured problem sets; akin to hand-held calculators.
7. *Distributed Intelligence*-local processing and storage of data accomplished by dispensing computer memory units throughout a firm.
8. *Electronic Data Processing (EDP)*-the transformation of data to information through electronic equipment; used to describe an automated data processing system.
9. *Environment*-anything outside a data processing system that affects or is affected by its operation.
10. *Feedback*-information explaining the variance between actual and potential operational experiences; a critical mechanism for monitoring a business system.
11. *Foodservice Information Systems (FIS)*-the movement of documentation and communication throughout a restaurant operation; analysis of a firm's most important resource, information.
12. *Human Engineering*-a change in job orientation away from clerical data processing functions to tasks requiring more decision-making capability.
13. *Information*-that which adds to what is known or alleged; resultant output of a data processing system.
14. *Input*-the initial phase of the data processing cycle; refers to the capture and coding of data for further processing.
15. *Knowledge*-something that adds to what is already known or alleged.
16. *Output*-the final phase of the data processing cycle; refers to the reporting and/or storage of information produced.
17. *Process*-the intermediate phase of the data processing cycle; refers to the arithmetic and logical manipulation of input data to yield output information.
18. *Source Document*-the original recording of a transaction; also serves as the basis for support documentation to prove a transaction.
19. *System*-an orderly arrangement of component parts necessary to accomplish some purpose; normally composed of subsystem components.
20. *Throughput*-a measure of computer system efficiency; describes the

DATA PROCESSING CONCEPTS

time required to transform input data to output information by the machine.
21. *Turnaround Time*–a measure of the time from when a user submits input data to a data processing system and receives output information back.
22. *Uncertainty*–deals with the improbability of outcomes related to a specific event; refers to an unknown variable in the decision-making process.

3

Computer Operating Systems

Chapter Objectives

1. To sketch the brief historical development of computer components and systems

2. To present the common characteristics and components of a computer system

3. To explain hardware and software concepts in a comprehensible manner

4. To illustrate various options for the participation of business firms in computer-assisted systems

Although the hospitality industry did not begin participating in computerized information systems until the late 1960s, some other businesses became involved in the early 1950s. The advent of the computer not only changed the field of data processing, but it also affected the entire workings of the business organization. In order to develop an appreciation of and understanding for the contributions, dynamic modifications, and extensions made by computer technologists, this chapter presents a brief review of computer operating systems and their effect on the business firm. Since only a general knowledge of computers is required for their use, the material presented here is not limited to any specific computer system.

Experts in the field of computer technology often refer to the continuous, on-going progressions of computers in terms of generations. The delineation of one computer generation from another is contingent on three factors: 1) the level of computer hardware and software; 2) the type of task and systems application; and 3) the organizational effect created by computer operations.

THE FIVE COMPUTER GENERATIONS

The Generations[1]

The first generation. This generation has been dated from 1953 to 1958 by Withington and is termed the "Gee Whiz" era. During this period, most of the larger American business firms sought to acquire computer machinery only to appear progressive. Few firms could cost-justify their expenditure, and the applications of the system were confined to the most formalized, easiest-to-program organizational functions (for example, payroll processing). Since the applications centered primarily around accounting procedures, the company's controller, or financial officer, was usually assigned to the system. The computers of this generation, limited to routine tasks, did not have much effect on the overall operations of the firm. They were very large, bulky units made up of heat-producing vacuum tubes that occupied a large room in an obscure part of the building. There was not much interaction between the computer specialists and the organizational management.

The second generation. Although the application technology remained primarily oriented to well-structured tasks, more rapid access to

---

[1] Frederic G. Withington, "Five Generations of Computers," *Harvard Business Review*, July–August, 1974, p. 100.

information was demanded. It was during this "Paper Pusher" period, 1958 to 1966, that software became recognized as an important resource, and the computers of this time could handle large volumes of input data and informational output. The business organization began to support programmer groups and developed internal computer centers. Managers benefited from the increased production of reports, the tighter monitoring and control over operations, and the company's increased ability to track and vary product lines. The first *on-line* systems appeared in the airline and stock-trading industries during this generation, and the transistor replaced the vacuum tubes of the first generation. These inquiry systems began a new approach to information handling, and the question of who should control the changing computer system and its operators arose.

The third generation. Advancements in integrated circuit technology, transistors, and related component parts made remote terminals feasible during the era of the "Communicators" (1966–1974). The centralized computer and its satellite terminals forced divisional managers and other organizational personnel to give up some control of their internal data processing. With the introduction of time-sharing, many users became capable of simultaneous interaction with the computer, allowing for the distribution of more timely information to all levels of the firm. This increased level of communications was accompanied by a centralization of control, reduced system-response times, and improvements in customer service.

The fourth generation. Begun in 1974 and expected to terminate in the early 1980s, this generation introduced the concepts of data-base management, floppy disk and bubble memory units, and the development and implementation of inexpensive satellite minicomputers. The "Information Custodians" of this time are concerned with the capture and storage of large volumes of information so that relevant data can be applied to more decisions, in a more timely manner than ever before. Increasingly, more raw data are being partially processed at their time of input and are being stored as finished bits of information, rather than as scattered pieces of alpha and numeric data. The application of remote terminals, with intelligence, has allowed for an increase in the decentralization of decision making and provides a more comprehensive knowledge of the overall business situation to personnel located in the field. The computers of this generation were faster, less expensive, and more compact than before.

The fifth generation. Easy-to-use programming and file manipulation languages are expected to follow in the "Action Aids" era starting around mid-1980. Computer experts envision personalized information systems in which individual users can program and have small summarized data files

COMPUTER OPERATING SYSTEMS

FIGURE 3-1 Technological Generations of Computing

FIRST GENERATION: VACUUM TUBES

Computer Hardware Characteristics:
- slow (1/1000 second)
- bulky (required lots of space)
- gave off lots of heat (required venting)
- a millisecond operating system (10^{-3})

SECOND GENERATION: TRANSISTORS

Computer Hardware Characteristics:
- faster than predecessor (1/1,000,000 second)
- improved amplification of system signals
- development of the transistor chip
- progress from miniaturization to subminiaturization to microminiaturization
- a microsecond operating system (10^{-6})

THIRD GENERATION: INTEGRATED CIRCUITS

Computer Hardware Characteristics:
- silicon chip technology
- very small (usually 1/1000 of sq. in.)
- required very little power to operate
- fast (1/1,000,000,000 second)
- a nanosecond operating system (10^{-9})

FOURTH GENERATION: LASER BEAM (LSI)

Computer Hardware Characteristics:
- distributed information systems using laser beams
- large-scale integration (LSI)
- combining voices, data, and graphics
- output printing in pages, not lines
- a picosecond operating system (10^{-12})

---

for independent analysis. Also, more realistic decision-making models are expected because of more data availability and an increased understanding of the relationships among the data variables. The system will most likely be composed of minicomputers that can perform many local operations and be tied into a central mainframe for centralized filing and production applications. Independent decision analyses based on a comprehensive awareness of the decision variables will be a routine procedure.

COMPUTER OPERATING SYSTEMS

Table 3-1 Facets of Computer Evolution

Name	Period	New hardware	New software	New functions	Organizational location	Effect on organization
Gee whiz	1953–1958	Vacuum tubes, magnetic records	None	Initial experimental batch applications	Controller's department	First appearance of technicians (with salary, responsibility, and behavior problems); automation fears among employees
Paper pushers	1958–1966	Transistors, magnetic cores	Compilers, input/output control systems	Full range of applications, inquiry systems	Proliferation in operating departments	EDP group proliferation, some workers and supervisors alienated or displaced; introduction of new rigidity but also new opportunities
Communicators	1968–1974	Large-scale integrated circuits, interactive terminals	Multifunction operating systems, communications controllers	Network data collection, remote batch processing	Consolidation into centrally controlled regional or corporate centers with remote terminals	Centralization of EDP organization; division data visible to central management; some division managers alienated; response times shortened

Information custodians	1974–c.1982	Very large file stores, satellite computers	General-purpose data manipulators, virtual machines	Integration of files, operational dispatching, full transaction processing	Versatile satellites instead of terminals, with control still centralized	Redistribution of management functions, with logistic decisions moving to headquarters and tactical decisions moving out; resulting reorganization; field personnel pleased
Action aids	c. 1982–?	Magnetic bubble and/or laser-holographic technology; distributed systems	Interactive languages, convenient simulators	Private information and simulation systems, intercompany linkages.	Systems capabilities projected to all parts of organization; networks of different organizations interconnected	Semiautomatic operating decisions; plans initiated by many individuals, leading toward flickering authority and management by consensus; greater involvement of people at all levels; central EDP group shrinkage.

Source: Reprinted by permission of the Harvard Business Review. An exhibit from "Five Generations of Computers" by Frederic G. Withington, (July/August 1974). Copyright © 1974 by the President and Fellows of Harvard College; all rights reserved.

FIGURE 3-2 Computer Information and Control Flow

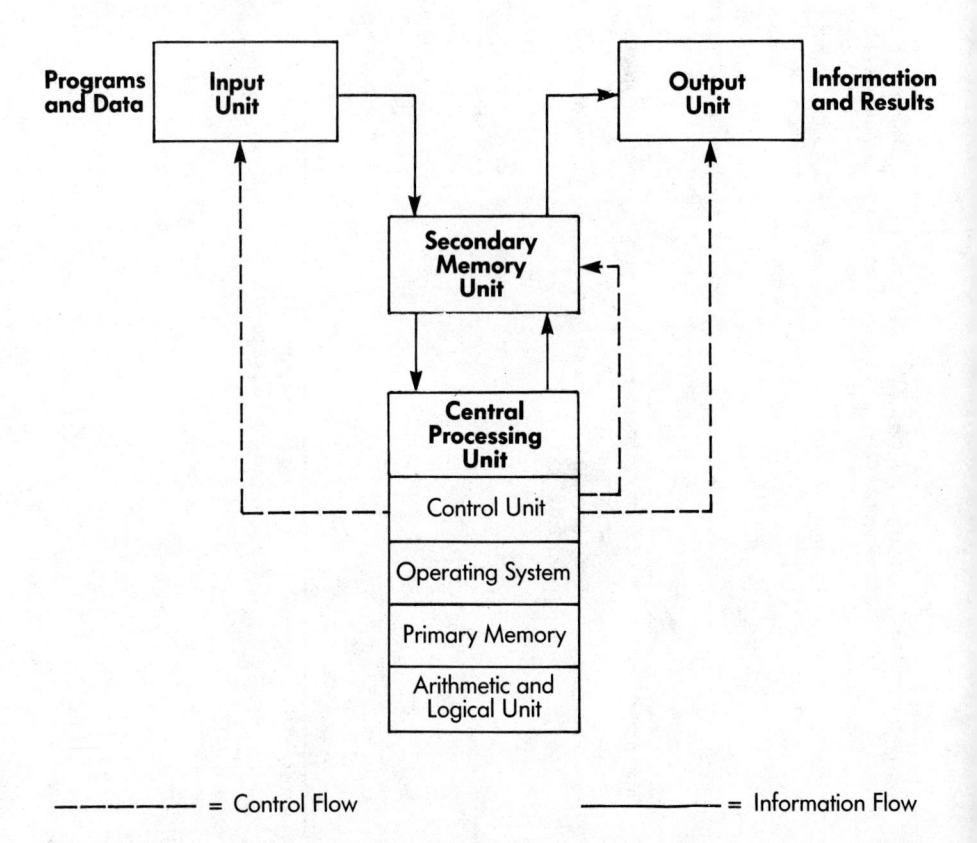

```
Programs      Input                          Output      Information
and Data      Unit                           Unit        and Results

              Secondary
              Memory
              Unit

              Central
              Processing
              Unit
              Control Unit
              Operating System
              Primary Memory
              Arithmetic and
              Logical Unit
```

———————— = Control Flow   ———————— = Information Flow

Throughout the evolution of the generations, Withington identifies a single ultimate objective: ". . . the machine that can collect, organize, and store all existing data, then apply them [the data] both to conducting routine operations in an optimum way and to supporting management actions."[2] The information contained in Table 3-1 is a classic summary of the past, present, and future characteristics of the facets of the computer evolution.

Special attention to the fourth and fifth generations is paramount for today's managers, as the state of the art proceeds to run its course. Figure 3-1 summarizes the characteristics of the technological advances made during the first four generations. The fifth has yet to occur, so no technological achievements are listed under that heading. The major areas of computer-design advancement have been in the following categories: 1) speed, 2) size,

[2]Withington, "Five Generations of Computers," p. 105.

3) cost, 4) operation, and 5) overall technology. Coincidentally, these same categories usually are cited as the advantages of a computer system over a manual or mechanical system.

BASIC COMPUTER FUNCTIONS

All computer systems are composed of three basic hardware component parts and five functional areas of operation (see Figure 3-2). These components are the *central processing unit* (CPU), the *memory unit*, and the *input and output unit(s)* (I/O). The functions are input, output, memory, control, and arithmetic and logical operations.

The CPU is made up of the *arithmetic and logical unit* (ALU) in which all calculations and manipulations of the data take place. A control unit in the CPU is responsible for directing the flow into and out of all *peripheral devices*. The CPU is the controlling unit of operation and the site of computational analysis. It also houses the *operating system*, of special importance to system design.

A memory unit is made up of addressable storage locations. Memory units can operate in *sequential access* or *random access* modes. A sequential access is much more time consuming and inefficient, since data are recorded in chronological order and must be retrieved through sorting (rewinding) and searching. For example, a tape recording of a speech would need to be rewound to recall what the speaker said ten minutes ago. Similarly, on the day a restaurant owner wanted to know sales figures for last year, that date would be have to be loaded into the proper memory component and begin the search for the proper sequence of data. This method would not facilitate rapid access or an effective means of conducting business. Typical sequential media include *magnetic tape* reels and smaller *cassette tapes*.

On the other hand, random access allows for data to be stored and retrieved in any order without regard to chronology. By definition, each piece of data stored in a random-access memory unit should be retrievable in the same amount of time. The data for last year, last week, the last shift, and yesterday should all be available on request in the same amount of time. Random-access memory units include *disks* and *diskettes*.

Information that is loaded (read from input to the memory unit) into the system will be either program instructions or input data and is held in memory until the CPU demands it. Following massaging, or manipulating, in the CPU, the processed information flows back to the memory unit until output, or storage, or both is determined. Storage formats include random access or sequential filing.

The I/O units serve as the communication link between the user and the system. Programs and data are inputed through these components and sent to the memory unit. Here the programs are converted to a machine-readable language for execution. After CPU processing, the output is available through the output devices. Recently, greater emphasis has been placed on the design and development of I/O hardware that is capable of inputing data and programs of variable formats. For example, a deck of computer cards and a terminal connected to the CPU by an *acoustic coupler* can both serve as inputing device formats to the same computer system. The output may also take various formats—for example, printed, punched, sketched, taped, or flashed on a screen. The details of computer hardware and software options are covered in a later section.

The User

Automated systems can be thought of as extensions of previous manual or mechanical processes, and the user's requirements should dictate the system requirements. Generally, the user's needs can be classified as:

1. minimization of costs (economy)
2. ease of system access (availability)
3. reproducibility of results (predictability)
4. simplicity of system operation (practicality)
5. quality of system design (reliability)
6. optimization of output (intelligibility)

The computer system should satisfy the user's demands, yet still afford practical, technical, and feasible machine configurations. The user should specify any special demands so that the system can respond quickly and accurately. The question of legitimacy of future commands, expansions, and reports rests with management.

HARDWARE CONCEPTS

Hardware Components

Although some of the basic hardware considerations have been generally discussed (in CPU devices), many options are available to a system user. The following section lists some of these options, and a later chapter presents possible applications to various aspects of the foodservice industry. Although many of these options require additional peripheral computer hardware, most of the critical devices will be mentioned.

Input Formats

The objective of the input function is to allow information to enter the data processing system as efficiently and as inexpensively as possible. The following devices are presently in use:

1. Punch card
2. Paper tape
3. Magnetic tape (reels and cassettes)
4. Disk packs (hard and floppy)
5. Magnetic ink
6. Cathode ray tube (CRT)
7. Video display terminal (VDT)
8. Graphic terminals (CRT)
9. Optical character recognition (OCR)
10. Mark-sense cards (OCR)
11. Key pad terminals (TTY)
12. Verbal recognition (VR)
13. Touch-tone telephones (TTP)

The punch card, the original input device, is relatively unpopular now as an input format. Although cards are cheap and versatile, paper tapes, also inexpensive, can be stored in small rolls. The use of tapes and disks has become popular with improved computer peripheral input that can be achieved at high speeds. Magnetic ink has the advantage of magnetic input speed and also can be read by the user. A bank check, for example, usually will have the customer's account number in magnetic ink for immediate inputing.

The use of CRT, VDT, and graphic terminals has intensified interest in the field of soft-copy input and display and has been a significant factor leading toward a paperless, or partially paperless, computer environment. The OCR and mark-sense formats are important developments in computer identification of simplified or partial input coding. The use of photoelectric cells within the hardware that recognize optical scanning formats, or printed input, is important to future computer system efficiencies. Similarly, the electric relays of the touch-tone phone pad and the POS terminal key pad have eliminated much of the complex, time-consuming functions involved in developing alternate input codes.

Recent experiments with verbal recognition, which may require a headset and use of a limited syntax (vocabulary), may indicate the future of input formating. All in all, much of the research done in the input area has led to faster and simpler formats for more efficient software loading. This efficiency is especially important in an industry like foodservice, which is described as very *front-end* (input) *loaded.*

CPU Options

The objective of CPU developments has revolved around increased speed in the arithmetic and control functions within the central processing unit. The CPU has undergone extensive technical revisions during the past two decades. Recently developed alternative CPU formats further enhance the processing capabilities of a computer system. A few of these options are:

1. *Macrocomputer (or mainframe)*–a large central unit; one of the older designs; is capable of handling several remote terminals and printers. This large unit usually contains the processor, the memory unit, and the system's power supply. This most expensive format can do *multitasking* and handle a variety of operating systems.

2. *Minicomputer*–An intermediate-size machine, presenting a sound cost/alternative design. Many computer specialists have noted the economic advantages of using a series of minis for branch processing, as opposed to one large computer. This branching is an example of the concept of distributed intelligence. In many branch processing systems, the minis communicate with each other, and if one machine should fail (i.e., go down), then another one can be picked up for immediate use.

3. *Microprocessor*–devices containing microprocessors (i.e., computers on a chip) are termed "smart" machines. Basically, the microprocessor is a silicone chip with an integrated circuit electronically etched onto it. The chip is inexpensive and comes preprogrammed. A microprocessor typically is used to control only one specific function and generally cannot be user-programmed.

4. *Microcomputers*–small-scale CPU, memory unit, and I/O device; also referred to as a personal or desk-top computer. Although initiated as a hobby for do-it-yourself computer enthusiasts, the microcomputer has become an important small-business data processing device. The main advantages of the micro system are the simplicity of operation and programming and its significant price/performance achievements over other systems. Although the microcomputer is not the equivalent of a minicomputer, it is beginning to receive some attention in the marketplace. Soon, some of the limitations of micros (memory size and processing speed) will closely approximate those of minicomputers.

Memory Units

Much research and development has been aimed at improving the memory capabilities of computer systems, since more storage of larger volumes of information is desirable. Recent memory-unit formats (and their access modes) include:

1. Paper and magnetic tape (sequential access)
2. Hard and fixed head disks (random access)
3. Flexible and floppy disks (random access)
4. Digital cassettes and cartridges (sequential access)
5. Bubble units (random access)
6. Silicon chips (random access)

The movement toward mass storage with a minimum of moving parts has produced storage on tapes, disks, and silicon chips. The portability of paper and magnetic tape storage has had many desirable cost benefits. The development of floppy disks and cassettes has further enhanced storage capabilities beyond previous expectations, but the development of the bubble unit has set new standards. The bubble unit works magnetically and can retain large amounts of stored information even when its power is turned off. Of solid construction, the bubble memory is high in access speed and low in power consumption. The bubble memory should make a significant impact on system design in the near future.

In addition to the mode of access, another important system consideration is volatility. A *volatile* memory unit loses all (or part) of its stored information during a power outage. *Nonvolatile* systems retain information even in an energy failure and therefore are more desirable for business system applications.

Output Formats

The purpose of a system's output is to report processed information in the most effective format and at the most efficient speed. The available options are:

1. Printed page (hard copy)
2. Terminal display (soft copy)
3. Graphics output (hard *or* soft copy)
4. Punched card (hard copy)
5. Magnetic tape (hard copy)
6. Paper tape (hard copy)

7. Disk packs (hard copy)
8. Voice synthesizer (spoken)
9. Microfilm and microfiche (hard copy)
10. Laser-beam printing (hard copy)

The printed copy, or *hard copy*, has been the most popular format since written records of output have been produced. Recent attempts at *soft copy*, information displayed on a screen, or verbal outputs (using a synthesizer) have made significant headway toward a paperless environment, an achievement still in the future. Microfilm and microfiche output are basically photo-reduced and super-reduced films of output that can be stored in a minimal space. The development and implementation of the laser beam as a line printer has revolutionized the format of the printed output page at remarkable printing speeds. Most business-system printers operate at 120 lines per minute (1pm), 300 lpm, or 900 lmp. Laser-beam printers supposedly can produce fifty-five pages of output per minute. System printers are either of an *impact* (strike-the-page) or *nonimpact* (heat process) nature. The nonimpact printer has the fewest moving parts, but the higher price tag.

SOFTWARE CONCEPTS

Algorithmic Design

An *algorithm* is a set of unambiguous rules specifying a sequence of operations that provide a solution to a problem. In other words, an algorithm is analogous to a formula. The design of the algorithm will facilitate effective programming.

Flowcharting is a common technique for algorithmic design. A diagram of the logic of a solution is defined as a flowchart. The flowchart not only depicts the solution to the problem, but it also simplifies the development of an eventual computer program. The three types of flowcharts are: 1) analytical (covers the entire business), 2) system (concentrates on interdepartmental transactions), and 3) program (deals with the requirements of a computer solution).

Programming

A computer program is a set of instructions for system operation or data manipulation and handling. The program is written in a computer language, and the selection of the language is at the discretion of the programmer. Language selection depends on the characteristics of a solution technique, the formulation of the problem, and/or the system design.

Depending on the requirements of the solution, a programmer may try to select the language needing the fewest *programming statements* (lines of code or instruction) and/or the least amount of system-operating time to solve the problem. Programming statements can be identified as being either:

1. processing statements (e.g., A + B = C)
2. control statements (e.g., Go Sub)
3. declaration statements (e.g., REM: this program calculates sales)
4. input/output statements (e.g., formats)

Many different languages and versions of languages exist, and new languages presently are being developed for future use. Some computer languages are machine oriented, others are procedure oriented, and some are problem oriented. Improvements in computer technology usually are accompanied by changes in programming languages. Languages may be referred to as high or low level, depending on how similar they are to the spoken language and how simple the language is to use. Present technology is aimed at producing more high-level languages, as these are the farthest from machine language (i.e., approximate the spoken language) and the easiest for the programmer to use.

Since computers can only handle low-level (object) codes, all high-level (source) codes must be converted to be machine-readable. A *compiler* is the hardware device that converts source code to object code in a computer system. Compilers are not inexpensive. An alternative to a compiler is an interpreter.

Frequently, users equate changing prices assigned to preset keys, for example, with programming. This procedure is really not programming but rather data file updating. A change in programming would enable a different routine to be followed once the price was picked up. Merely changing the price (data) does not alter the logic (program).

Operating Systems

An *operating system* is basically a program, or series of programs, that is part of a piece of hardware designed to maintain the continuous operation of a computer system. If the computer system had to be monitored and controlled by a human operator at all times, most of its speed and economic advantages would certainly decrease. The operating system is an automated collection of program components designed to control the use of system resources, track system use and charges, and to maintain overall control of the system's operation. Because operating systems are comprised of both hardware and software, they are often called *firmware*. The operating system is housed in the CPU and contains the logic of the system. It is created by the manufacturer and differentiates one system from another. A system that operates on multiple job streams with high levels of efficiency is obviously more desirable than one that is constrained and restrained.

Software Systems

The term *software* incorporates both instructions and data in a computer system. The two types of software are *system software* and *application software*. System software is the responsibility of the manufacturer. Application software is at the discretion of the user.

A program has been defined as a set of instructions designed to direct the computer to perform certain operations in a predetermined order. However, programming is not a simple task. The instructions must be in a code that the computer can understand, requiring the use of a machine language. No two computers have the same machine language, and user programs are generally not transferable from system to system. In fact, because of the complexity of machine languages, programs are written in either an assembly language or in a translation language, to be converted to the machine format by an internal computer-system device. An object program, written in a machine-readable language, is essential for computer processing.

Application software. An *assembly language* is machine oriented and closely related to machine language. Because of this machine orientation, this system language is thought of as hardware oriented, not problem or people oriented. Assembly programs are read into the computer system through a processor that converts the program instructions into the proper machine language. The machine language program is then operated upon. The assembly language is simply an abbreviated machine language that is less complicated and requries much less rigorous detail. These languages are referred to as "low-level" languages since they are more closely akin to machine requirements.

A translating system is based primarily on a problem application, rather than on the specifics of the computer hardware. The languages of a translating system are "high-level" languages in that they are located farthest away from the eventual machine code requried by the computer for execution. Since most of these languages closely resemble the spoken languages (i.e., BASIC, COBOL, FORTRAN, and APL), the computer system requires a compiler for conversion. The compiler operates similarly to the processor discussed in the assembly system. As mentioned earlier, the source program leaves the compiler in an object format for execution.

The main advantage of a translating system is that it is easier and quicker to learn, since it most closely parallels the spoken language. The time needed to write and edit programs is greatly reduced; and because translation languages are basically machine independent, programs can be written for use with more than one computer system.

System software. Additional software found within a computer system includes a series of utility programs (used to perform loading, printing, and other routine operations) and a set of diagnostic programs (used to assist the programmer in error detection). Most computer systems are designed so that their operating systems assist the programmer during program creation, loading, and execution. A computer system comes equipped with system software that will identify the strengths and weaknesses of the system.

Problem Solving

The computer is capable of handling problems that occur only once and those that occur frequently. The rate of occurrence determines the precise approach and programming techniques for solution. The isolation and analysis of a problem area are prerequisites for the identification of problem variables. In other terms, determination of the facts in a situation dictates its programming algorithm. Data gathering, coding, and inputing are performed in a consistent format to the specifications of the program. Processing of the data renders information for output. Problem solving is a function of both the algorithmic design and the programming.

COMPUTER PROCESSING MODES

The three basic computer mode systems are *batch processing*, *real time*, and *time sharing*. In addition to these systems, a special-purpose system may be designed for specific application.

All operating systems have the following common characteristics: a) they handle all input and output operations; b) they handle the scheduling of the system's resources; c) they control the operation of the system's resources; and d) they chart the use of the system's components for accounting and analysis purposes.

Batch Processing

A batch-processing system is best for routine jobs that occur at regularly scheduled times. The system groups programs and data together and then handles them sequentially. Keypunched cards, sorters, and readers are characteristic of this mode. The user has no interaction per se with the computer and must wait until the job is requested, loaded, and executed by the computer operator before obtaining feedback. The time differential between program request, or the beginning of a run, and the availability of the output is the *turnaround time*. The batch-processing system has had inherent time delays in its turnaround, since jobs are processed in succession and on a priority scheduling basis. The decision of which job to mount and when is under the direct control of the systems operator, not the user. Information does not flow directly into a computer device but must await a request. Recent advances have created shorter turnarounds and allow for remote job entry (RJE) batch-processing systems.

Real Time

A real-time system allows the user to interact somewhat directly with the computer. An outstanding characteristic of a real-time operation is that it generates information fast enough to affect the decision-making process involving the input data. Whenever information is available very shortly after inputing, the system is operating in a real-time mode. The real-time device need not be directly connected to the computer and usually does not allow the user to enter programs or alter existing cataloged or library programs. Only input data and outputs from cataloged programs can be found in a genuine real-time system. Situations such as changing status in inventory and/or availability lend themselves well to a real-time mode. The terms *on-line* and *off-line* describe the system's state with regard to direct CPU connection or no connection, respectively.

Time Sharing

Time sharing is distinguished from other forms of computing by its input/output devices, not by what happens at the computer. The I/O devices in a time-sharing system are connected directly to the computer and allow the user to interact directly. This direct connection enables programming and immediate feedback from the computer to the user. Time sharing is rendered somewhat unique in that it allows several users to interact simultaneously with the computer, without any one user knowing what the other users are doing.

Time sharing is possible because of the extremely fast CPU hardware in the computer network. I/O devices are relatively slow and thereby allow simultaneous users to be hooked up. Characteristics of the time-sharing system include:

a) simultaneous access to many users
b) remote terminals located away from central unit
c) simplifed software
    1. Languages are usually a combination of words and elementary mathematics (i.e., high language).

2. Programs are available from a library or can be quickly written.
d) suitability to problems frequently occurring at irregular times
e) cost effectiveness
   1. may require no computer team
   2. terminals may be rented
   3. may require no capital commitment
   4. CPU, hook-up, and file storage costs are usually variable

COMPARISON OF MODES

Although all operating systems have a number of common characteristics, each has specific operational capabilities. The batch-processing system has had inherent problems with its turnaround time, since it uses rather complicated software. Because the system serves each user in sequence, an invalid program will not be detected immediately, and even when it is, it must be debugged and re-entered into the waiting sequence. An example of proper use of a batch system is in the area of payroll. Payrolls normally are produced at regularly scheduled time intervals and can be executed in a routine manner.

In real-time systems, the emphasis is on maintaining a series of programs and data bases. No direct link may exist between the computer and the user, but the user can obtain a relatively quick system response (throughput). This system has been proven especially effective in monitoring inventory, as the status of available stock is well suited to this mode.

Time sharing, on the other hand, involves a direct connection to the computer, and the immediate response of the system makes it all the more attractive. Time sharing can be cost effective and can handle several users simultaneously. A time-sharing design is found in point-of-sale terminals, which are beginning to replace the traditional cash register.

COMPUTER SYSTEM OPTIONS

Computer options involve *in-house systems, service bureau systems,* or *shared systems.* The term *in-house system* describes the situation in which all the required system components (I/O, M and CPU) are located on the premises of the user. In-house systems require that users take sole responsibility for their staffing, use, and maintenance. A service bureau system implies that all the system components are located off the premises of the user. For example, a bank or bookkeeping service that computes and monitors a restaurant's payroll serves the eatery as a service bureau. The cost and responsibility for continuous system operation is purely in the hands of the service bureau management. A third alternative involves the cost and time-sharing of a central system by several users. One site will house the CPU and perhaps a large memory unit. Several peripheral devices will be interfaced for optimum system use. All users pay a percentage for system costs and maintenance and receive automated capabilities at a discount. This option has not been extremely popular in the foodservice industry to date, but it is forecasted to be a future trend.

PERSONNEL IN COMPUTER SYSTEMS

In-house systems that require on-the-premises personnel may employ all, or some, of the following:

1. *Data Recorders*–keypunch operators and typists; in a restaurant the cashiers, service personnel, and secretarial staff that compile data for inputing.
2. *Computer Operator*–person in charge of the overall hardware operation. In most in-house foodservice systems no need for a computer operator exists in this context. The personnel that provide systems maintenance and assume responsibility for systems continuity are closest to this job description.
3. *Programmer*–people who convert data and instructions into language the computer understands. Some foodservice systems come with already-written library routine programs for typical foodservice functions (i.e., service and special functions). Frequently, the foodservice system does lend itself to customized programming by management personnel.
4. *System Analyst*–person responsible for the overall design of the computerized system. The foodservice system is usually designed by both restaurant people and computer systems people. Some of the prepackaged systems modules have been designed for general industry consumption.

USER'S MANUAL

The written instructions that specify the system's operating procedures are called the *user's manual*. This manual usually includes the system's rules and policies, sample data entry forms and output reporting formats, detailed operating instructions, error correction procedures and a trouble-shooting guide for emergency situations. The operating procedures typically cover all the necessary functions required for normal computer use, data handling, resource scheduling, and recovery procedures in case of system failures. Accompanying the user's manual may be a set of training materials designed for employees who will operate the system. Included also may be a separate set for management who will interpret the output and use the system as part of a decision-making process.

SUMMARY

The field of computer technology can be analyzed in terms of its computing generations. Experts delineate five distinct time frameworks and identify significant system characteristics for each.

The first generation applied computer technology to routine, well-understood tasks; although the systems were not cost justified, firms acquiring this hardware were viewed as progressive.

The second generation dealt with the demand for more rapid access to information. During this generation, software became an important resource, and the first on-line systems were applied in the area of airlines and stock market trading.

The next generation benefited from advances in the electronics field. Remote terminals, cabled to a central processor, became reality.

Fourth generation technology is involved with satellite minicomputers and the development of enormous data bases. Decision making is becoming more decentralized because of distributed intelligence and a better comprehension of the business environment.

Predictions for fifth generation systems include personalized information systems in which individual users can program and maintain summary files. Even more realistic decision models are expected as a result of more data availability and an increased understanding of the relationships among decision variables.

Computer systems are composed of three component parts: the CPU, memory unit, and I/O devices. Through the input component, the user requests programs and data for execution. The input is received by the memory unit that assigns it to a storage area. The CPU controls the flow of information and messages within the system and directs the program and data from the memory to the CPU for processing. Following the computational run, the CPU directs the program and output back to the memory unit for storage and/or outputing. The CPU then controls the movement from the memory unit to the output component. The user receives the output from a prespecified output device. The overall system requirements are essential for network continuity of the system controls.

The user's needs are essential for the design of a feasible computer system. Considerations of economy, availability, predictability, reliability, and intelligibility are important for a system that can respond to the user's requests. The computer programmer normally chooses the language requiring either the fewest number of programming statements to execute or the minimum operating time to generate a desired output. Similarly, the development of a flowchart depicting the algorithm also can facilitate the programming. The computer's approach to problem solving is a function of the algorithm and the programming technique.

The three computer-operating modes are batch processing, real time, and time sharing. Each mode has special characteristics that make it more suitable to a given situation than either of the other two.

Batch processing is best for routine problems that occur frequently. The inherent problem with the batch system is that only one program is executed at a time. Requested programs must wait in sequence until the operator calls for them.

A real-time mode allows the user to employ a set of cataloged programs and to update the status of the data in the programs at almost any time. The real-time system may not afford the user direct interaction with the computer, but it does permit a reasonably quick systems response.

The time-sharing system is composed of satellite terminals directly linked to the central computer. The user can interact with the computer to program or operate existing programs with instantaneous feedback. Time sharing has been shown to be potentially cost effective, since a capital outlay may not be required and only variable rentals and operating expenses may be incurred.

KEY CONCEPTS

The following concepts were introduced in this chapter. Their meanings should be completely understood.

1. *Acoustic Coupler*–a system device used in a telecommunications application; a modem unit through which computer signals are transported to a telephone line and vice versa.
2. *Algorithm*–a formula for solution; a computerized approach to problem solving.
3. *Application Software*–instructions oriented toward user needs, not system needs. Application software is under the control and discretion of the user. Typical application software includes spreadsheet analysis, word processing, and data base management.
4. *Arithmetic and Logical Unit (ALU)*–the component part of the CPU responsible for the mathematical and sorting capabilities available through a computer system.
5. *Assembly Language*–a low-level language easily interpreted by a computer system. Assembly language programs operate at the highest levels of efficiency and power.
6. *Batch Processing*–a method of data processing in which all input data must be grouped together and entered simultaneously for processing to take place.
7. *Casette Tape*–a magnetic, sequential storage medium.
8. *Central Processing Unit (CPU)*–the most important component of a

computer system; referred to as the "brains" of the system; contains the ALU, control unit, operating system, and primary memory.
9. *Compiler*-a device required to convert a high-level language computer program to a machine-readable, low-level language.
10. *Disk*-a random-access storage medium.
11. *Diskette*-a removable, random-access storage medium; also called a floppy disk; usually available in 5¼ in. and 8 in. diameter sizes.
12. *Firmware*-describes the operating system component of the CPU; responsible for system logic, priorities, and optimal use of system resources.
13. *Flowchart*-a schematic drawing detailing the flow of documentation and information in a data processing system.
14. *Front-end Loaded*-describes an information system that has a large volume of input data compared to a relatively small amount of output.
15. *Hard Copy*-a printed page output format.
16. *Impact Printer*-a hard copy device that prints by punching letters onto a page; a device with a large number of moving parts.
17. *In-house System*-a computer system in which all required component parts are located on the same premises.
18. *Input Unit*-the hardware component used to communicate user data and instructions to the CPU; can be on-line or off-line.
19. *Macrocomputer*-a very large computer system that can handle numerous peripheral devices, users, and programmable options; also termed a mainframe computer.
20. *Magnetic Tape*-a magnetic, sequential storage medium.
21. *Memory Unit*-the hardware component responsible for storing data and instructions in a computer system; correctly labeled as the secondary memory if located outside the CPU.
22. *Microcomputer*-a small version of the macrocomputer; restricted number of peripherals, users, and capabilities available.
23. *Minicomputer*-an intermediate-sized computer system; characteristics range between the micro- and macrocomputer system specifications.
24. *Multitasking*-describes the ability of a CPU device to process more than one stream of data at a time; multiple job execution.
25. *Nonvolatile*-describes a memory device that does not lose stored data when its power is lost.
26. *Nonimpact*-a line printing technique depending on heat exchanges between heat-sensitive surfaces and paper. A key does not strike a ribbon to print.
27. *Off-line*-refers to an electronic state in which an input device is not directly connected to the CPU device.
28. *On-line*-refers to an electronic state in which an input device is directly connected to the CPU device.

29. *Operating System*–see Firmware.
30. *Output Unit*–describes the hardware device responsible for displaying or printing an information system's output.
31. *Peripheral Device*–a hardware component located outside the CPU.
32. *Programming*–the production of logical, unambiguous instructions for operating computer hardware; also called software.
33. *Programming Statements*–lines of computer code used to direct and control the flow of operations within a computer system.
34. *Random Access*–the ability to store or retrieve any piece of data stored in a system in the same amount of time as any other piece of data.
35. *Real Time*–describes a computer operating mode in which output is received quickly enough to affect the decision-making process; instantaneous output.
36. *Sequential Access*–the ability to store or retrieve data from a storage medium via chronological or rank ordering only.
37. *Service Bureau System*–describes a computer use option in which all the required component parts are located outside the user's premises.
38. *Shared System*–a computer use option in which computer components are located on and off the user's premises.
39. *Soft copy*–a displayed output format.
40. *System Software*–instructions oriented toward continuous system operation, not user applications. Typical system software includes diagnostics and self-testing routines. System software is provided by a system's manufacturer.
41. *Time Sharing*–a computer system that gives many users simultaneous access to a CPU device without any one user being aware of what any other one is doing.
42. *Turnaround Time*–a measurement of system efficiency. Computation of elapsed time between data input and informational output.
43. *User*–person using a computer system.
44. *User's Manual*–guide for a computer system user detailing specific operating procedures.
45. *Volatile*–describes a memory device that loses part or all of its stored data when its power is lost.

Cash Register Concepts

Chapter Objectives

1. To present a brief overview of the evolution of cash register technology including manual, mechanical, electronic, and computer-based networking

2. To identify common cash register component parts and their interrelated functions

3. To present an overview of peripheral cash register system equipment

4. To review some of the conceptual and operational procedures involved in effective cash register system design

More growth and technological improvements have occurred in the cash register industry than in any other foodservice-related supplier market. Until recently, the only automated application equipment available to the foodservice industry was the *cash register*. The cash register, originally designed to maintain cash balances, evolved from a mechanical framework, to an electronic format, to a computer-based terminal in a relatively short time. As the register's primary focus shifted away from individual transactions and toward analytical reporting, the cash register became an increasingly more powerful tool. Accompanying the advancements in cash register technology has been the restaurateur's departure from the historic emphasis on menu and meal planning to an emphasis on improving bottom-line profitability. Large, integrated cash register networks containing precheck machines, remote slip printers, automatic change dispensers, and intelligent processor-based components appear desirable to foodservice operators.

This chapter contains a brief overview of cash registers, a discussion of their component parts, and background information about sophisticated system configurations. Although not found in the same style, location, or quantity, most registers typically contain a *keyboard, accumulator windows, customer display, cash drawer, receipt printer,* and *change plate*. These common components are introduced in this chapter. Electronic cash registers (ECR), which can be designed as stand-alone units, master-slave devices, or processor-based systems, are presented in the following chapter. Gaining some understanding of basic computing system components (see preceding chapter) is advisable before beginning this and the next chapter.

AN HISTORICAL OVERVIEW

The first generation registers, identified as pre-1960, were primarily manual in design and operation (see Table 4-1). Keys were very difficult to use, recording required some physical effort, and machine controls were nonexistent.

The second generation improved the operation by implementing mechanical components that increased the speed of transaction completion, while

TABLE 4-1 Cash Register Generations

Time Frame	Generation	Orientation	Technology
pre-1960s	First	Cash Transaction Recording	Manual
1960s	Second	Cashier Reconciliation	Mechanical
1970s	Third	Menu and Meal Monitoring	Electronic
1980s	Fourth	Aggregated Report Management	Automated
post-1980s	Fifth	Enhanced Operational Controls	Teleprocessing

establishing some auditable controls over the register operator (cashier). Management could review recorded transactions and determine the balance of cash expected to be in the cash drawer at the close of business. This improvement was perceived as a major enhancement to the development of cash register products.

As foodservice personnel continued to monitor menu and meal patterns, the third generation of registers evolved with electronic features. Preset recording, detailed tapes, improved control over drawer operations, and electrical wiring to other devices became readily available. Management concerns centered around the menu, and the register more closely tracked the day's transactions via specialized keyboards and peripheral devices.

The current (fourth) generation of registers exhibit both *forward* (customer-service) and *backward* (production) *integration* within the foodservice environment. Descriptive customer displays, automatic tendering functions, interfaces to beverage-dispensing equipment, automatic transfer of credit card settlement, and the development of processor-based technology have reshaped the role of the cash register. Registers can generate aggregated, comprehensive operational reports and track employee time and attendance. They can segment revenues by food groups within month, week, day, hour, and fraction-of-an-hour time intervals. The linking of stand-alone terminals to intelligent, redundant memory networks is also a significant characteristic of fourth-generation cash register systems.

Although not fully developed, the fifth generation of cash registers will take management beyond the standard expectations for the areas of service and control procedures. Customer service will be enhanced by communication equipment that enables two-way dialogue between the server and the production station (kitchen). This format will require an expediter to transport prepared items from the kitchen to the correct server station in the dining room. Since servers need not leave their service areas to dispense production orders, customer service should be greatly expanded. Operational controls over such critical areas as cash, inventory, receivables, and fixed assets will be the other focal point of fifth-generation hardware. An ability to interface large format printers with graphics capabilities, CRT terminals with color tuning, and smart remote access-entry devices will change the way restaurants do business. Many vendors will spend millions of dollars for these and additional developments within the next decade.

CASH REGISTERS: BASIC COMPONENT PARTS

The cash register was designed primarily to record sales transactions and to house cash balances. Somewhat later, a printing device for producing detailed transaction tapes and sales receipt slips was added. Inventory and price controls were added by preset keys, price look-up keys, function keys, and computerized memory. The engineering design of registers shifted from a large number of moving parts requiring much maintenance to a machine composed of relatively few or no moving parts. Many specialized features have been designed to modernize the keyboard, the cash-drawer operation, the computing capabilities, and the information-retention qualities of the device. Computer-based registers can be cabled together to form interactive terminal systems through IRC (interregister communications) technology. Electronic cash registers (ECR) and point-of-sale terminals (POS) are recent register devices that clearly illustrate the extent of advancement in cash register technology. Although cash register designs and capabilities vary widely, the following discussion of basic component parts is representative of registering devices in general.

Keyboard

All keys on the keyboard are arranged systematically to insure proper operation and designed to enhance simplicity of operation. In addition, the keyboard is slanted or tilted (at an angle with the counter on which the register is located) to increase an operator's speed and productivity and to help locate special feature keys. Usually, keys are grouped into these categories:

1. *Amount Keys*–used to record the amount of a transaction. The single largest dollar amount that can be entered from the keyboard is a function of the number of amount keys found on the keyboard. Selection of an appropriate register partially depends on the anticipated size of the largest dollar transactions.
2. *Department Keys*–used to record transactions by departments or by designated units within the restaurant. A department key is depressed in combination with the amount keys to record a departmental amount.
3. *Transaction Keys*–used to record the type of transaction being made. Since there are basically only four types of business transactions, registers usually have a maximum of four transaction keys. These keys usually are labeled cash, charge, paid out, and received on account. Most registers require that the cashier simultaneously depress either a departmental or transaction key when recording a purchase with the amount keys, guaranteeing the creation of a properly documented transaction.
4. *Cashier Keys*–a set of keys used to log the identity of the cashier ringing up a transaction. Normally cash registers carry alpha-coded keys (A, B, C, D, E, etc.) that can be assigned to each cashier. This individual cashier code is recorded for all transactions rung by a given cashier, enabling the restaurant to have an audit trail on all business entered by each cashier.

This key can either be locked on during a cashier's shift or be depressed each time the amount keys are used. Registers that allow the cashier key to be locked in will require that only one cashier works any register during a given shift. The basis for a thorough cashier-reconciliation analysis is provided, since the cashier's code is logged automatically each time the register is used.

5. *Clear/Correction Key*–key, or lever in some cases, used to release all depressed keys before ringing. If the operator should realize that an error has been made, the clear key resets all depressed keys to their full, upright position. The cashier then depresses the correct keys and completes the transaction properly. This feature allows the operator to correct a potential error before it is entered into the register.

6. *Total Key*–used to complete the recording of a transaction. After all the components of a sale have been rung, it is pressed. On most registers, the cash drawer automatically opens when the total key is depressed.

7. *Cash Tendered Key*–used to compute change due the customer. After completing the sales transaction with the total key, the cashier enters the amount of cash the guest has paid and activates the cash tendered key. In the indicator window, the register then displays the balance due the customer. This feature, although not available on all keyboards, does eliminate arithmetic errors by the cashier in computing change that should be removed (disbursed) from the cash drawer.

A simple schematic diagram of the logical flow of keyboard operations is shown in Figure 4-1. Note the order of procedures and the options available to the cashier throughout this process.

Figure 4-2 shows the keyboard of a sophisticated electronic cash register. Many of the concepts discussed here still apply even though the technology has progressed rapidly.

Indicator Panel

The indicator panel provides feedback information while a transaction is being recorded. The indicator panel, typically located at the top of the register, should be visible to both the customer and the cashier. This feature enables the guest to follow all register ringings and provides the operator with an index of the transaction in progress. Each time a sale is rung into the register, the keyboard input appears in the indicator unit. The indicator panel may be composed of simple mechanical number and name plates or may be a sophisticated LCD (liquid crystal display). See Figure 4-3 for an electronic indicator panel display. The indicator panel provides an immediate verification of individual recordings while the cashier proceeds through a series of transactions.

CASH REGISTER CONCEPTS   65

FIGURE 4.1 The Flow of Cash Register Keyboard Functions

FIGURE 4.2 Sample ECR Keyboard

Source: Courtesy of Sweda International

CASH REGISTER CONCEPTS

FIGURE 4-3 Electronic Indicator Panel

Source: Courtesy of Sweda International

Cash Drawer

The cash bank of the register is maintained in the cash drawer, separated into denominational money compartments. The decreasing order of the bills and coins from left to right aids in the careful handling of cash. Registers often will have removable drawers, allowing cashiers to bring their initial bank to the register and to remove their ending bank. This method of cash management usually results in increased accuracy and care in cashier activities. The responsibility for correct cash balances is placed directly on each cashier. Since each bill and coin is assigned a specifc location in the drawer, cashiers who properly sort and store currency will be able to cash out, or reconcile their cash drawer, faster and with fewer errors.

Change Plate

The change plate, also referred to as the change shelf, is an intermediate holding place for cash received from a guest while change is being made from the cash drawer. The cashier places the tendered cash on this shelf (usually located just above the cash drawer) during the transaction in order to recount exactly the amount of cash the guest has tendered. If the cash had gone directly into the drawer, and a discrepancy arose about how much the guest had tendered, the cashier would have no recourse in identifying the amount of cash presented. The use of a change plate significantly enhances the cashier's ability to make change and reduces the chance for a discrepancy.

Accumulator Windows

Accumulator windows display the volume of dollar activity for each classification of sales. The information collected in these registers is a function of the keys on the keyboard that are assigned accumulators. Although most registers have a transparent plastic cover on their accumulator windows, some manufacturers place these displays inside the cabinet to forbid cashiers from seeing them. The assumption is that the information stored in the accumulators could be useful to a cashier interested in falsifying cash balances. If a cashier knew which accumulations were tracking which transactions, cash thefts would be possible. However, the accumulators are usually visible and are used by management to analyze cashier productivity, departmental sales volumes, sales trends, number of customers, and volume of paid-outs.

Receipt Printer

The customer's receipt for each sale is printed and dispensed in the upper left-hand portion of the register. The specific information printed on the paper tape is a function of managerial judgment and the register's capabilities. The printed slip contains abbreviated notations and dollar transaction amounts. This slip is a valuable proof of transaction for the guest and assists the guest in verifying the correct recording of transactions by the cashier. Figure 4-4 is a photograph of a cash register device.

FIGURE 4-4 Sample Cash Register Device

Source: Courtesy of TCA, Morrisville, PA

ELECTRONIC REGISTER ANATOMY

The preceding comments were primarily oriented toward first- and second-generation hardware. Just as the function of the machine became more valuable to managers, so, too, did the application of electrical engineering become critical to the register design.

Third-generation machinery featured many tender key options, expanded clerk/cashier key pad, operator authorization switches, and alpha-character operator displays. The ability to transact cash, credit cards, house account, discount, coupon sales, and checks renders this cash register a broad-scope settlement machine. No longer does management focus attention only on cash reconciliations. Now, the entire spectrum of transactions receives closer monitoring.

Evolving register designs maintain expanded clerk/cashier keys by offering eight to ten where previously only two to four were present. Enough flexibility is provided to allow twice as many employees to work from the same machine, each with his or her own accountability. Operation authorization via key switching, a necessary security enhancement when combined with mode and access switches, offers management a safeguard against register tampering. The implementation of easy-to-read light-emitting diodes (LED) or liquid crystal display (LCD) panels brings customer and *operator displays* to a more understandable level. Transactions become easier to follow and fewer operator errors improve customer service and cashier productivity.

As the register continued to advance to the latest ECR technology, many sound intermediate stages prevailed. Figure 4-5 contains two vendor-developed cross-sectional views of a basic electronic register. The location of a journal printer, receipt printer, and cash drawer should be noted carefully. In the following chapter (on ECR configurations), the reader may be surprised to learn of the many significant alterations register manufacturers have made during their transition to state-of-the-art designs.

Special notice should be given to the keyboard layout and design. Although not a very recent innovation, micromotion keyboards began to appear before the release of a full line of ECRs. The following section introduces this concept as an early ECR application.

CASH REGISTERS WITH ADVANCED KEYBOARDS

Cash registers may be described as intelligent or nonintelligent devices, depending on whether they contain resident memory. They may be capable of one-way or two-way communications depending on how they are interfaced. But, regardless of the characteristics of any specific manufacturer's system, most systems have some form of micromotion keyboard.

CASH REGISTER CONCEPTS

FIGURE 4-5 Cross-Sectional Register Analysis

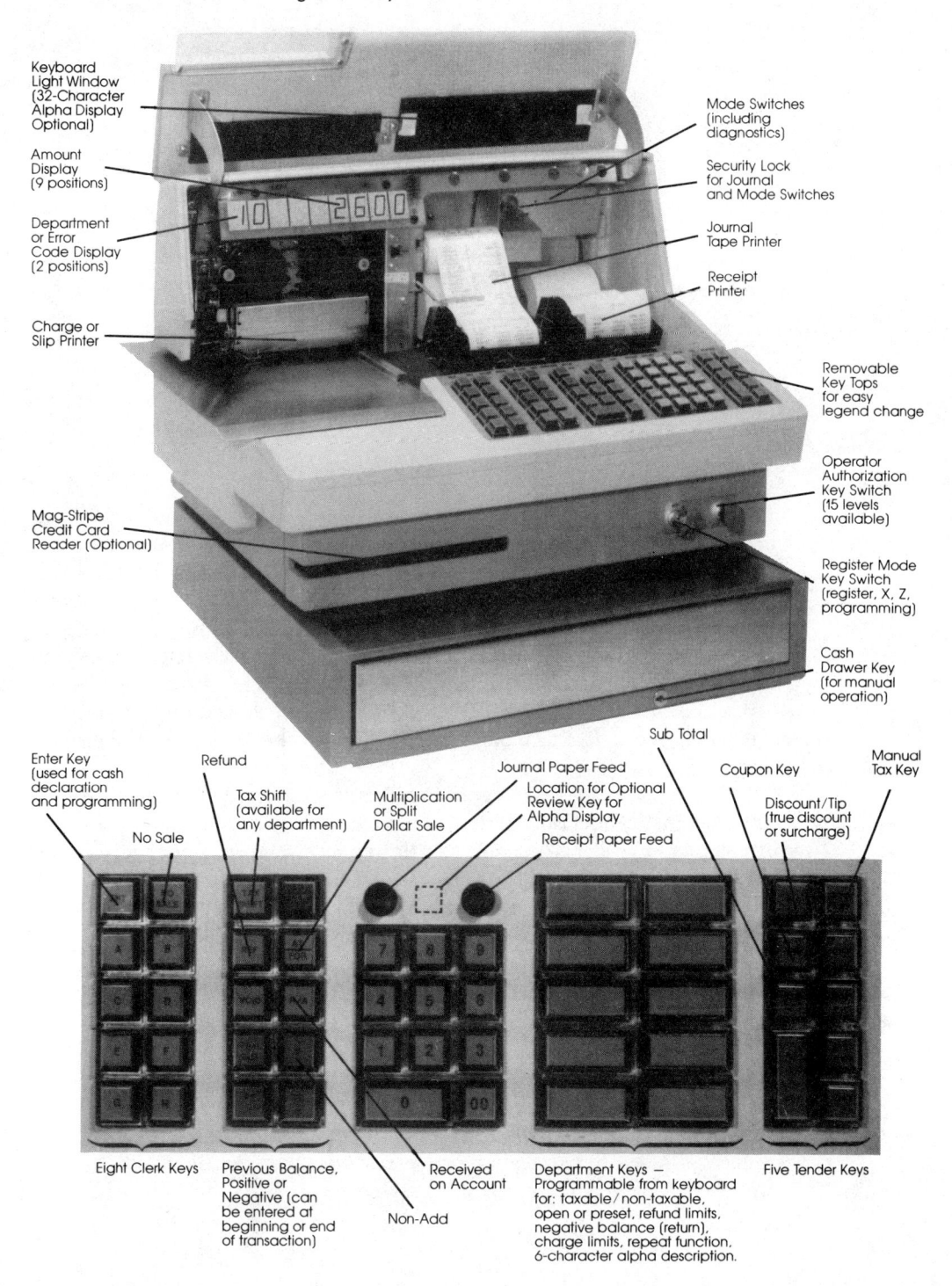

- Keyboard Light Window (32-Character Alpha Display Optional)
- Amount Display (9 positions)
- Department or Error Code Display (2 positions)
- Charge or Slip Printer
- Mag-Stripe Credit Card Reader (Optional)
- Mode Switches (including diagnostics)
- Security Lock for Journal and Mode Switches
- Journal Tape Printer
- Receipt Printer
- Removable Key Tops for easy legend change
- Operator Authorization Key Switch (15 levels available)
- Register Mode Key Switch (register, X, Z, programming)
- Cash Drawer Key (for manual operation)
- Enter Key (used for cash declaration and programming)
- No Sale
- Refund
- Tax Shift (available for any department)
- Multiplication or Split Dollar Sale
- Journal Paper Feed
- Location for Optional Review Key for Alpha Display
- Receipt Paper Feed
- Sub Total
- Coupon Key
- Discount/Tip (true discount or surcharge)
- Manual Tax Key
- Eight Clerk Keys
- Previous Balance, Positive or Negative (can be entered at beginning or end of transaction)
- Received on Account
- Non-Add
- Department Keys — Programmable from keyboard for: taxable/non-taxable, open or preset, refund limits, negative balance (return), charge limits, repeat function, 6-character alpha description.
- Five Tender Keys

Source: Courtesy of MICRO-Z Corporation

FIGURE 4-6 Sample Micromotion Interchangeable Menu Keyboard

Source: Courtesy of NCR Corporation

The implementation of various key pads (preset, price look-up, and function) has been accompanied by simplification processes in mechanical operations. No longer is it necessary to depress a register key with a heavy hand in order to initiate a transaction. In fact, with some keyboard mask designs, the operator's only indication of data entry is the register's display window. Micromotion keyboards minimize the processing time of transactions (by altering physical effort required), offer the foodservice operator a waterproof approach to register maintenance, and allow for the use of multiple menu boards.

Figure 4-6 contains a photograph of a micromotion keyboard with interchangable menu-selection panels. This feature facilitates a quick menu/meal change. In order to accomplish this change, management replaces the register mask and turns a price mode key. These simple procedures allow a registered item to be associated with the proper food or beverage price.

The variety and simplicity achieved from micromotion technology has been of significant advantage to the foodservice industry. Compare this advancement to the flip card menu keyboard pictured in Figure 4-7.

SUMMARY

A heavier emphasis has been placed on cash register developments for the foodservice industry than for any other industry-related product. Cash registers have evolved from mechanical design, to electromechanical construction, to electronic circuitry, to interfacable point-of-sale devices. Although

FIGURE 4-7 Flip Card Menu Keyboard

Source: Courtesy of Standard Logic, Inc.

their design has varied, their purpose still remains the tracking of settlement transactions and cash balances. Registers have six common component parts: keyboard, accumulator windows, customer display, cash drawer, receipt printer, and change plate.

Cash register technology for the foodservice industry can be segmented into five distinct time periods. The first generation, pre-1960, featured manual registers that required the operator to direct the machine's functions. Nothing was automatic, and the register had no controls to allow for cashier monitoring.

The second generation of registers improved in all of these areas. Registers were redesigned for speed of transaction entry, and auditable controls became standard equipment.

The 1970s ushered in the third era. Menu and meal period monitoring became the focal point for internal register operations. An ability to generate menu mix and revenue reports was indicative of the machine's new emphasis from charting transactions to financial reporting.

The current generation of registers offers a multitude of ECR configurations capable of both forward and backward integration. Alpha-numeric customer displays, automatic tendering functions, preset and price look-up keys, and automatic change dispensers have again redirected managements' use of the register.

Fifth-generation registers are forecasted to have built-in telecommunication capabilities (on-line teleprocessing), to use wireless communications, and to be part of a totally integrated foodservice system. Such concepts as electronic store and forward (ESF) and interregister communications (IRC) might become commonplace with fifth-generation hardware.

KEY CONCEPTS

The following concepts were introduced in this chapter. Their meanings should be completely understood.

1. *Accumulator Window*-the component part of a cash register responsible for displaying the journal tape and/or an aggregated transaction total for like items.
2. *Backward Integration*-a reverse movement in the foodservice production cycle beginning with service and going through preparation to purchasing.
3. *Cash Drawer*-the component part of a cash register responsible for maintaining cash balances.
4. *Cash Register*-a piece of hardware designed to monitor transactions and generate managerial reports.
5. *Change Plate*-the component part of a cash register designed to hold tendered currency during a settlement transaction.
6. *Customer Display*-the component part of a cash register that shows the customer what is being rung up in the register during a transaction.
7. *Forward Integration*-a progressive movement in the foodservice production cycle beginning with service and going to revenue analysis and sales mix forecasting.
8. *Keyboard*-the component part of a cash register that the cashier uses to record transactions and/or respond to system prompts.
9. *Operator Display*-the component part of a cash register that shows the operator what is being rung up in the register during a transaction.
10. *Receipt Printer*-the component part of a cash register responsible for producing hard copy documentation of a transaction.

Electronic Cash Register Configurations

Chapter Objectives

1. To delineate the three broad categories of electronic cash register (ECR) configurations

2. To identify the major characteristics of ECR hardware units and system networks

3. To describe configuration design techniques within foodservice operations

4. To highlight essential safeguards and back-up system techniques for computer-based ECR systems

The design and layout of a computerized cash register system may appear rather complex at first. On closer inspection, it becomes apparent that register networks can be categorized into three broad types, based on the location, capability, and interrelationships of component parts. These types of configurations are stand-alone, master-slave, and processor-based.

STAND-ALONE CONFIGURATION

A *stand-alone* configuration is the easiest to distinguish of the three ECR designs. A single piece of hardware contains all the required component parts of a computer-based system. The register keyboard serves as the input unit. The operator (and customer) display, along with any printer options, function as output devices. The register also houses the central processor and memory units.

Figure 5-1 presents a schematic diagram of a simple stand-alone design. Figure 5-2 shows a photograph of a stand-alone device and a receipt printer (interfaced to it). Stand-alone units can be interfaced together to form a restaurant-wide network. Even though stand-alone registers may be cabled together, each still maintains its independence of operation. Since each device has its own CPU and memory and I/O unit, interconnecting them generates a *redundant memory* network. No other form of ECR has this same networking capability. Any transaction entered into one register automatically is entered into the memory of all registers in the network. Each terminal contains a complete memory of all transactions recorded at any entry point. In the case of an individual unit failure, all other devices remain functional and can be used for back-up and/or reconstruction of the memory

FIGURE 5-1 Stand-Alone Configuration

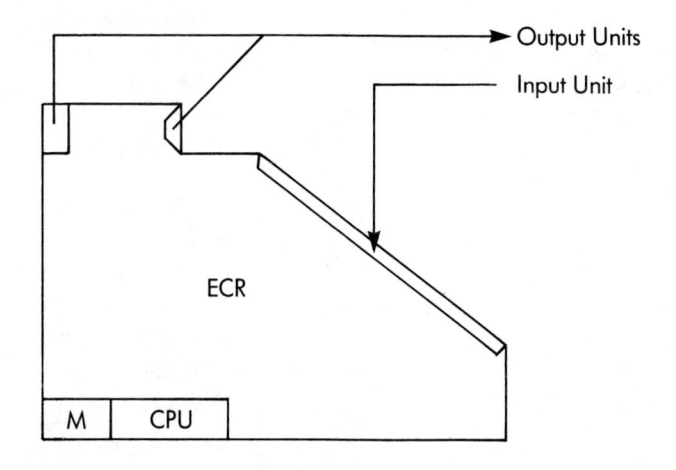

FIGURE 5-2 Stand-Alone with Remote Printer

Source: Courtesy of NCR Corporation

of the replaced or repaired unit. This is not the case with either a master-slave or processor-based system.

Connecting terminals together is termed *interregister communication* (IRC); *distributed intelligence* refers to each unit in the network having its own memory. (Recall that the word *intelligence* denotes memory in an automated system). Figure 5-3 depicts a distributed intelligence, stand-alone network. Because each register in a network contains similar or identical component parts, the cost of stand-alone units tends to remain constant (on a per unit basis). This situation presents a better cost-effective alternative to the operator requiring five or fewer register devices.

Stand-alone units, like other register units, can offer preset, price-lookup, and/or function keys in a variety of keyboard designs. Each design can function as a *precheck* or cashiering terminal (or both) depending on the presence of a cash drawer and slip printer. Typical peripheral devices for stand-alone registers include remote printers (slip, receipt, kitchen, and journal), change dispensers, and multiple cash drawers. Stand-alone devices can also be interfaced to other systems as well as to each other. Even when several stand-alone terminals are interconnected, the total system's memory capacity is

FIGURE 5-3 Stand-Alone Terminal Network

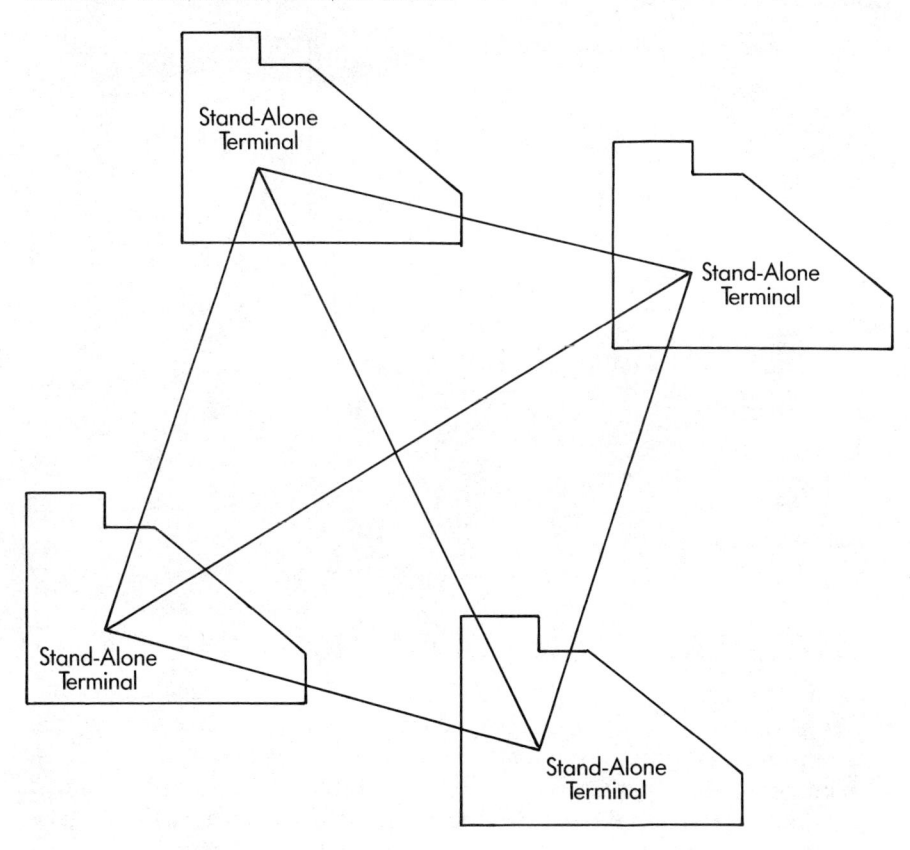

no greater than the smallest memory of any device. Redundant memory does not mean expanded memory!

In fact, to maximize communication and memory capability, a cassette tape recording unit can be built right into the stand-alone device. The cassette tape, which is in addition to the register's basic secondary memory, will also record all transactions rung for a specific period. The tape is then removed and placed onto a cassette playback unit for input to a larger memory device. Holding information inside the register and later transporting it to a consolidating, expanded memory unit is commonly referred to as *electronic store and forward* (ESF). This technique provides an additional memory support for each terminal and allows decentralized foodservice operations more easily to develop centralized data bases. Figure 5-4 illustrates the concept of ESF.

FIGURE 5-4 Cassette Tape ESF Application

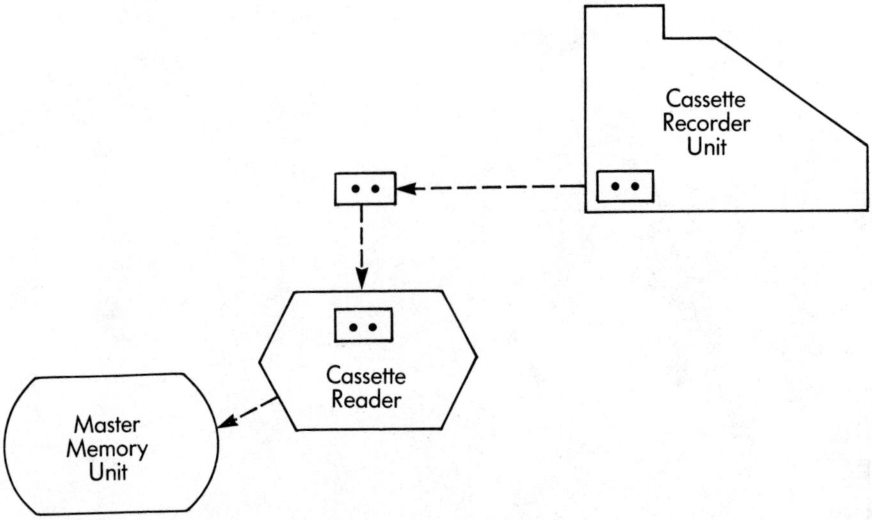

MASTER-SLAVE CONFIGURATION

Although not a particularly popular ECR design, the *master-slave* configuration is an alternative to the stand-alone unit. In a master-slave system, the host terminal resembles a stand-alone unit in that it contains all the requisite computer component parts. In other words, the input/output, memory, and central processor units are all resident in the master terminal. To make the best use of the capacity of this device, several remote terminals can be connected to the master. These slave units typically do not contain memory units themselves and few, if any, processing capabilities. They are basically interfaced to the master register to serve as additional, nonintelligent input/output (I/O) units and depend on the master for transaction processing.

This form of *remote job entry* (RJE) places a heavy burden on the master, which is also a working register itself. The entire network is rendered vulnerable to system failure should anything happen to disrupt the master. The loss of the master will take the entire system down. For this reason, and the fact that processing time may be relatively slow when compared to the two other ECR options, the master-slave configuration has not been widely adopted. Figure 5-5 contains a schematic diagram for a basic master-slave design. Because each slave unit must be connected to the master unit's processor to function, each slave unit is referred to as a *point-of-sale (POS) terminal*. By definition, a POS device must be interfaced to a remote processor in order to function.

FIGURE 5-5 Master-Slave Configuration

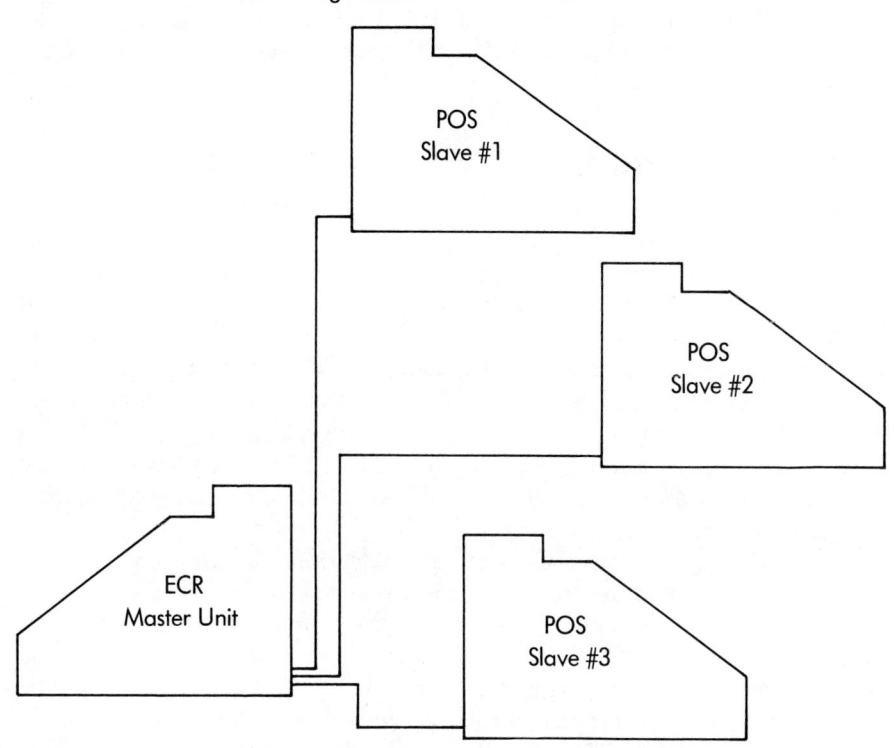

[Diagram showing ECR Master Unit connected to POS Slave #1, POS Slave #2, and POS Slave #3]

Although the master unit may carry a relatively high price, each of the slave units (basically empty boxes) can be obtained at a much lower cost. The master-slave network may present cost savings to those operations requiring more than three, but fewer than seven, terminals. Because each slave unit depends on the master for its processing needs, the master-slave configuration is an example of a *distributed processing* system.

The major distinction between a distributed processing system and a distributed intelligence network, both of which have a one-terminal memory capacity, is the location of the memory unit or units. A stand-alone network involving four terminals has four memory units (one inside each terminal). A corresponding four-terminal master-slave system has only one memory unit (located in the master terminal). The master-slave design thus tends to be less expensive than its stand-alone counterpart. The master-slave network critically depends on its master unit to survive. Master-slave systems can also make effective use of electronic store and forward (ESF) technology.

Because of the nature of its component parts (master terminal performing like a stand-alone and operating as a distributed processing system), the master-slave configuration has some strengths and weaknesses of each of the other two ECR configurations.

PROCESSOR-BASED CONFIGURATION

In comparison to the limited memory and processor power found in the stand-alone and master-slave designs, the *processor-based configuration* is superior. Although significantly more expensive as a network, these systems tend to be especially cost effective in multiple-dining-room restaurant operations. In this system design, each register must be connected to a central CPU to operate and is called a (POS) terminal. Whether or not each POS device has intelligence, the processor-based configuration features a large central memory. Similar to the slave units in the master-slave design, each register serves as a remote I/O device also. The CPU and memory units are housed together, away from the register workstations. Figure 5-6 contains a simple schematic of this configuration.

The expense of a powerful CPU and expanded memory unit renders a system purchase of fewer than four or five terminals difficult to cost justify. The true advantages of a processor-based system are not often found at the front end (input), but rather at the back end (output) of a system application. The ability to monitor a wide range of transactions closely through a central site presents opportunities for greater managerial and operational control.

Similarly, the use of CRT and LPT (large format printer) units can signficantly extend the capabilities of a *data base system*. Along with these strengths come the greatest weakness. Because of the inherent dependence on a central processing and memory unit, a component failure could leave the entire system inoperable. Traditional methods of information and energy back-up may simplify computerless operations, but they will not replace on-line processing capabilities. The only system configuration with independent unit status is the stand-alone device.

Because of the capacity of various system components, processor-based systems offer extensive application software packages. The foodservice operator has a considerable array of store-wide controls and reporting capabilities with this cash register system, even more than some back-office systems. Applications such as time in attendance, financial reporting, inventory management, and menu engineering can be accomplished through a processor-based ECR configuration. Figures 5-7 and 5-8 contain photographs of processor-based configurations. Note the various component parts of each system and the relative size of their processing units. Table 5-1 contains a comparative table summarizing the three ECR configurations.

ELECTRONIC CASH REGISTER CONFIGURATIONS 81

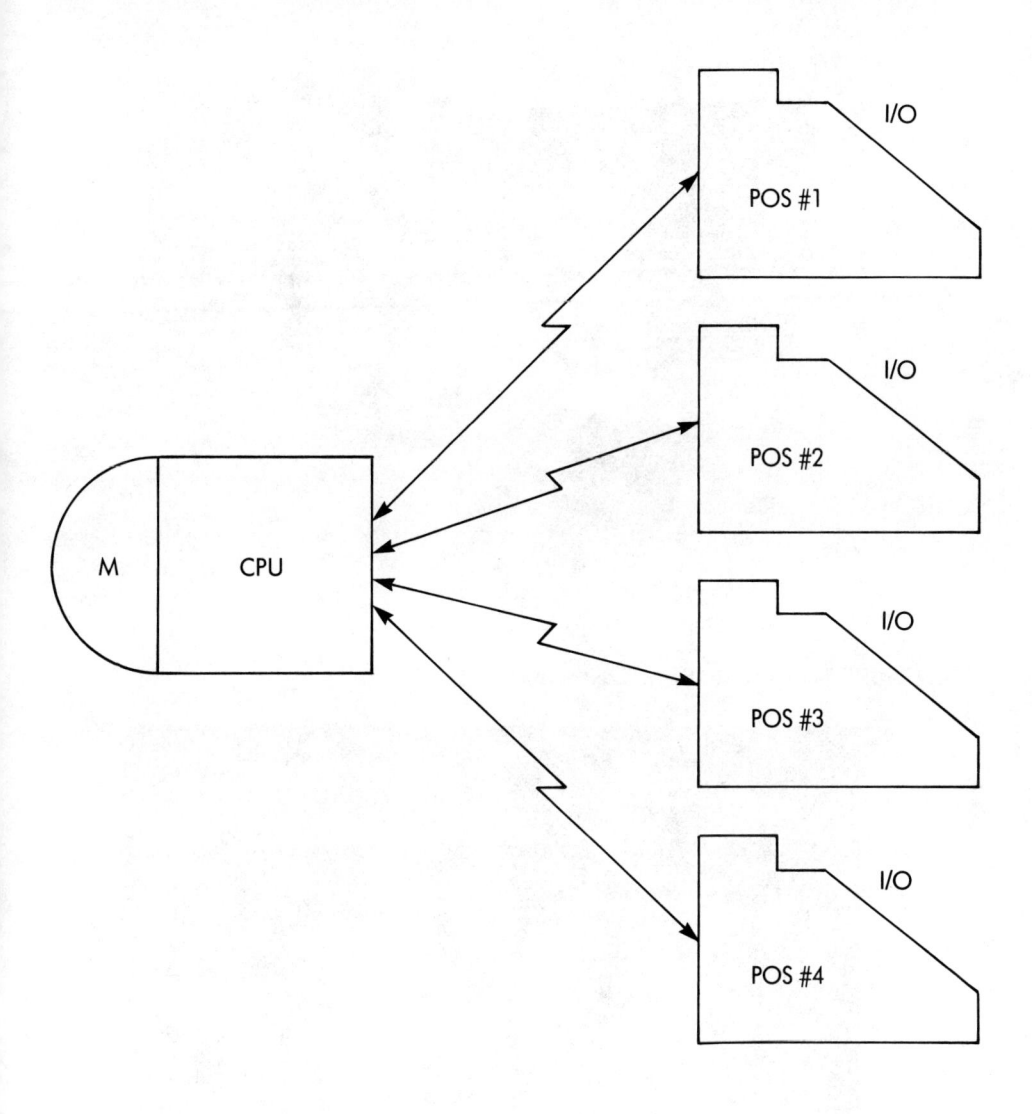

FIGURE 5-6 Processor-Based Configuration

ELECTRONIC CASH REGISTER CONFIGURATIONS

FIGURE 5-7 Processor-Based Configuration I

Source: Courtesy of Remanco Systems, Inc.

FIGURE 5-8 Processor-Based Configuration II

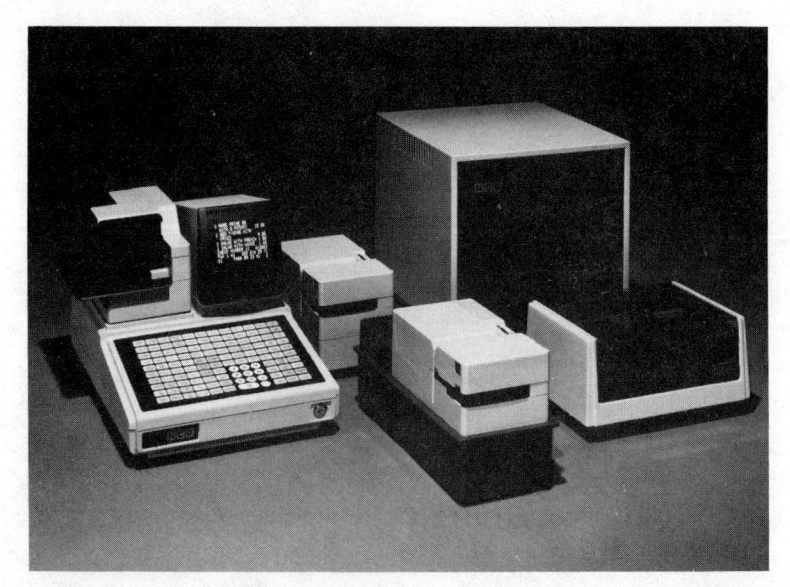

Source: Courtesy of NCR Corporation

TABLE 5-1 ECR Configurations: A Comparative Study

ECR Configurations	Component Parts Central	Component Parts Remote	Key Characteristics	Operating Mode	Network Features
I. Stand-Alone	I/O Memory CPU	None	a. Can operate as a single unit system	Distributed Intelligence	a. Redundant Memory b. Terminal Independence
II. Master-Slave	I/O Memory CPU	I/O Memory (optional)	a. Master terminal is a working register b. Remote slaves may or may not be intelligent	Distributed Processing	a. Limited Memory b. Terminal Dependence
III. Processor-Based	CPU Memory	I/O Memory (optional)	a. Possesses powerful CPU and expandable memory b. Can service large number of peripherals	Distributed Processing	a. Expanded Memory b. Terminal Dependence

SELECTION OF ECR CONFIGURATIONS

The determination of which ECR configuration is most appropriate for a given operation is a function of several factors. Perhaps the most important criterion should be one of microeconomics. The number of points of purchase determines how many registers will be required to satisfy the workload for the foodservice establishment. Given this number, a wise operator should survey vendors by a *request for proposal* (RFP) and determine the break point for stand-alone hardware versus either of the other system designs. Should five or more terminals be necessary, it is very likely that the use of stand-alone equipment will be eliminated. Processor-based technology will probably be chosen. Additional decision factors include ease of operation, reliability of system design, and effectiveness of operation.

The system most closely aligned with preautomated procedures is likely to be the easiest to operate. Beyond this requirement, however, the hardware itself must be simplified and lend itself well to the foodservice environment. Such important *user-friendly* techniques as preset, price look-up, and function keys, as well as interactive programming that leads an operator through a predetermined routine (see Figures 5-9 and 5-10 for a sample of actual system prompts and keys) may be critical. The ability to input the same data into a system and receive the same output is indicative of one type of system reliability. Also essential is the percentage of operating time a system is likely to provide. A system that has a history of poor operations and/or high failure rates should not be considered.

FIGURE 5-9 Sample of User-Friendly Prompts

```
ENTER SERVER ID

ENTRY TOO LARGE

1 T-BONE STEAK

INSERT NEW CHECK
```

Source: Based Upon the MICROS Systems

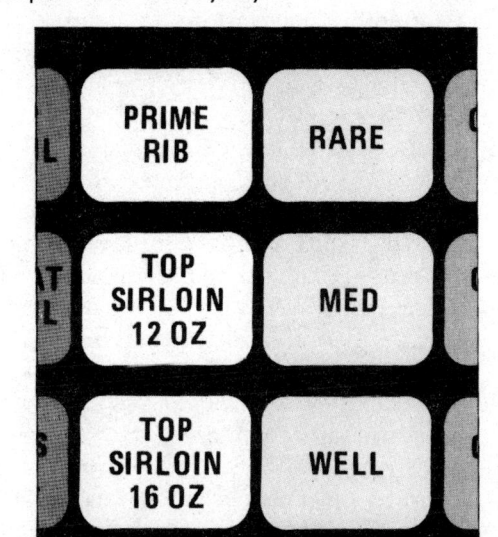

FIGURE 5-10 Example of User-Friendly Keys

The effectiveness of a system is difficult to measure. The two criteria usually applied to this area of evaluation are feasibility and achievement. A system that is operationally and economically feasible receives a more favorable review than one that is not. Similarly, assessing the level of achievement depends on how much more effective management is with the system as opposed to being without it. In essence, system selection is difficult and requires an analysis of numerous factors.

SYSTEMS IN ACTION

Given the preceding overview of the three major ECR configurations, some additional needs should be addressed. Such important considerations as peripheral equipment options and the availability of telecommunications deserve mention.

Peripheral Equipment Options

Although a complete list of peripheral equipment would be endless, most operators focus primarily on *remote printing units, cash-handling equipment,* and *guest-check numbering*. There are four families of remote printers: 1) workstation printers, 2) receipt printers, 3) slip printers, and 4) journal

ELECTRONIC CASH REGISTER CONFIGURATIONS

printers. Each is differentiated by its location, printing capabilities, and principal function. Workstation and journal printers tend to be located away from the register units they serve. Receipt and slip printers usually are located alongside or atop their register devices.

Remote printing units. Most of the expanded capabilities of sophisticated ECR registers can be found in their larger memory storage and superior communication capabilities. One of the greatest advantages of communication enlargement (achieved through remotes) involves improved guest service, efficient productivity, and enhanced management reporting. The ability to print at a remote location, or locations, allows kitchen personnel and management to receive information concerning all transactions at the same time.

Medium- to large-size restaurants typically opt to place workstation printers (also referred to as kitchen printers) directly in food preparation areas. Normally, one printer is placed at the hot food production station and another in the cold foods section. This placement enables an intelligent distribution of hot and cold food item orders to the appropriate kitchen staff.

Figure 5-11 shows a photograph of a workstation printer and a sample of its output. These printing units may be located up to 1,000 feet from a register terminal. Register keys are preprogrammed to trigger printing at a designated printer and/or in a specific ink color. For example, an operation with only one remote kitchen printer may identify cold food items in red ink and hot food items in blue ink on the same piece of paper. Or, all hot food items can be printed in blue and special preparation instructions in red. Having

FIGURE 5-11 Remote Workstation Printer

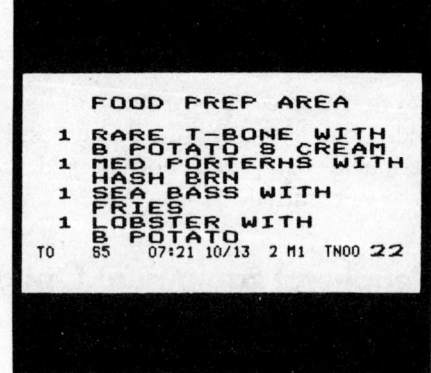

Source: Courtesy of NCR Corporation

multiple ink colors on the same printer enhances the intelligibility of output.

A dedicated unit has only one remote attached to a register network; two or more printers necessitate the addition of a *network controller*. This controller, also called a print controller, buffers transmitted orders waiting to be printed. Figure 5-12 contains a sample schematic depicting the role of a network controller. Figure 5-13 illustrates its use in an ECR configuration. An order is communicated from the dining room to the kitchen without requiring a server to carry it there. Time is saved and customer service enhanced. Operations that employ this precheck technology are referred to in detail in the following chapter.

Remote workstation printers enable a rapid dissemination of information that initiates more efficient foodservice preparation and service. Following preparation, an *expediter* may be used to facilitate efficient service and reduce kitchen traffic. Not only are potential communication problems between server and cook avoided, but foot traffic patterns also are altered. Workstation printers can also be placed at bars, service bars, cashier, and other preparation areas.

Receipt printers are available in a variety of styles and with a number of print head options. Receipt printers normally are attached to an ECR device and serve to generate hard-copy guest checks. See Figure 5-14 for an example of a hardware device.

A legible, neat guest check reduces discrepancies and improves efficiency. Most foodservice operators redesign their existing guest check formats to adapt to an ECR-produced documentation, a minor compromise compared to the benefits derived.

FIGURE 5-12 Role of a Network Controller

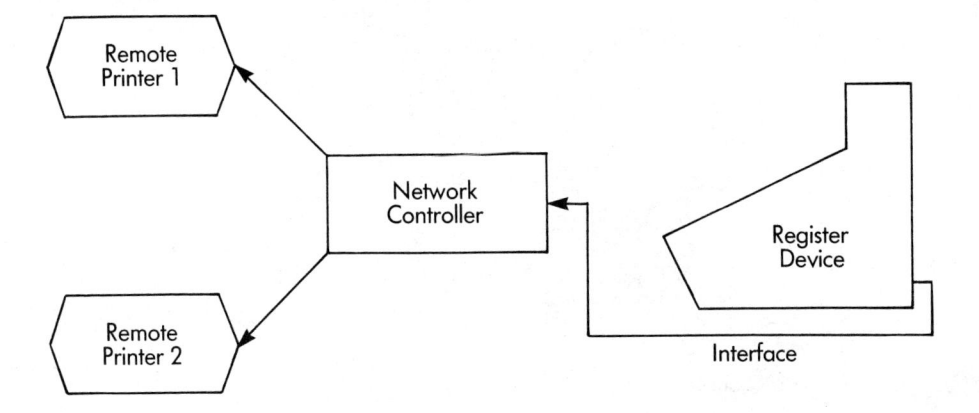

88 ELECTRONIC CASH REGISTER CONFIGURATIONS

FIGURE 5-13 Remote Printer Configuration

Source: Hospitality Financial Consultants

FIGURE 5-14 Typical Receipt Printer

Source: Courtesy of Sweda International

ELECTRONIC CASH REGISTER CONFIGURATIONS

A slip printer also tends to be located relatively close to the register device and can serve a variety of purposes. Fast food restaurants may only invoke a slip printer to print special order requests. Table service restaurants might use slip printers to supplement remote printing units.

Suppose a restaurant requires the prechecking of all ordered items but only uses hot and cold food workstation printers. How could beverages and desserts be handled? These items can be monitored with a slip printer that is dedicated to their printing. When a drink or dessert item is entered into the

FIGURE 5-15 Sample Remote Printer Output

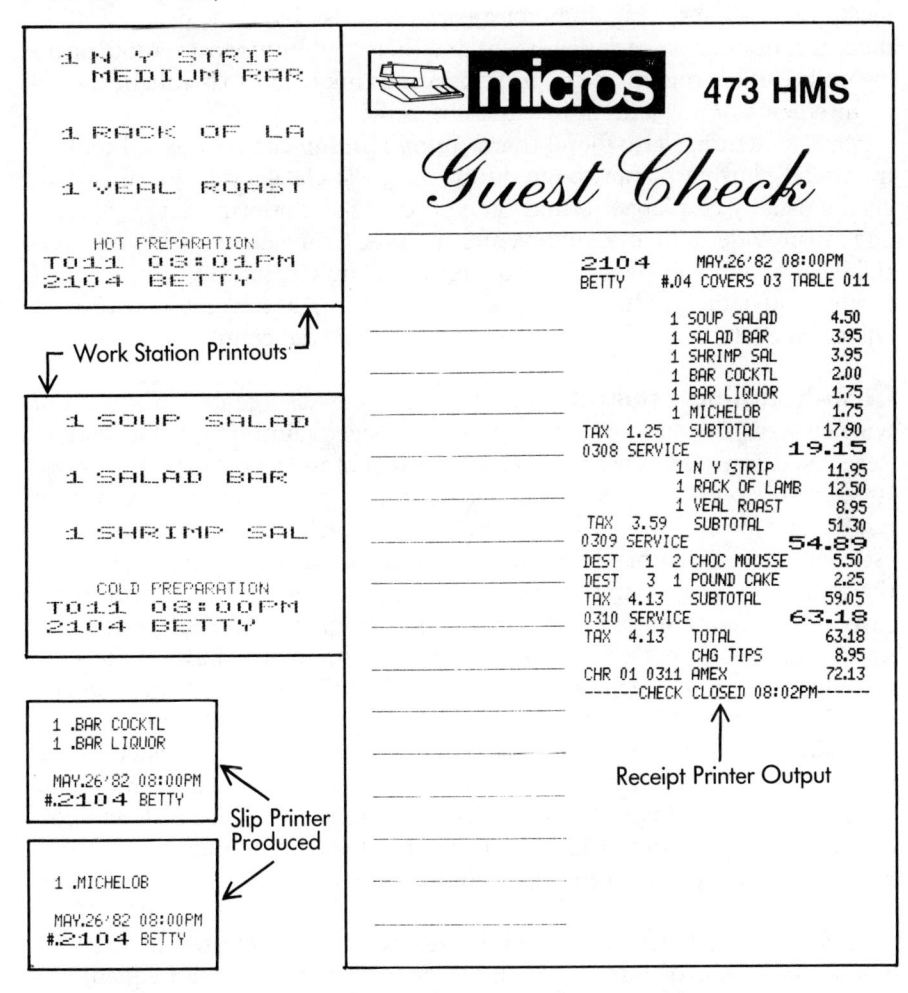

Source: Courtesy of MICROS Systems, Inc.

register, the slip printer outputs those items not communicated to a workstation unit. The server must then hand carry this slip to the correct production area (bar or pantry) for authorized requisitioning. The prechecking gap is closed and tight control over all food leaving a preparation area is insured.

Although the cost of printing units varies among vendors, workstation printers tend to be the most expensive since they require additional hardware (network controller) to function. Receipt printers are the next highest priced, followed by slip printers. Some restaurateurs believe that they need only a series of slip printers in order to gain many advantages of prechecking at about half the normal cost.

Figure 5-15 contains actual systems-generated output from workstation, receipt, and slip-printing units for a party of three. Note the detailed information contained on each document and their legibility. Most remote printing units can be constructed to print in various ink colors to highlight special requirements or preparation instructions.

Management has also found that a *journal printer* can be a useful tool for monitoring business at any point during the guest-check cycle. Journal printers are usually of a larger format than other register-printing device options and can provide audit journal, revenue analysis, financial, and other managerial reports. Major gains from remote printing units include minimization of production time, reduction in kitchen traffic, better table turnover, enhanced customer service, and improved managerial control.

Cash-handling equipment. Cash registers can be designed with or without cash drawers. Many operators consider eliminating this option. Registers designated as precheck terminals do not use a cash drawer. For registers that serve primarily as cashier terminals, management may opt for remote and/or multiple cash drawers. Singular cash drawers offer the greatest control over cash-handling procedures. Operators can place them below the counter or away from the register. Singular cash drawers are connnected to a cash-tendering station. Often, fast-food restaurants have one person ring up an order while another handles the cash. Multiple cash drawers allow for simultaneous cashiering out of one register by several persons. In addition, specific activities can be separated to facilitate future auditing routines.

Vendors claim that the drawer was made a separate entity because of the popularity of cashless precheck machines, server banking, and the increased use of credit cards. Regardless of where the cash drawer is located, an *automatic change dispenser* is another available add-on. Automatic change dispensers are believed to speed up account settlement and reduce cash-handling errors.

To date, most foodservice establishments have not elected to use this device. This lack of interest might stem from the fact that frequently a

FIGURE 5-16 Automatic Change Dispenser Unit

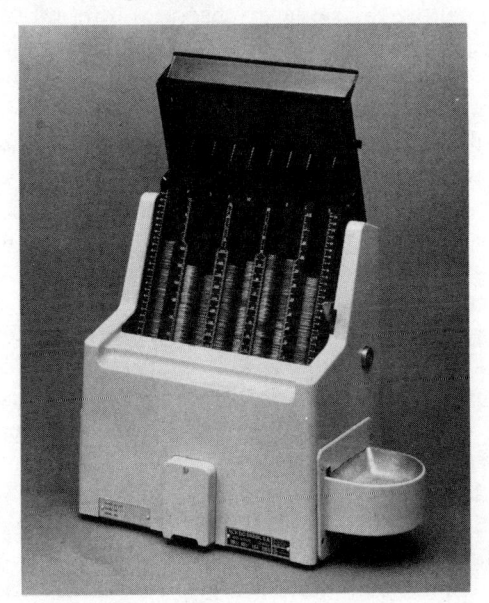

Source: Courtesy of NCR Corporation

check is settled tableside, not at a cashier stand. In addition, most advanced registers are designed to accommodate several different forms of settlement (e.g., cash, credit card, house charge, and discounts), but few involve cash-handling procedures. Figure 5-16 contains a photograph of an automatic change dispenser.

Guest-check numbering. The requirement that a guest check be inserted into a register to enable initiation or settlement of an account is not new to the cash register industry. However, the use of various methods for serially numbering source documents is a new requirement. Guest-check serial codes can be preprinted and distributed in batches to service personnel. At the end of a shift, unused checks, along with all issued checks, need to be collected and audited.

Preprinting guest-check numbers offers tremendous control not available with uncoded checks. The problem with the coded check technique is that the server is required to enter the check serial code each time a transaction involving that account occurs. This procedure can be a time-consuming task, especially if a *check digit verification* number, randomly assigned by the system, must also be entered.

ELECTRONIC CASH REGISTER CONFIGURATIONS

To avoid the bottlenecking that could arise out of this lengthy input procedure, some vendors allow the server to insert an unnumbered check into a register. In this instance, a check number is generated by the system, stored in memory, and printed on the check. The server can initiate this account more quickly than when a preprinted code has to be entered, but a similar entry procedure will be required for all subsequent account activity.

For example, a customer orders a glass of white wine and the server opens a new check by inserting an uncoded form into a register terminal. Before the transaction is completed, the terminal prints a check number in a designated location. The need to batch-issue server checks is eliminated and the work involved in creating an open check is reduced. Now, assume that the guest orders an appetizer, and later, dinner. The server must enter the system-produced serial number with each transaction relative to this account, twice in this example. The guest may also want dessert and after-dinner cordials, all of which will require reentry of the check number. How can this process be improved?

The fastest way to access and/or create a guest account is through the preprinting of a machine-readable optical character code. This code, similar to the universal product code found on grocery store items, can be interpreted by the register and will not require server entry. Each time an additional transaction occurs that affects a particular account, that check is slid under

FIGURE 5-17 Automatic Form Number Reader (AFNR)

Source: Courtesy of NCR Corporation

the code reader located along the normal passage found for check insertion on or near the register. See Figure 5-17 for a pictorial view of an automated form number reader (AFNR).

In each of the check number options described, the system stores the serial number of the guest check as part of a total control system. Other features (such as check tracking and mandatory check insertion) depend on this basic element for monitoring of outstanding as well as settled transactions. In addition, most guest-check printers recall the last line number they printed and are capable of automatic slip feeding (ASF).

Telecommunications and Foodservice

The fastest-growing dimension of the ECR industry is in the area of *telecommunications*. With telecommunications, a central computer can survey participating remote computer devices over telephone lines. This technique is commonly referred to as *polling*.

Since computer systems operate on signals that cannot be transmitted over the phone lines, a *modem* device must be placed between the host computer and its telephone. The modem (which is an abbreviation for modulator-demodular) enables the requisite signal conversion. At the receiving end, there also must be a modem placed between the phone line and the satellite

FIGURE 5-18 Telecommunications Polling Application

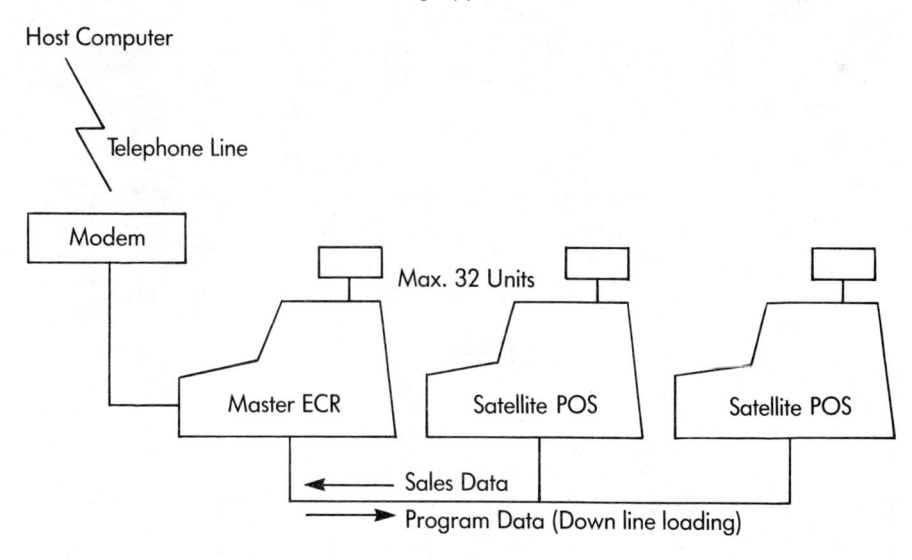

Source: Courtesy TEC America, Inc., Torrance CA

94 ELECTRONIC CASH REGISTER CONFIGURATIONS

FIGURE 5-19 Simplex and Duplex Communication Networks

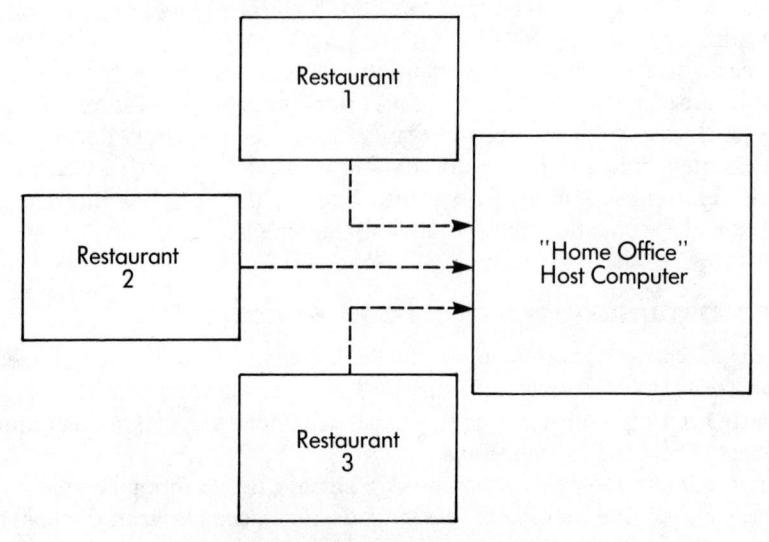

One-Way (Simplex) Communication

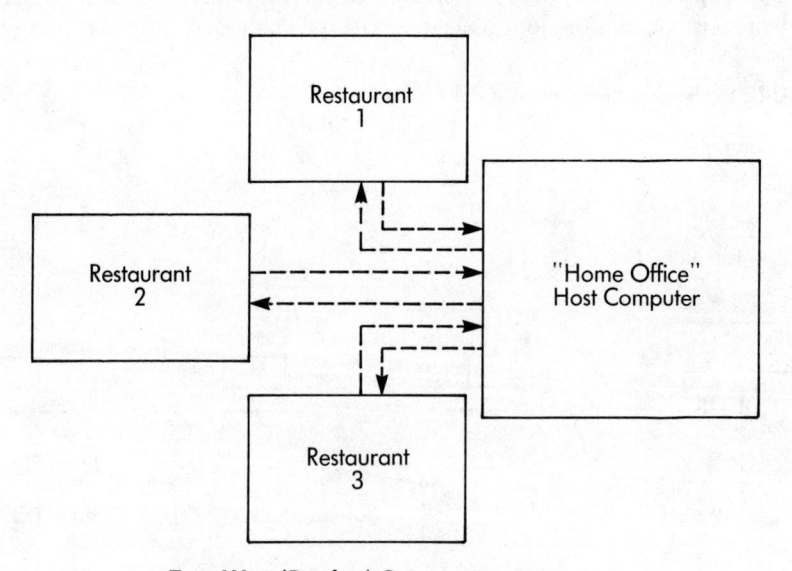

Two-Way (Duplex) Communication

computer. Both autodial and autoanswer modems allow computers to converse, at predetermined times, without any human intervention. Currently, only the largest chain restaurant operators are involved with telecommunications technology (store reporting), but as information needs change, it is anticipated that a majority of foodservice companies will be users. Soon, telecommunications also will reach the foodservice industry in the form of vendor order-entry systems, on-line credit verification, and electronic banking. Its future appears bright.

Figure 5-18 depicts an in-store master-slave (satellite) system designed for polling to a host computer via telecommunications. Note the use of a modem for transmission.

Figure 5-19 contains schematic drawings differentiating one-way communications with a host (simplex) from two-way communications (duplex).

Another use of telecommunications involves the interfacing of a magnetic strip (credit) card reader to a cash register terminal for settlement procedures. On-line verification and authorization screening lead to instantaneous attainment of approval ratings and acceptance codes. Credit card settlement is used by a majority of foodservice customers and is forecasted to be an even more dominant force in the future. The ability to check a guest's card status over phone lines is a valuable innovation. As electronic fund transfer (EFT) programs become more popular, there may be a movement from traditional credit card use toward debit card use. The transfer of cash balances between customer and retailer accounts by teleprocessing will significantly affect the future design of cash-registering devices and business systems.

SUMMARY

The three major classifications of ECR configurations are stand-alone, master-slave, and processor-based. The three types differ based on the location, capability, and interrelationships of component parts. A stand-alone device houses all of its required components in a single, free-standing unit. Although stand-alone registers function independently, they can be interfaced to form redundant memory networks. This redundancy in memory is for information protection, not for memory expansion. The memory capacity of a stand-alone network is not greater than the capacity of the smallest register. Foodservice operators may opt to use electronic store and forward techniques for enhanced data collection, but these tapes must be reentered into an additional memory unit.

The master-slave configuration is not very popular because it creates a critical dependency on one register. The master unit is similar to a stand-alone ECR, except that it has remote slaves cabled to it. The slaves serve as

I/O devices only and depend on the master for all data processing functions. In the case of the stand-alone network, the system's intelligence (memory) is distributed to each register; in the master-slave set-up, the memory is centralized but the processing is distributed to each register. The terms *distributed intelligence* and *distributed processing* apply to the stand-alone and master-slave configurations, respectively. Another distributed processing application is the processor-based configuration.

The processor-based configuration features a powerful CPU and large memory unit, located away from the register units they service. Because of the cost economies of each register network, only operations requiring five or more terminals will find this system easier to cost justify than a corresponding stand-alone series. Processor-based sysems offer extensive software packages and maintain a large data base for analysis. CRT and LPT peripherals can be interconnected to the CPU for large format printing and soft-copy display. A comparative analysis of the three ECR configurations reveals their relative strengths and weaknesses.

In addition to each system's required components, several optional pieces of hardware are available to the user. Remote printers are a popular feature of most ECR networks, particularly in precheck applications. Workstation printing units transmit order information from the service area to the production area without requiring a server to leave the dining room. Receipt printers can reduce potential guest discrepancies significantly and present an important customer service. Slip printers are useful for interdepartmental communications and as supplemental equipment in a precheck system.

Restaurateurs may be puzzled that cash drawers are not standard equipment on many vendor-designed systems. The popularity of prechecking, server banking, and deferred payment plans has kept manufacturers from assuming that every machine will maintain a cash bank. But for operators requiring several drawers at a variety of locations, the cash register industry is prepared. Along with the option of cash drawers is automatic change-dispensing equipment. The change dispensers are designed to eliminate cash-handling errors and to speed up guest settlement. However to date, this has not been a very popular restaurant application.

Perhaps the greatest potential of any system concept available to the foodservice industry is represented by telecommunications. The ability to poll remote computer systems over telephone lines will continue to expand system capabilities and provide management with better information. As smaller chains and multiple-unit operators begin to adopt telecommunications to achieve centralized information, a large portion of the industry will subscribe to on-line credit verification services, vendor order-entry systems, and electronic banking. ECR development in the area of telecommunications is forecasted to be phenomenal.

ELECTRONIC CASH REGISTER CONFIGURATIONS

KEY CONCEPTS

The following concepts were introduced in this chapter. Their meanings should be completely understood.

1. *Automatic Change Dispenser*–a device that interfaces to an ECR and dispenses coins as part of a change-making procedure dealing with an amount of sale and the amount of tender.
2. *Automatic Form Number Reader (AFNR)*–an optical character recognition device capable of reading preprinted guest-check codes. Eliminates the need for a user to key in a guest-check serial number.
3. *Cash Handling Equipment*–mechanical device designed to maintain cash banks or drawers. Used to control access to money and to track transactions affecting its balance.
4. *Check Digit Verification*–complicated mathematical formula used to verify that a legitimate guest-check serial number has been entered into a cash register system.
5. *Data Base System*–large collection of information stored in a central memory unit for future use. An invaluable collection of addressable storage locations.
6. *Data Collector*–a magnetic tape medium used as part of an electronic store and forward memory system application.
7. *Distributed Intelligence*–the dispersion of memory units among several hardware elements in an automated network; for example, stand-alone devices.
8. *Distributed Processing*–the centralization of data-handling procedures, but with a dissemination of output; for example, master-slave and processor-based networks.
9. *Electronic Store and Forward (ESF)*–the storage of transactional data for reentry to a larger memory unit at a later time; related to data collector.
10. *Expediter*–a person who carries prepared items from production to service, thereby enabling service personnel to remain out of the kitchen.
11. *Guest-Check Numbering*–use of serial numbering (or coding) to permit accurate and efficient tracking of all sales source documents.
12. *Interregister Communications (IRC)*–the process of connecting register units together, or to a remote processor, for interactivity.
13. *Journal Printer*–remote printing terminal that produces a continuous output of all recorded transactions in a cash register system. Anything input into a computerized register system will be printed on a journal printer.
14. *Master-Slave Configuration*–an ECR network in which the master unit resembles a stand-alone and the slaves are nonintelligent POS devices.

15. *Modem*-a system component required to achieve direct connect telecommunications; related to the acoustic coupler.
16. *Network Controller*-mechanical device designed to temporarily hold and direct the flow of data within a multitasking computer system. Often referred to as a buffer memory unit.
17. *Point-of-Sale (POS) Terminal*-a register device that will not function unless connected to a remote CPU; serves as a remote I/O in an ECR configuration.
18. *Polling*-the surveying of another computerized device from a remote location via telecommunications.
19. *Precheck*-technique in which no food or drink leaves a production area unless its sale is first accounted for (through a register device).
20. *Processor-Based Configuration*-an ECR network in which a powerful CPU and large memory unit are interfaced to a series of nonintelligent POS devices.
21. *Redundant Memory*-a computer system technique in which interconnected memory units each mirror one another (all retain identical information).
22. *Remote Job Entry (RJE)*-refers to a satellite I/O device sending data to a host computer for processing.
23. *Remote Printing Unit*-an output device located outside an ECR terminal capable of one-direction communication.
24. *Request for Proposal (RFP)*-part of the system-selection process; the method in which an operator solicits a system design suggestion from a vendor.
25. *Stand-Alone Configuration*-an independent ECR device that contains the necessary computer system components in a single piece of hardware.
26. *Telecommunications*-computer system technique involving use of telephone equipment for the control of data flow within an automated network. See *Polling*.
27. *User-Friendly*-describes system techniques that minimize user training and comprehension; prompts that lead a user through the system's logic.

Automated Precheck Systems

Chapter Objectives

1. To describe the steps necessary in computerized prechecking procedures
2. To present the prechecking cycle as a cash-register-based application area
3. To discuss the relative strengths and weaknesses of a precheck system
4. To identify the control aspects of a precheck system with regard to open checking, check tracking, and check settlement

Although prechecking systems primarily depend on a cash register application, they are one of the most popular service-oriented control techniques. The concept of *prechecking* requires that there be a written requisition to the production area (kitchen) before the dispensing of any food item (service). This written record establishes accountability in the service area and authorization in the production area. In other words, unless a server has written proof that he or she intends to charge a guest for a particular item, the server will not be allowed to remove that item from the kitchen. From a control perspective, prechecking may be the best means of operation.

But what does prechecking imply that some other systems may not? Prechecking implies slower service, since everything must be in writing to be acceptable. Second, prechecking appears to foster a cumbersome communication link between the service personnel and kitchen staff because of the variability in legibility and completeness of written orders. Third, prechecking assumes a large volume of kitchen traffic because everyone must first submit an order and then return later for pick-up. With all these inherent problems, why are precheck systems such popular cash-register-based applications?

The use of cash register terminals as order-entry devices solves the legibility problem, since machine-printed output is uniform and therefore easier to read. The cabling of remote printing units from the dining area to the production area(s) enables a previously entered order to be disseminated to the proper remote printer for rapid, automatic communication. This procedure does not require the servers to go to the kitchen to place orders. Instead, the servers have more time to spend with the guests because they do not have to leave the floor to place the order.

Upon completion of production, many operators employ an expediter to bring the items from the kitchen to the correct server station in the dining room. With this system, the server stays in the dining room and communicates easy-to-read prechecked orders to the kitchen. Prechecking is used in a fine dine, tableservice operation much more than in a fast-food environment. Often, however, a fast-food restaurant may use remote printers to relay special orders quickly to the production area. Usually this is the extent of the prechecking process in fast-food restaurants.

PRECHECKING SYSTEMS

A prechecking system is composed of both hardware and software designed to control the production and service link. Typical hardware requirements include *precheck register*, check printer, network controller, remote printer, receipt printer, and journal printer. Requisite software usually involves *open checking*, *check tracking*, *check preparation*, and *check settlement*. Each of these system components is discussed in the following sections. Although prechecking is not a new concept, automation has significantly altered and expanded its capabilities.

Hardware Components

The most critical hardware device in a precheck system is the *precheck terminal*. A precheck terminal, or register, normally is constructed as a modified cash register. The major distinguishing features are that the precheck machine does not need to have a cash drawer and/or a receipt printer built into it. Because this terminal is located typically in an inconspicuous section of the dining room, it is not used for settlement and does not need to produce a receipt or contain a cash bank. These components could, of course, be cabled to the precheck terminal (as peripherals) if necessary. Precheck terminals that contain many preset keys are more efficient input devices than those that are limited. Price look-up keys are also useful for remote communications. Similarly, interchangeable cash register keyboard masks and price-change mode keys further extend the capabilities of a precheck unit. All the server needs to do is depress the appropriate item keys and the respective quantity desired for each item to initiate a transaction. This system has enhanced production efficiencies otherwise unavailable. The implementation of sophisticated keyboards and function keys streamlines the local, in-house order-entry process.

Although some precheck machines have built-in check-insertion tables, most tend to have a peripheral *check printer* for this purpose. A system safeguard may require that a check be inserted before keyboard operation, as an additional element of the internal control process. No matter where the check printer is located, it is an integral part of the system. Guest checks are normally stored in hard copy outside the system; inside the system, only the perpetual, running balance for an open check is stored. Should a check be misplaced, or lost, only its last balance may be found, and this is a function of access via serial number. The specifics of check preparation may vary among vendors, but at some time in the guest-check cycle a hard copy is essential for account monitoring and settlement.

Remote (kitchen) printers are extremely beneficial to a successful precheck scheme. Remote printers receive orders entered at scattered precheck terminals, and their output is used to communicate orders to the production staff. The preceding chapter presented illustrations of remote printers; Figure 6-1 contains an assortment of remote printer formats. Note that one printout illustrates the handling of a voided item, and all three highlight accompaniment items and preparation instruction (rare, medium, well). The check number and server codes are used as responsibility indicators while the time and date of order placement become extremely helpful in an analysis of production.

AUTOMATED PRECHECK SYSTEMS 103

FIGURE 6-1 Assorted Report Printer Formats

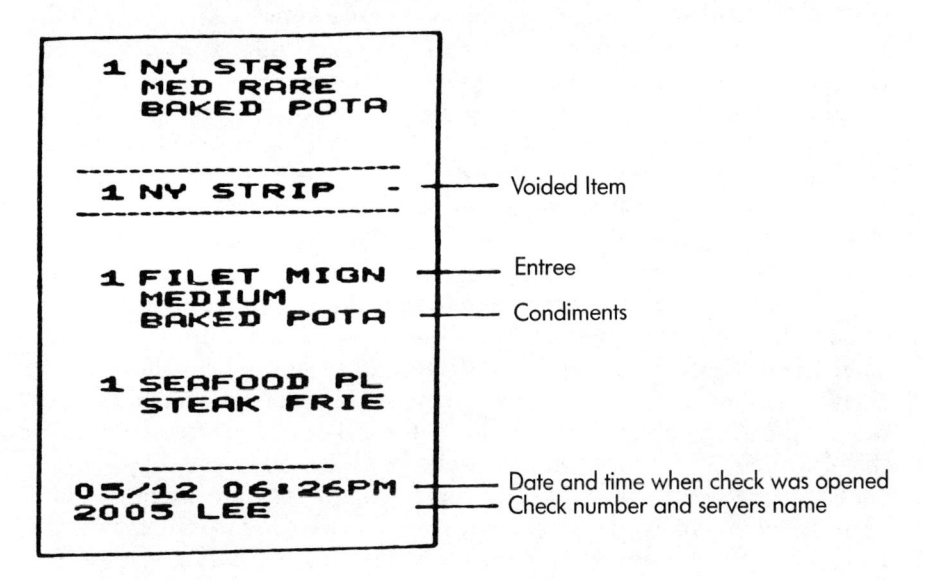

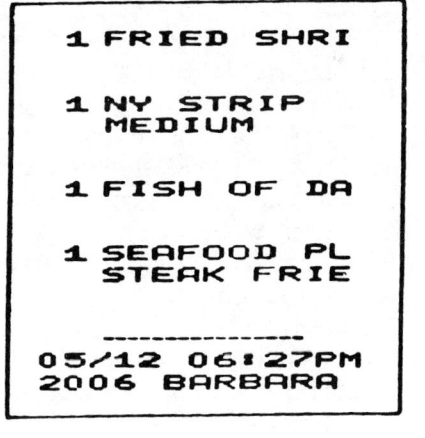

```
1 NY STRIP
MED RARE
BAKED POTA
-----------------------
1 NY STRIP      -           ——— Voided Item
-----------------------
1 FILET MIGN    ——— Entree
MEDIUM
BAKED POTA      ——— Condiments

1 SEAFOOD PL
STEAK FRIE

-----------------
05/12 06:26PM   ——— Date and time when check was opened
2005 LEE        ——— Check number and servers name
```

```
1 FRIED SHRI
1 NY STRIP
MEDIUM
1 FISH OF DA
1 SEAFOOD PL
STEAK FRIE

-----------------
05/12 06:30PM
2009 BARBARA
```

```
1 FRIED SHRI

1 NY STRIP
MEDIUM

1 FISH OF DA

1 SEAFOOD PL
STEAK FRIE

-----------------
05/12 06:27PM
2006 BARBARA
```

Source: Courtesy of MICROS Systems, Inc.

Unless one remote printer is dedicated to each precheck terminal, a *network controller* is required to establish effective interregister communication flows. The major function of the controller unit is to prevent bottlenecking through a *buffered memory*. In other words, if two or more precheck machines simultaneously are trying to print an order at one printer, the system might jam or lock up. Likewise, if one precheck terminal communicated split orders (hot foods versus cold foods) to two or more remote printers, control of the process would need to be maintained. This supervisory position is the responsibility of the network controller.

How does the controller unit work? It is a memory device capable of holding transmitted orders for distribution to the printers. If a printer is currently in use, it will store sequential transmissions and distribute them to the appropriate printing unit as it becomes available. This system alleviates the delay that could arise at terminals if they had to remain inoperable while a remote printer completed prior order output. Basic schematic drawings of the placement of network controllers can be found in Figure 6-2.

In a precheck system, *receipt printers* or *slip printers* are often used for a purpose not originally intended. Some operators have found it more effective to use their remote printers only at major kitchen preparation stations and allow servers to hand-carry inexpensive, machine-produced slips to other areas for requisitioning. For example, a restaurant may place a remote hot food and cold food station printer at their respective kitchen workstations. Should a dessert item or beverage be ordered, it is also entered into the precheck terminal. However, a receipt is produced at the slip printer located adjacent to the precheck machine, not at the remote unit. This slip is then taken to the designated distribution station, or person, for order initiation. Because adjacent receipts or slip printers do not require extensive cabling and are less expensive than remote printers, some operators report significant savings in both system design and on-going operations.

A *journal printer* is an essential component of a precheck system. A journal printer produces a hard copy of all transactions recorded at any terminal location within the precheck network. This continuous printing of all activities provides management with an audit trail for monitoring all recorded business. Without a journal printer, there is no support document by which to cross-reference transaction authorization and verification. It is important to note that any printer located more than 13 to 15 feet from a precheck terminal is considered a remote (off-board) printer. The usefulness of additional hardware components should not be precluded by the preceding description. The hardware described here is not assumed to be exhaustive.

Figure 6-3 depicts a hardware configuration for a coffee shop, lounge, and fine dine restaurant all located under the same roof. Note that emphasis should be placed on the overall system design, more than on the specifics of any one device.

FIGURE 6-2 Sample Placement of Network Controllers

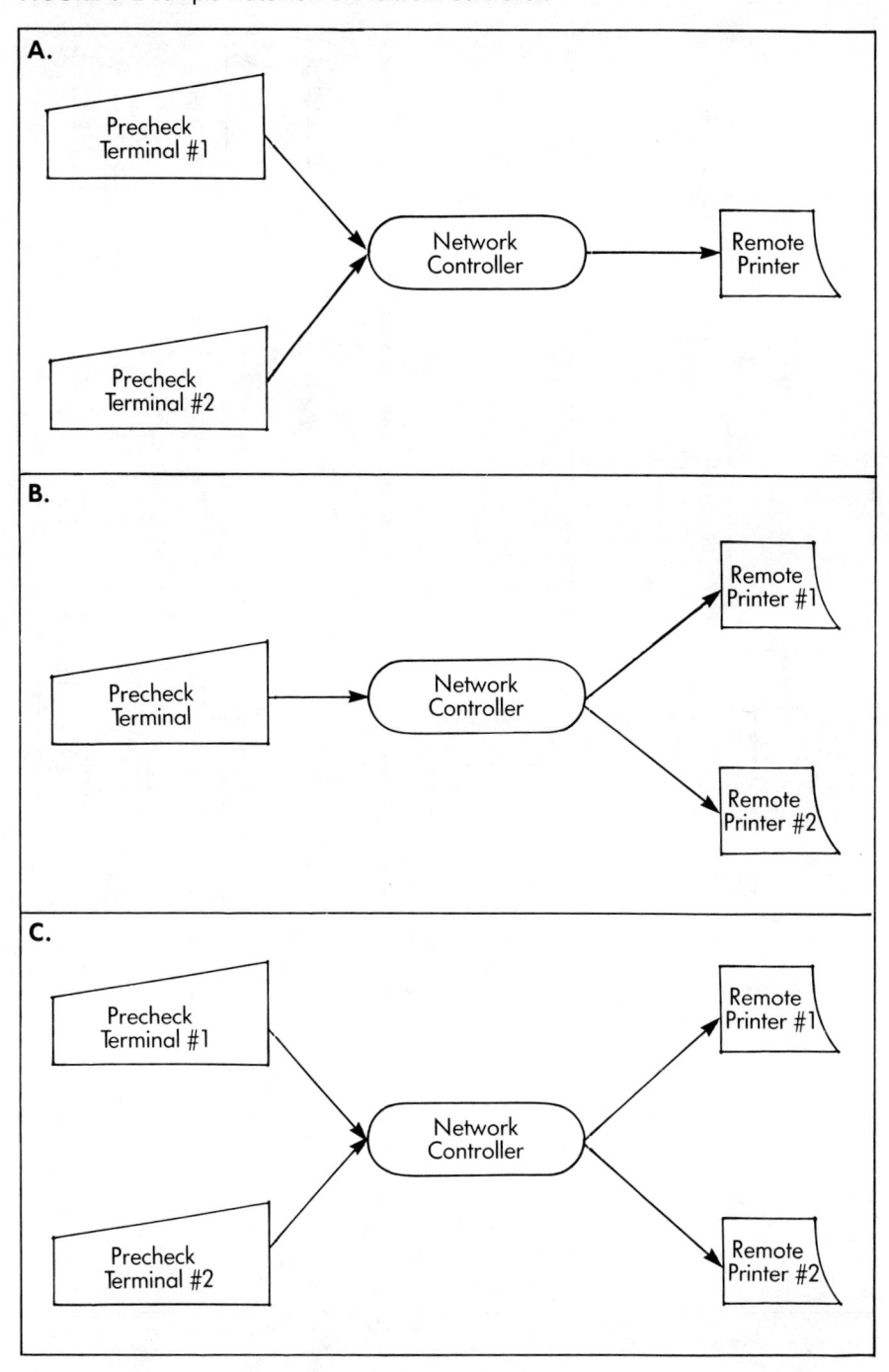

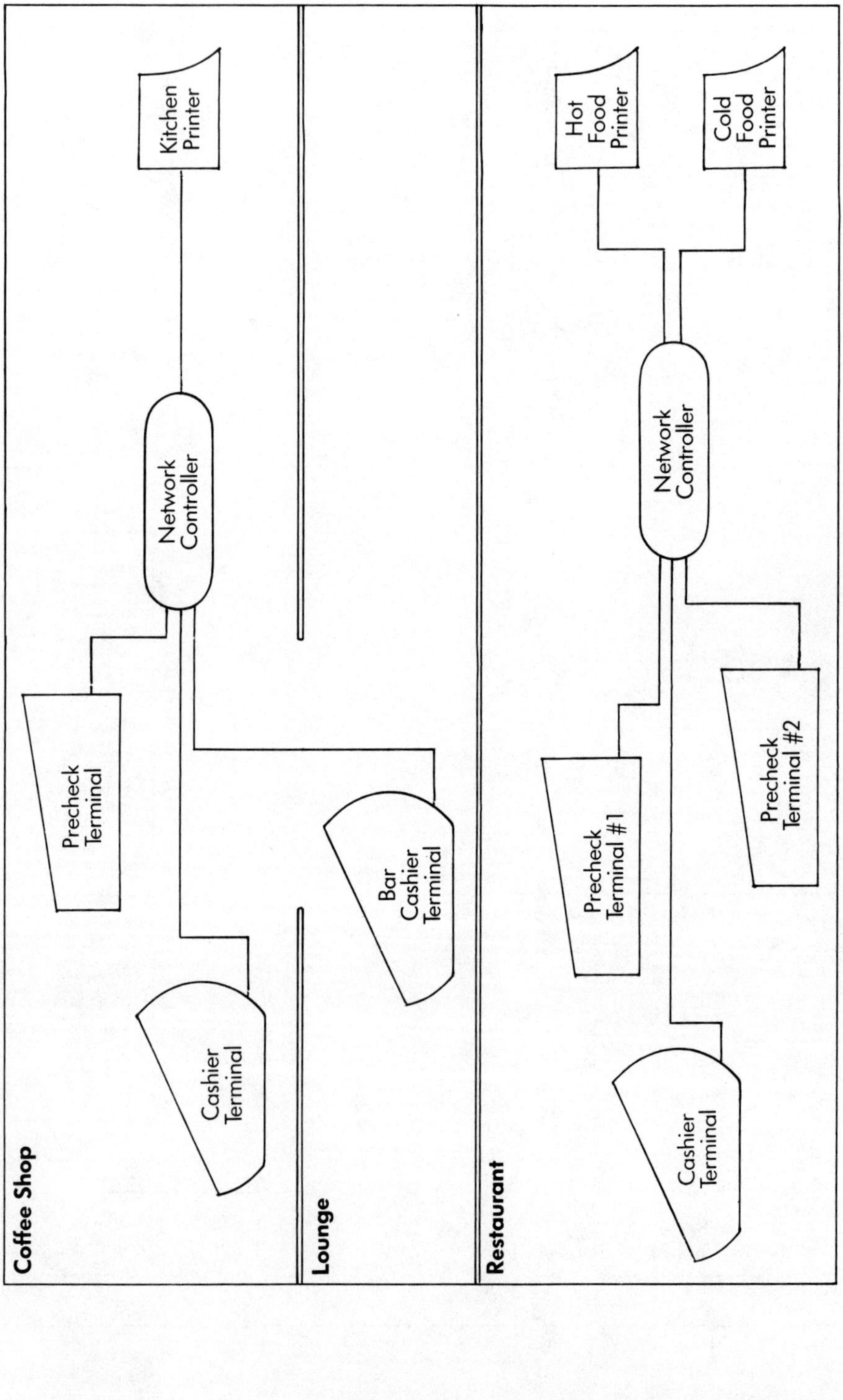

106 AUTOMATED PRECHECK SYSTEMS

FIGURE 6-3 Multiroom Restaurant Configuration

Software Components

In addition to the communication of orders taken in a service area and sent to the production area, a precheck scheme has other features. One of the most highly regarded characteristics of prechecking is the concept of open checking. Open checking enables the posting of unrelated transactions to an outstanding guest check from several remote order entry points.

From the time a guest check is initiated until it is closed out, additions and/or authorized modifications can be made from a qualified register terminal. For example, a guest waiting for a dining room table may order a drink in the lounge. The server establishes an account for this guest by beginning a new check. Entering the check's serial number, table number, and server identification code creates an open-check record in the system's memory. This customer continues to run a tab in the lounge. This same check may later be transferred to the dining room to track additional purchases.

When a table becomes available in the dining room, the restaurant may request that the bar bill be settled then or may offer superior guest service by allowing the open check to be transferred to the dining area. The open-check transfer can be accomplished in a variety of ways. In any case, the dining room server's identification code replaces the lounge server's number. A new check serial number may be assigned in the dining room or the same serial number may be carried over. This check allows for continued reference in the service bar, lounge, and dining room areas. Whether food or beverage is ordered, the server can access the correct open check from any precheck machine. Significant controls for the foodservice operator are achieved, while the guest receives one-check service. To ask a guest to settle the bar bill before moving to the dining room may upset the guest and would require the restaurant to produce two checks for the same customer. See Figure 6-4 for a sample open-check report.

Determining the status of any guest check resident in a precheck system can be achieved through check tracking. Check tracking describes a software application package that can report the serial number, time of creation, server code, account balance, and table number for every open check in the system. This system capability has been credited with a reduction in walkouts/skippers and with providing rapid feedback on service times and patterns. A server who repeatedly has missing or unaccountable checks requires closer monitoring, and this monitoring can be accomplished through a check-tracking system. At any time, an open-check report can be printed to highlight checks that have been open too long (potential walkout) and/or checks that have a large outstanding balance (high risk accounts).

The preparation of a guest check can be performed piecemeal, as an order is constructed, or at the completion of service. In any case, the final preparation of a guest check leads to settlement (closed checks). The closing of pre-

FIGURE 6-4 Sample Open-Check Report

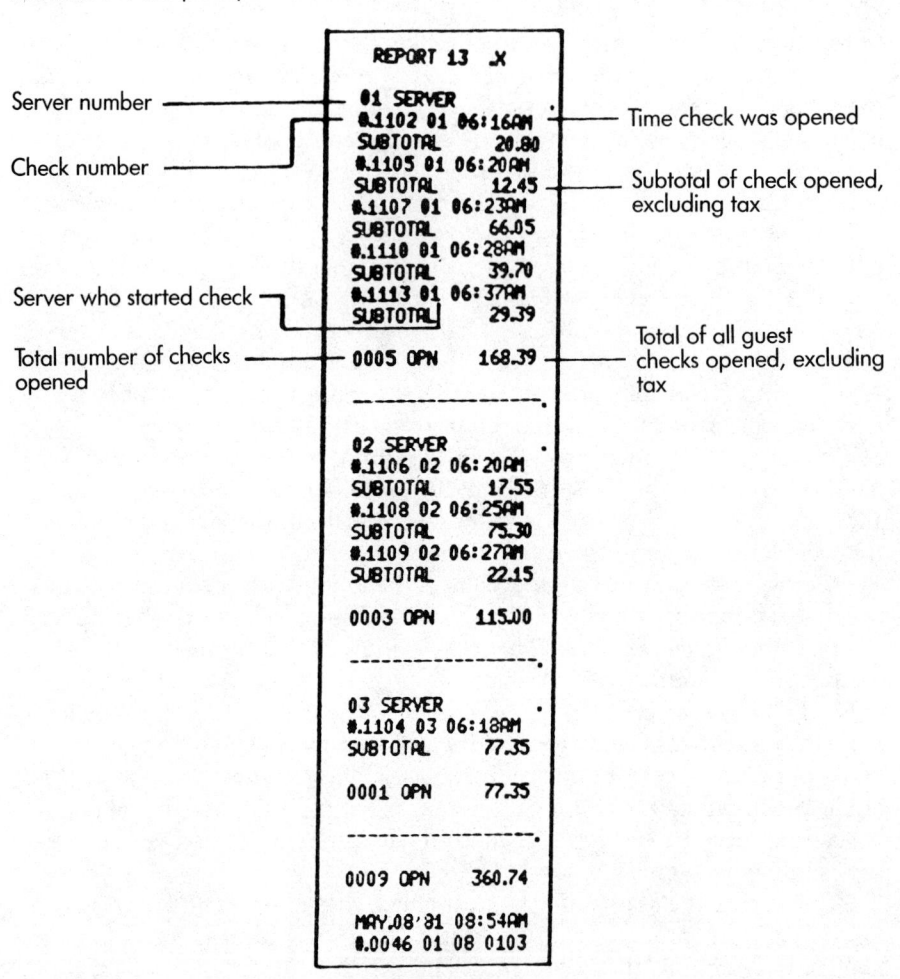

```
                    REPORT 13   X

                    01 SERVER
Server number ————— #.1102 01 06:16AM ——— Time check was opened
                    SUBTOTAL     20.80
Check number —————— #.1105 01 06:20AM
                    SUBTOTAL     12.45 ——— Subtotal of check opened,
                    #.1107 01 06:23AM        excluding tax
                    SUBTOTAL     66.05
                    #.1110 01 06:28AM
                    SUBTOTAL     39.70
Server who started check ——— #.1113 01 06:37AM
                    SUBTOTAL     29.39
                                                  Total of all guest
Total number of checks ————— 0005 OPN    168.39 ——— checks opened, excluding
opened                                              tax

                    ——————————————————

                    02 SERVER
                    #.1106 02 06:20AM
                    SUBTOTAL     17.55
                    #.1108 02 06:25AM
                    SUBTOTAL     75.30
                    #.1109 02 06:27AM
                    SUBTOTAL     22.15

                    0003 OPN    115.00

                    ——————————————————

                    03 SERVER
                    #.1104 03 06:18AM
                    SUBTOTAL     77.35

                    0001 OPN     77.35

                    ——————————————————

                    0009 OPN    360.74

                    MAY.08'81 08:54AM
                    #.0046 01 08 0103
```

Source: Courtesy of MICROS Systems, Inc.

viously open accounts terminates access to those accounts and requires a reconciliation and settlement. A closed-check report (see Figure 6-5) can be extremely important in monitoring employee check accountability and in evaluating server productivity (number of tables served). The area of prechecking is an important one that requires constant review by management to remain a strong control technique.

AUTOMATED PRECHECK SYSTEMS

FIGURE 6-5 Sample Closed-Check Report

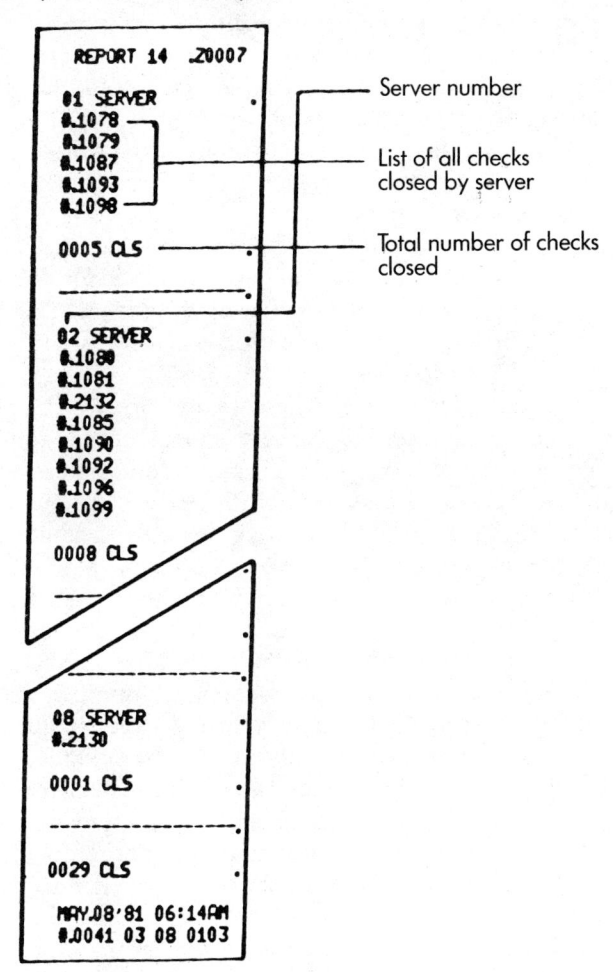

```
REPORT 14  Z0007

01 SERVER                    ── Server number
 #1078
 #1079
 #1087                       ── List of all checks
 #1093                          closed by server
 #1098

0005 CLS                     ── Total number of checks
                                closed

02 SERVER
 #1080
 #1081
 #2132
 #1085
 #1090
 #1092
 #1096
 #1099

0008 CLS


08 SERVER
 #2130

0001 CLS


0029 CLS

MAY.08'81 06:14AM
#.0041 03 08 0103
```

Source: Courtesy of MICROS Systems, Inc.

Automated precheck application. The following steps are based on a survey of vendor systems:

1. Server records order on scratch or order pad, noting all instructions associated with menu items requested.
2. Server proceeds to a POS precheck terminal to record the order, open the guest check account, and validate the transaction.

3. Server enters his or her server I.D. number (usually two digits), table number, number in party, and the preprinted serial number found on the guest check. (Note: Some systems automatically assign a guest-check identification number at the time the order is recorded, thereby eliminating preprinting, but not the subsequent entry of the serial number. Other systems may employ an OCR reader to pick up preprinted codes.)
4. These procedures create a new open account that will be tracked by the system until the balance of the account is settled.
5. Server inserts a guest check into the check printer and enters the desired menu items via preset keys, price look-up files, and/or dollar amounts. Also, many systems provide a modifier option for entering preparation instructions, micromotion keyboards for versatility, and function keys for simplicity of operation.
6. The system automatically prints the date and time of the order on the guest check (from its internal real-time clock). In addition, the guest check may include the server's name, I.D. number, number of covers, table number, all menu items ordered, price extensions, and tax.
7. Simultaneous to check printing (at the time a new check is opened), systems with remote printers begin communicating production requirements to the proper preparation station. Individual menu items with corresponding preparation instructions are sent to the designated slip printer. Production slips might also carry the table number (for expediting), the time the order was placed, guest check number, and the server code. In terms of mechanical function, at the time a complete order is entered into a POS terminal, all information is forwarded to a remote buffer controller unit, freeing the terminal for immediate use by the next server. The controller unit, in turn, relays the appropriate production information to the proper remote kitchen printer or remote bar station.
8. Following service, the printed guest check is presented to the customer for settlement. If a guest orders additional menu items, the server enters the serial number of the check into the POS terminal and presses the pick-up or open-check balance button. The system then provides access to the correct check and allows the server to enter the additional items ordered. The original guest check is reinserted into the terminal and the new documentation in printed on the check and disseminated to the proper remote printer(s). The new, updated check is now available for presentation. Refer to Figure 6-6 for a flowchart depicting these transactions.

Guest-check considerations. The problems associated with guest-check serial numbering were covered in the preceding chapter. Recall that preprinted codes are beneficial for control purposes but require that the server enters the number to open a check and reentry to post items to the

AUTOMATED PRECHECK SYSTEMS

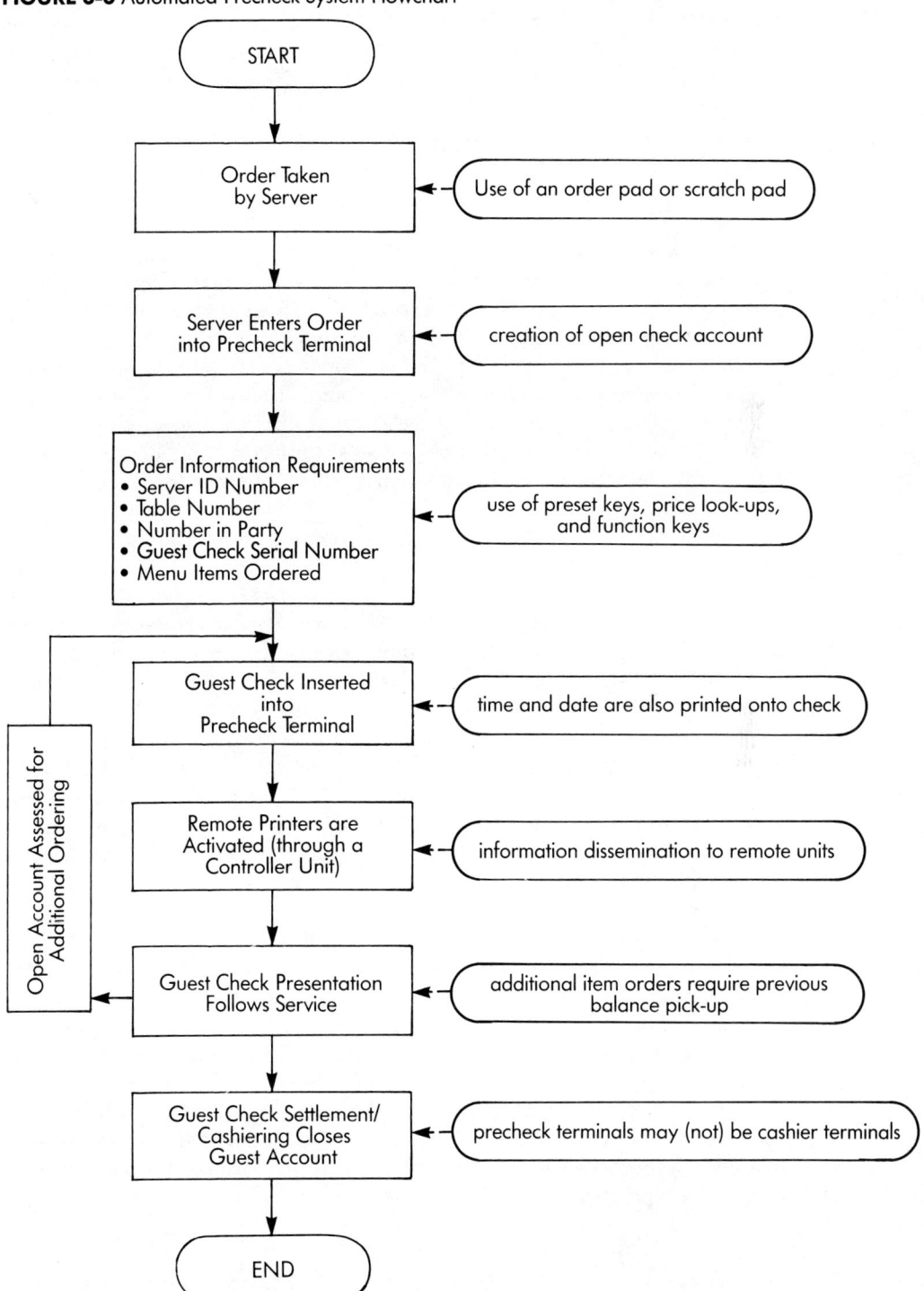

FIGURE 6-6 Automated Precheck System Flowchart

```
                    START
                      │
                      ▼
            ┌──────────────────┐
            │  Order Taken     │◄──── Use of an order pad or scratch pad
            │  by Server       │
            └──────────────────┘
                      │
                      ▼
            ┌──────────────────┐
            │ Server Enters Order │◄──── creation of open check account
            │ into Precheck Terminal │
            └──────────────────┘
                      │
                      ▼
      ┌──────────────────────────────┐
      │ Order Information Requirements │
      │ • Server ID Number            │◄──── use of preset keys, price look-ups,
      │ • Table Number                │        and function keys
      │ • Number in Party             │
      │ • Guest Check Serial Number   │
      │ • Menu Items Ordered          │
      └──────────────────────────────┘
                      │
                      ▼
            ┌──────────────────┐
            │ Guest Check Inserted │◄──── time and date are also printed onto check
            │      into            │
            │ Precheck Terminal    │
            └──────────────────┘
                      │
                      ▼
            ┌──────────────────┐
            │ Remote Printers are  │
            │ Activated (through a │◄──── information dissemination to remote units
            │ Controller Unit)     │
            └──────────────────┘
                      │
                      ▼
            ┌──────────────────┐
            │ Guest Check Presentation │◄──── additional item orders require previous
            │ Follows Service          │        balance pick-up
            └──────────────────┘
                      │
                      ▼
            ┌──────────────────┐
            │ Guest Check Settlement/ │
            │ Cashiering Closes       │◄──── precheck terminals may (not) be cashier terminals
            │ Guest Account           │
            └──────────────────┘
                      │
                      ▼
                    END
```

(Open Account Assessed for Additional Ordering — loop back from Guest Check Presentation to Guest Check Inserted into Precheck Terminal)

account. System-generated serial numbers also have advantages but again require the server to key in the code each time the account must be accessed. Preprinted, machine-readable codes alleviate the code-number entry problem but are more expensive to purchase. Obviously, there is a trade-off between service and economies.

Other potential problems revolve around 1) picking up previous balances and 2) multiple checks for a single account. Previous balance pick-up can be accomplished through guest-check serial number entry and, if necessary, combined with a *check digit verification* code. Check digits are system generated and simply assure that a server cannot accidentally pick up an incorrect balance. Figure 6-7 contains an example of a guest check showing a previous balance pick-up. Note that the balance was accessed from the system's memory via the automatic check number displayed in the upper right-hand portion of the check. This code number is also printed in the space labeled "previous check number" on the body of the check. Atop the second group of charges is a reiteration of the check number, as an addtional verification of proper retrieval. Although not all systems function identically, this previous balance pick-up routine is fairly typical (except for the use of an optical code).

Whenever a system-generated check contains more transactions than lines it can print (on one page), a second check is created. How does the information on the second check relate to the first? How does the server know there is more than one check? What assures management of proper balance tracking? Normally, the system manufacturer devises some means that allows the server to insert any serially numbered check into the register for multiple check printing. Regardless of the serial number preprinted on the second check, the serial code of the first check is machine printed, as a monitoring feature, on the second check. The first check also displays a message to the server advising that the original check is contained on another document. Some vendors advocate the use of blank, unnumbered checks for multiple check accounts. Their use is probably not a sound technique, as any gains achieved through a tight serial numbering scheme may be compromised.

Figure 6-8 contains a sample multiple check for one open account. The original source document (check number 124222 on the left) contains the statement "continued on next slip" as its last transaction entry. The supplemental check (serial number 124097 on the right) was inserted into the terminal to be used as page two for the original record. Notice that under the heading previous check number (prev. chk. no.) on the second form, the serial number of the first check is printed in double-size type to show that the second document is tied to the first. This linkage is an important consideration in a precost system and deserves attention during system design.

AUTOMATED PRECHECK SYSTEMS

FIGURE 6-7 Previous Balance Pick-Up

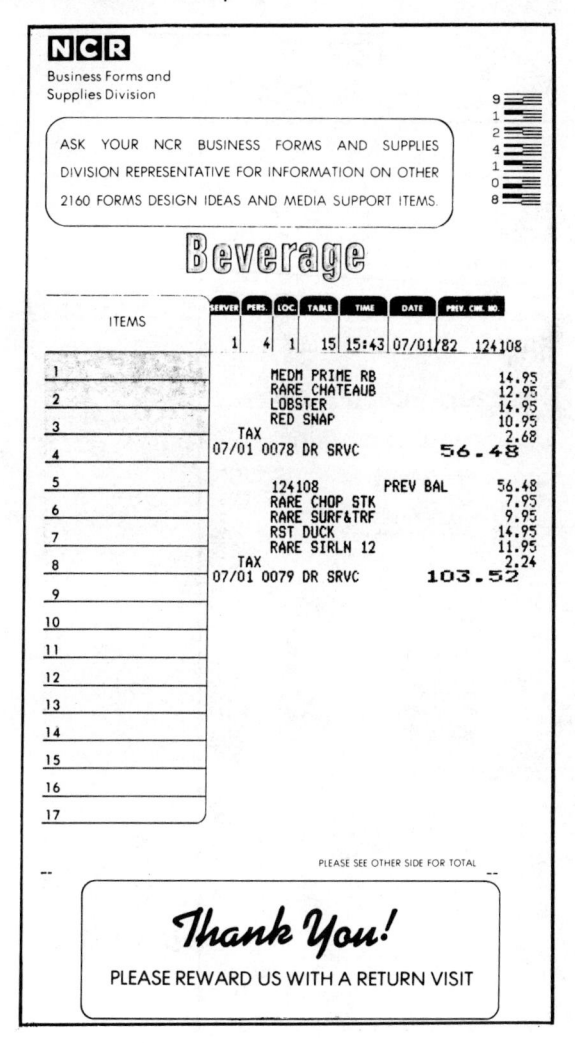

```
NCR
Business Forms and
Supplies Division

ASK YOUR NCR BUSINESS FORMS AND SUPPLIES
DIVISION REPRESENTATIVE FOR INFORMATION ON OTHER
2160 FORMS DESIGN IDEAS AND MEDIA SUPPORT ITEMS.

                    Beverage

        ITEMS    SERVER PERS. LOC. TABLE  TIME   DATE    PREV. CHK. NO.
                    1    4    1    15   15:43  07/01/82   124108
  1              MEDM PRIME RB                    14.95
  2              RARE CHATEAUB                    12.95
                 LOBSTER                          14.95
  3              RED SNAP                         10.95
                 TAX                               2.68
  4      07/01 0078 DR SRVC              56.48

  5              124108        PREV BAL          56.48
                 RARE CHOP STK                    7.95
  6              RARE SURF&TRF                    9.95
  7              RST DUCK                        14.95
                 RARE SIRLN 12                   11.95
  8              TAX                              2.24
         07/01 0079 DR SRVC             103.52
  9
 10
 11
 12
 13
 14
 15
 16
 17
                              PLEASE SEE OTHER SIDE FOR TOTAL

                    Thank You!
         PLEASE REWARD US WITH A RETURN VISIT
```

Source: Courtesy of NCR Corporation

AUTOMATED PRECHECK SYSTEMS

FIGURE 6-8 Sample Multiple Check Order

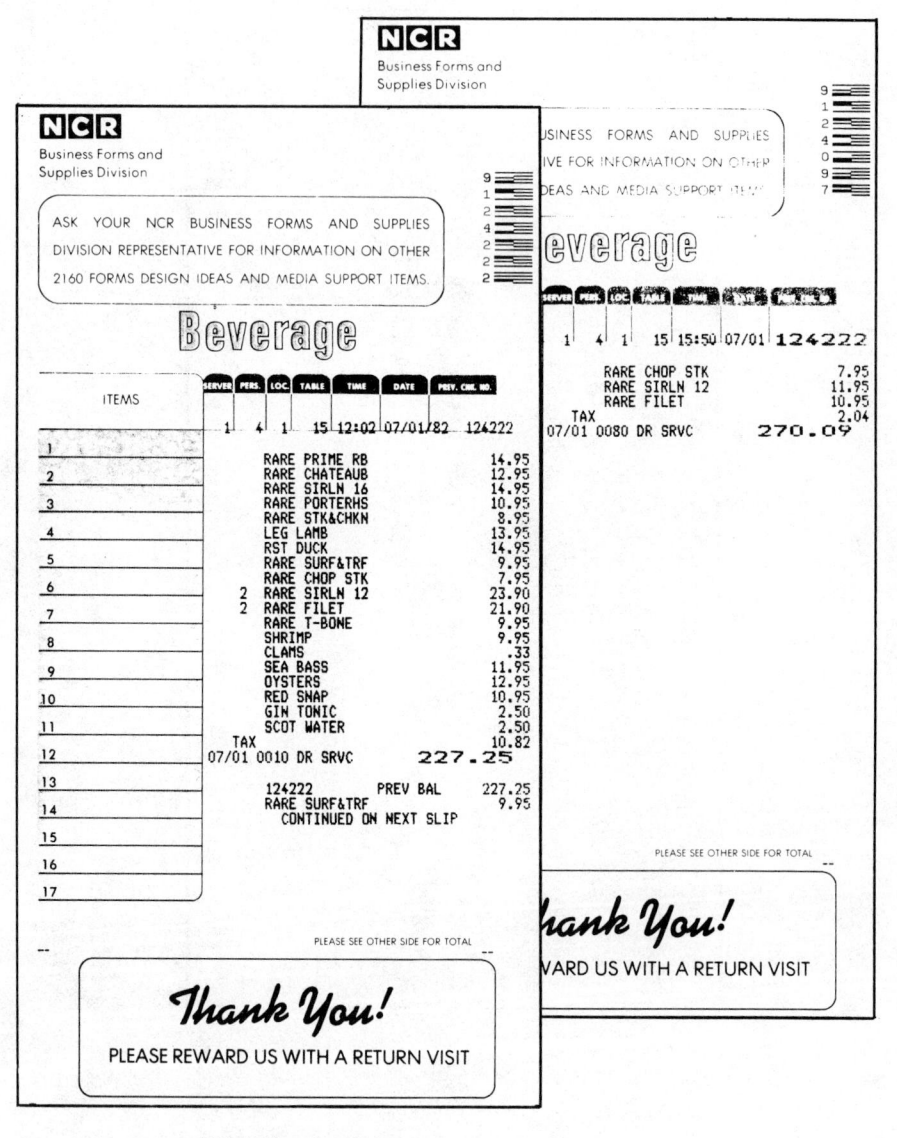

Source: Courtesy of NCR Corporation

SUMMARY

Prechecking systems are cash-register dependent, control techniques designed to relate production quantities to sales activities. This concept requires the writing of a requisition to a production station before any food item is dispensed. This requisition establishes accountability and authorization and insures that all items served will be recorded. Prechecking systems are assumed to provide slower customer service (because of processing activities), awkward service-production communication linkage (between server and kitchen staff), and heavier volumes of kitchen traffic (item ordering and pick-up).

None of these assumptions has much validity when one considers the characteristics of an automated system. Remote information dissemination, uniform system-generated output, and interregister communication capabilities provide an efficient, effective precheck design. Tableservice operations derive the most benefit from a prechecking application, while fast-food restaurants may use only a small fraction of a system's capabilities. Note that the concept of prechecking is not revolutionary. For many years, restaurants have employed food checkers and generated volumes of paperwork to accomplish these objectives.

An automated precheck system uses both dedicated hardware and software to control the production and service network. Typical hardware includes precheck register, check printer, network controller, remote printer, receipt printer, and journal printer. Most of this hardware has been introduced in preceding chapters. Application software features open checking, check tracking, check preparation, and check settlement. All of the features of a precheck system make it an effective monitoring device that is of interest to a majority of foodservice operators.

KEY CONCEPTS

The following concepts were introduced in this chapter. Their meanings should be completely understood.

1. *Buffered Memory*–that component of a network controller unit responsible for retaining information to be communicated to a remote printer.
2. *Check Digit Verification*–a random-generated number used to verify the correct entry of an open-check serial number insuring proper account balance pick-ups. Prevents a server from entering only the sequential check serial number, while presenting a security feature.
3. *Check Preparation*–describes the actual printing and totaling of a foodservice check for presentation to the guest.

4. *Check Printer*-peripheral unit used to generate hard copy records of guest transactions, for settlement.
5. *Check Settlement*-a receipt of payment for an outstanding guest check.
6. *Check Tracking*-the ability of a system to monitor outstanding, open-guest checks (accounts).
7. *Network Controller*-device used to regulate the movement of information between a cashier and/or precheck terminal and remote printing unit(s).
8. *Open Checking*-the creation of an account for the purpose of posting transactions and achieving proper settlement.
9. *Prechecking*-a method of operation that requires requisitioning before the dispensing of any food or beverage from a production area.
10. *Precheck Register*-also called a precheck terminal; a cash register device modified to function as an I/O device (without cash drawer or receipt printer).
11. *Precheck Terminal*-a cash-register-like device that contains no cash drawer or receipt printer; basically serves as an input device.
12. *Receipt Printer*-similar to a check printer.
13. *Remote (Kitchen) Printer*-output device used to communicate orders from a service area to a production location.
14. *Slip Printer*-similar to a check printer in operation, but used for in-house communication and authorization.

7

Precost Systems

Chapter Objectives

1. To introduce the concept of a precost system and its component subsystem files
2. To describe the contents and characteristics of file data elements required in precosting
3. To illustrate the functions and usefulness of precost system reports and displays
4. To discuss the advantages and disadvantages of computer-assisted precosting

The determination of potential food costs before the actual production and service of a meal is called precosting. A *precost system* simply enables management to revise or abandon a menu plan that appears to violate budgetary constraints. A system's capacity to produce valuable precost information is predicated on three types of data. The first data element required is cost figures. An accurate cost of every food item purchased by a foodservice operation must be known. Without current costs, the eventual precost is of limited application.

The second important component in the precost process is a set of standardized recipes. Every menu item served in an operation should be prepared from a tested and well-documented *standard recipe*. A standard recipe contains a list of all required ingredients, their quantity, and a description of prescribed procedures necessary to produce a predetermined batch and portion size of a menu item. For example, a standard recipe for the production of one hundred egg salad sandwiches includes 200 slices of white bread and 12.5 pounds of egg salad. The procedure required to produce these sandwiches reads: place a two-ounce scoop of egg salad evenly across the bread; place another slice of bread over the egg salad; cut the sandwich in half and place into a waxed paper bag. By following these instructions and using only the allowed ingredients, one hundred sandwiches, each containing two ounces of egg salad, are produced.

The third data requirement involves a *menu plan*. The name of each menu item and the number of portions expected to be consumed (of each) must be specified. Although institutional foodservice operators may use a repeating, cyclical menu, the portion projections are likely to be different even though the same menu items are served. On the other hand, commercial restaurants having a fixed menu can also use standard recipes and ingredient costs to forecast their precost information. The techniques used to generate a precost may vary. A general overview of precost systems follows.

PERFORMING A PRECOST

Precosting is achieved through a series of mathematical procedures aimed at computing both total menu and individual menu item food costs. A schematic relationship between the input data (costs, recipes, and menu plan) and the resultant precost is presented in Figure 7-1.

Since some menu items appearing on the menu plan may simply be served in their "as purchased" condition, they most likely do not require a standard recipe. For example, whole milk can be served without any modification or additions and therefore can be costed out directly from its ingredient cost record. The lack of a standard recipe card for milk tends to simplify a manual

FIGURE 7-1 Precost Data Elements

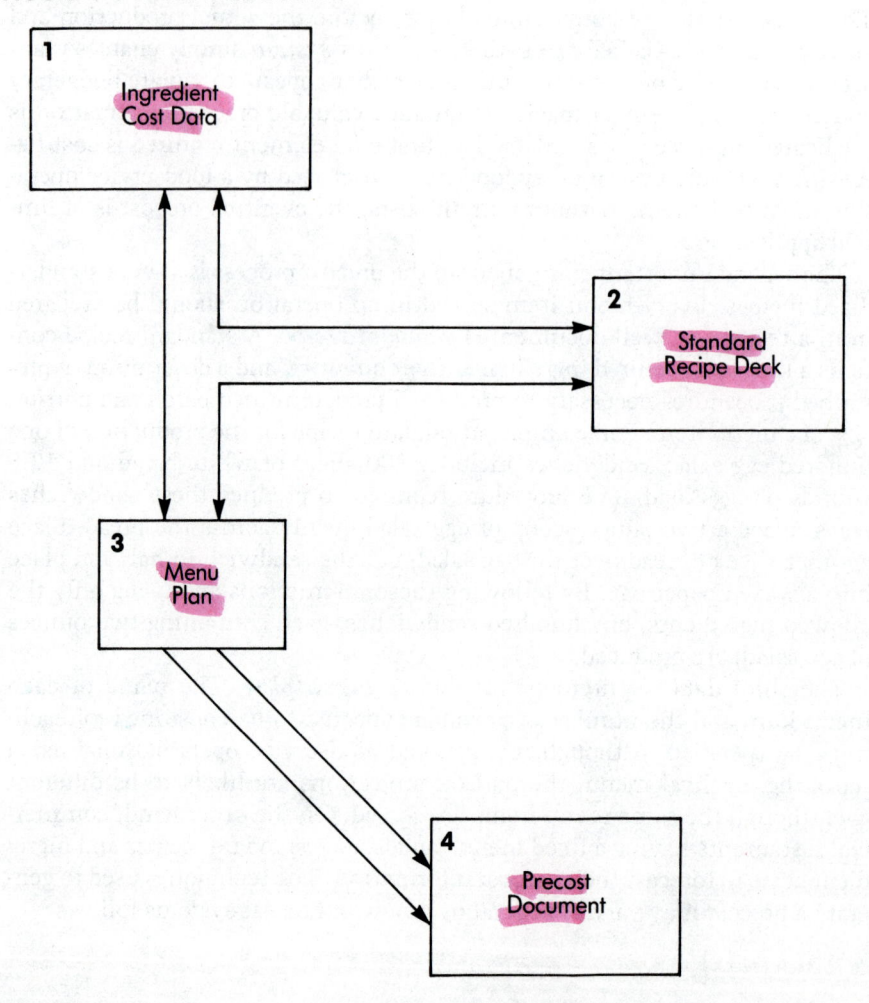

```
┌─────────────┐
│ 1           │
│  Ingredient │
│  Cost Data  │
└─────────────┘
       ↕           ┌──────────────┐
       ├──────────→│ 2            │
       │           │   Standard   │
       ├──────────→│   Recipe Deck│
       ↕           └──────────────┘
┌─────────────┐
│ 3           │
│   Menu      │
│   Plan      │
└─────────────┘
       │           ┌──────────────┐
       └──────────→│ 4            │
                   │   Precost    │
                   │   Document   │
                   └──────────────┘
```

computation of the precost document. The ten steps involved in a manual precost are:

Step One. Develop a list of all food items currently purchased by a foodservice operation.

Step Two. Record the price of all purchased food items listed in Step One.

Step Three. Investigate the purchase unit of all purchased food items to determine their net weight and issue unit contents.

Step Four. Calculate a cost per pound (net weight) for every food item (ingredient) listed in Step One. Be sure that all item costs are on a per pound basis. (Note: The terms *cost/pound* and *price/pound* can be used interchangeably).

Step Five. Establish a set of standardized recipes for all menu items the foodservice operation is likely to serve.

Step Six. Cost out every standard recipe (by batch and portion) using the ingredient cost-per-pound values determined in Step Four.

Step Seven. Develop a sound menu plan, by meal period, day, week, and cycle. Be aware that competing menu items influence the number of portions taken of any one menu item.

Step Eight. Forecast the number of portions to be consumed for each menu item on the menu plan.

Step Nine. Compute the cost of all meals by multiplying each menu item's projected count (Step Eight) times its respective portion cost (Step Six).

Step Ten. Complete the precost document by determining all costs per meal, per day, per week, and per cycle on both a meal-period and menu-item basis (by batch and portion size).

The manual completion of a precost is time consuming and monotonous. The work required to maintain updated cost and recipe records can be perceived as demanding. The ability to accurately forecast and design a satisfactory menu plan often appears overwhelming. By the time most operators have updated their data records, designed their plan, and followed the ten steps outlined above, their cycle may be more than half over! Because precosts must be accurately performed in a timely manner and involve a large amount of quantitative computation, the best method may be one involving automation. Computer-based precost systems, containing updated, on-line files, can free the operator to concentrate on designing a sound menu plan without getting mired in repetitive costing and clerical procedures.

COMPUTERIZED PRECOST SYSTEMS

The operations of computer-based precost systems are similar to the manual procedure outlined previously. The major differences between automated precosting and manual precosting are 1) the amount and type of work performed by the foodservice operator, and 2) the number and types of by-product reports and applications that can be achieved from the data files. The foodservice manager simply becomes a conduit for updating cost data on file and for monitoring standardized recipe ingredients and quantities. All the mathematics are performed internally by the system and at extremely high speeds (in nanoseconds).

Perhaps the major gains for the foodservice operator are the by-products and applications available through the computer. Although not all systems

122 PRECOST SYSTEMS

are alike, most can produce such additional items as food group analysis, menu group analysis, disposable standard recipes, and extensive precost report packages. Food and menu group analyses are available since food items and recipes are entered into the system in accordance with input coding specifications. These coding specifications detail addressable number locations, by categories, and assign different data to unique sectors within the data base. For example, to analyze vegetables, the computer system searches the reserved vegetable code number files and generates a report.

Disposable standard recipe sheets are helpful in some operations because they contain expanded recipe cards. In other words, if a standard recipe is designed to produce sixty six-ounce portions of beef stew, and 660 portions are projected on the menu plan, the automated system will multiply the basic recipe by a factor of eleven (660/60). The computer-printed recipe for 660 portions is sent to the issuing clerk for requisitioning and to the production chef for cooking. The assumption is made that the mathematical capabilities and printing speed of the computer are assets in streamlining kitchen production processes and reducing production errors. A computerized precost report package contains a multitude of reports such as percentage cost reports, food group cost reports, food purchasing reports, food usage reports, and nutritional achievement reports.

All in all, a computer-assisted precost system exceeds the expectations of most foodservice operators. The computerized precost system is composed of four subsystem component parts: the ingredient file, the recipe file, the menu file, and the precost file. Figure 7-2 contains a diagram of the relationships among these files.

Ingedient File

The *ingredient file*, also referred to as the food item data file (FIDF), contains a complete list of all inventory food items purchased by a foodservice operation. The ingredient file serves as the primary data base for precosting and inventory control applications. Standard recipes, menu cycles, and inventory explosions are constructed from data stored in this file. Within the context of a precost system, a user has four ingredient-file options: 1) add an item to the file, 2) delete an item from the file, 3) update data currently on file, or 4) list information stored in this file. By selecting the add option, a first-time user who needs to create an ingredient file can do so or can add an individual food item to an existing file. However, note that system specifications limit users to a predetermined, maximum-ingredient file size. This maximum file-size constraint is a function of the number of additional files required by the system and the type of computer hardware used.

A precost system that shares the same computer with payroll, general ledger, account receivables, and account payables applications may not per-

FIGURE 7-2 Automated Precost Data Files

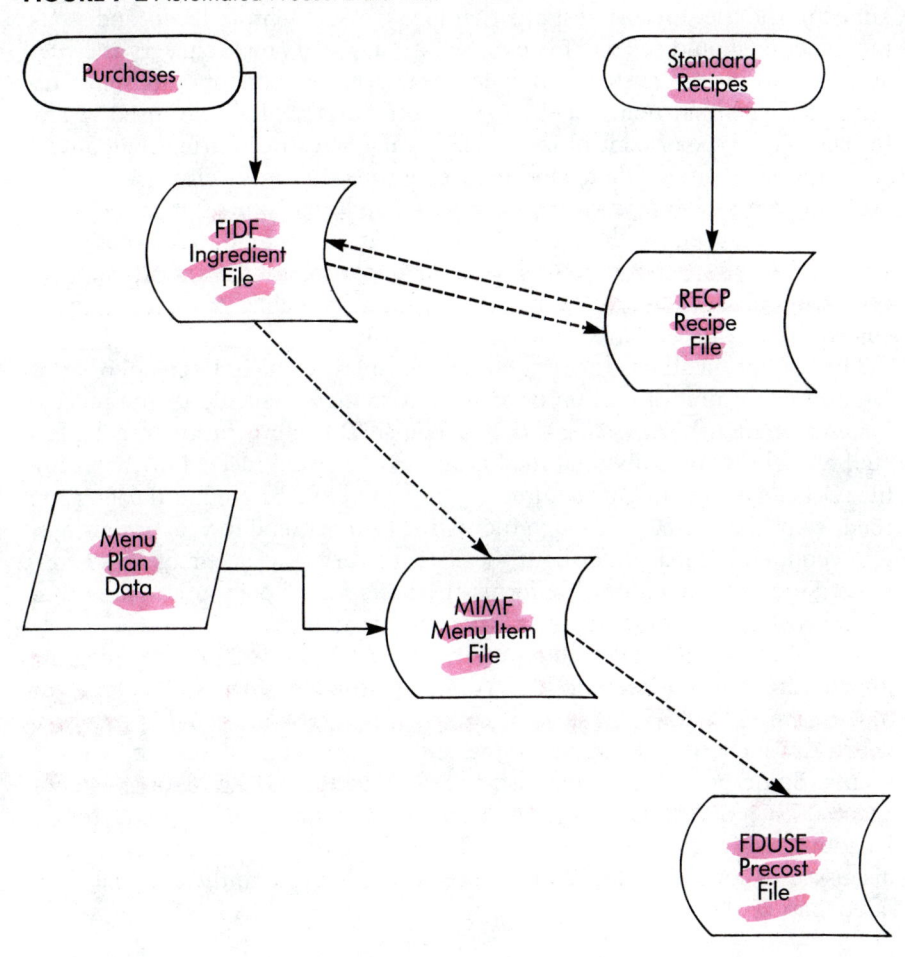

mit as large a file space for ingredients as a dedicated, single application system might. Similarly, a microcomputer-based system may contain fewer than 1,500 food items in its file, whereas a large-scale macrocomputer might allow in excess of 8,000 items to be stored. In any case, be aware of file constraints and system parameters, since the size of the ingredient file surely is a finite entity.

The delete option permits a system user to remove items currently on file. This option allows for the discarding of unnecessary file records associated with food items no longer required in inventory. Therefore, the delete option serves to monitor the accuracy and size of the ingredient file.

Only ingredients currently used to produce menu items should be maintained in the file. Precost systems that also track inventory levels and stock movements should reflect this consideration. Dead stock clutters the files and reduces overall system efficiency. Foodservice operators often are surprised to learn that many of the ingredients purchased are not used in any recipes. This type of control information may be gained during the conversion process required when adopting a computer-based system.

The update option is perhaps the most frequently used ingredient-file function. Because ingredient costs and purchase units tend to fluctuate constantly, the updating of an item's cost and purchase unit data is critical to an effective precost system. The update option also enables the user to make changes to any other data elements kept on file.

The list option allows the user either to display (on a CRT screen) or print (on an LPT printer) a portion of or the entire ingredient file. Some precost systems segment the ingredient file by food group coding (meats, vegetables, etc.) and allow for individual food groups to be listed instead of the entire file. Other systems might require that the whole file be produced each time the list option is used. Although file-listing formats tend to vary among system vendors, the reason for listing a file is to verify the accuracy of its contents. Since the inventory file forms the basis for all computations within the precosting, its contents must be verified regularly.

In general, the ingredient file contains at least five essential data elements for each food item placed on file: 1) ingredient code number, 2) ingredient description, 3) unit of purchase, 4) weight of purchase unit, and 5) purchase unit price. These five entries represent minimal ingredient-file requirements. Some precost systems also use such additional file data as vendor code number, date of last purchase, amount of inventory purchased, storage location, and length of safe shelf life. Each of the five basic elements will be discussed in some detail. (Additional reference is made to these concepts in later chapters.)

Ingredient code number. Every food item to be placed in the ingredient file must be assigned a unique *ingredient code number*. Although the most common length for a code number is four digits, some systems use eight- or even ten-digit numbers. Number assignment should not be achieved through an arbitrary or random process. When a four-digit number is used, the code number normally assigned falls within a block of numbers allocated to a specific food group. For example, the number 0201 might be assigned to fresh asparagus, since the 0200–0275 block may be reserved for fresh vegetables only. In systems using an eight-digit code number, a meaning is given to specific digits in the number. Usually the first two digits represent an item's food group, the next two digits are associated with a dominant food code, and the last four digits are a product's unique code number.

For example, in coding fresh asparagus, the eight-digit code number assigned might be 30150204. Here, the first two digits (30) represent the fruits and vegetable food group, the next two digits (15) correspond to the asparagus-dominant food code, and the last four digits are the item's unique code number (0204). The use of large code numbers creates relative difficulties in accurate assignment but provides significant descriptive information when the name of an ingredient is not given. From a practical standpoint, most operators find a four-digit code number allocated from a food group block satisfactory. Once a directory of food groups and unique item code numbers exists, the next data element of concern is the product's description.

Ingredient description. The *ingredient description* is composed of the food item's name and a brief statement of its condition at the time of purchase or issue. Normally, precost systems limit the user to a thirty-space description field. In this space, the item should be described as clearly and as fully as possible. A clever use of this space involves reference to the item's issue unit. Since a description of the purchase unit is allowed elsewhere, and since there is no place to mention the breakout or issue unit, this is an appropriate location. For example, ingredient number 0310 has been assigned to corn that is purchased by the case. A description of this item might read—

0310 Corn, Canned

or it could be expanded to read—

0310 Corn, Canned 6 #10 Cans

The incorporation of issue units might be valuable information in the determination of recipe quantities, food usage requirements, or be helpful if the purchase unit (case), or issue unit (#10 can), should change. To illustrate this point, consider tomato ketchup that is purchased by the case. Although the ketchup is purchased by the case, some cases contain one-ounce packets, others contain fourteen-ounce bottles, and others contain #10 cans. The assignment of one ingredient code number and description to this product does not represent these different food item purchases. Hence, three separate ingredient code numbers and three separate descriptions, are required to handle this product adequately. The correct assignments might appear like this—

0351 Ketchup, tom. 100-1 oz. packets
0352 Ketchup, tom. 48-14 oz. bottles
0353 Ketchup, tom. 6-#10 cans

The more accurate and complete the ingredient description, the easier data-coding procedures will be in the other precost files.

Unit of purchase. The unit of purchase, also referred to as the *purchase unit*, is important to precost systems for two reasons. It provides a quick index to the purchase price of an ingredient. Should an invoice be received for an item delivered in a 50-gallon drum versus a four-gallon case, this would signal a different ingredient record.

The unit of purchase also is important during the final summation phase of the precost cycle where ingredients are being summed and converted back into originating units for purchasing. If during a precost cycle it was determined that forty-two #10 cans of corn were needed, the system, which eventually converts these issue units back to case lots, would show a six-case purchase requirement. Purchase units have no real internal meaning to an automated system, since all conversions are based on net weight of the purchase unit and can be adjusted to the user's liking. Although most precost systems limit purchase unit descriptions to six spaces, some may allow for up to ten spaces. The reason for this is that the description is never operated on during system processing; it is merely carried along for communication to the user. Common purchase units are case, drum, block, lb., loaf, bag, and dozen.

Weight of purchase unit. All costing in a precost system must be performed using a common denominator. This common denominator traditionally has been price per pound. In order to establish this base, a *net weight* of each purchase unit must be determined and input into the system. The use of a net weight, rather than gross weight, assures that the price per pound is only on the usable portion of the product.

The net weight describes the purchase unit by its edible quantity, not including its packaging and shipping containers. For example, a case of canned fruit punch might weigh thirty pounds, but its net weight (drinkable quantity) may only be twenty-four pounds. If this product is purchased for $22.56 per case, then its correct price per pound would be 94 cents ($22.56÷24), not 75 cents ($22.56÷30). Net weights should be used because all costing is gravely distorted by any other weight measure. Net weights are not difficult to determine, since most purchased products carry their net weights on their labels. Net weights should be easily obtainable from a reputable vendor.

With growing interest and steady change in packaging toward the metric system, the price-per-pound costing base may evolve into price per gram and/or liter. Many precost systems have been designed to accommodate both metric and imperial units, and therefore conversion to the metric system should not be traumatic.

PRECOST SYSTEMS

Purchase unit price. Because precosting is predicated on an accurate price per pound, the *purchase unit price* becomes the most critical input data to the system. Without a correct purchase unit price in the system, all subsequent costs are computed incorrectly. Every price change must be inputed to the ingredient file via the update option. Price changes may occur because of an increase in the cost of goods or a change in the unit of purchase. For example, canned fruit punch may cost 94 cents per pound when it is purchased by the case (6 #10 cans), but the cost may change to 84 cents per pound when the purchase unit changes to gallons.

Products purchased in different packages must be considered as separate ingredients. The example of ketchup should further clarify this point. Individual portions of ketchup (one-oz. packs) may cost more per pound than does ketchup purchased in large #10 cans. If all recipes containing ketchup were incorrectly coded with the ingredient code number of packets, all of those recipes would carry inflated costs. Furthermore, consider the compounding by product costs that can occur when thousands of ingredients are used to code hundreds of standardized recipes. Once the ingredient file data elements are entered into the system, recipe file work can begin. Figures 7-3 and 7-4 contain sample printouts from two vendor precost systems.

Recipe File

The *recipe file* contains the ingredient requirements for the set of standard recipes used by the foodservice operation. The recipe file program allows the user the same four options that the ingredient file does: 1) an add option for creating or building the file, 2) a delete option for purging an existing file record, 3) an update option for performing changes to data already on file, and 4) a list option for printing or displaying recipes in the file. By selecting the appropriate option, the user can achieve control over the recipe file contents and can experiment with cost structures for recipes in development.

Each recipe is coded and entered into the system in two parts. The first part of the recipe coding involves completion of the recipe header data fields. The header information consists of 1) recipe code number, 2) recipe description, 3) number of portions, and 4) recipe portion size (optional). The second part of the recipe-coding procedure involves 1) ingredient code numbers, 2) ingredient names, 3) ingredient quantities, 4) ingredient yields, and 5) production procedures. Each of these phases will be discussed in detail.

Recipe code number. Every recipe is assigned a unique (four-digit) *recipe code number.* The code numbers are usually assigned according to a prespecified allotment scheme. For example, recipes numbered 3202 to 3250 depict sandwich recipes, and recipes numbered 5100 to 5500 can be used only for desserts. Whatever number allocation scheme is used, ingredient

FIGURE 7-3 Sample Ingredient File Output

Code No.	Ingredient Item Name	Purchase Unit	Price of P. Unit	Weight P. Unit	Price Per Pound
501	FLOUR CLEAR	BAG	15.00	100 LBS	0.15
502	FLOUR BREAD	BAG	22.00	50 LBS	0.44
503	FLOUR GOLD MEDAL	BAG	5.00	25 LBS	0.20
504	FLOUR MIX BASIC MUFFIN	BAG	22.20	30 LBS	0.74
505	FLOUR PANCAKE HUNGRY JACK	BAG	17.10	30 LBS	0.57
506	FLOUR BREAD CORNFLAKE CRUM	BAG	21.90	30 LBS	0.73
507	SUGAR BEET	BAG	8.00	25 LBS	0.32
508	SUGAR GRANULATED	BAG	15.50	50 LBS	0.31
509	SUGAR LIGHT BROWN	LB	16.32	32 LBS	0.51
510	SWEETNER LO CAL	CASE	12.00	12 LBS	1.00
511	MILK NON-FAT DRY	BAG	55.00	50 LBS	1.10
512	STARCH CORN	BAG	5.75	25 LBS	0.23
513	SYRUP CRYSTAL	CASE	12.48	32 LBS	0.39
514	SYRUP BLUE KARO	CASE	14.72	32 LBS	0.46
515	SYRUP RED KARO	CASE	13.72	30 LBS	0.46
551	MUSTARD	GAL	6.72	32 LBS	0.21
552	COCKTAIL SAUCE	CASE	5.67	6 LBS	0.95
553	SAUCE WORCHESTERSHIRE	CASE	18.93	42 LBS	0.45
554	VINEGAR CIDER	GAL	8.16	48 LBS	0.17
601	CEREAL RAISIN BRAN	CASE	26.00	25 LBS	1.04
602	CEREAL CORN FLAKES	CASE	26.73	27 LBS	0.99
603	CEREAL RICE KRISPIES	CASE	17.00	19 LBS	0.89
604	CEREAL QUICK OATS	CASE	14.57	31 LBS	0.47
605	CEREAL CREAM WHEAT	CASE	11.04	16 LBS	0.69
606	CEREAL MALTO MEAL	CASE	10.24	16 LBS	0.64
607	SPAGHETTI	LB	7.80	20 LBS	0.39
651	SPICE GRD BASIL SWEET	LB	2.03	1 LB	2.03
652	SPICE GRD CELERY SALT	LB	0.82	1 LB	0.82
653	SPICE GRD CHILI POWDER	CAN	15.56	5 LBS	3.11
654	SPICE GRD CINNAMON	LB	2.68	1 LB	2.68
655	SPICE GRD GARLIC POWDER	CAN	2.40	12 OZS	3.20
656	SPICE GRD NUTMEG	LB	2.41	1 LB	2.41
657	SPICE GRD OREGANO	LB	4.08	1 LB	4.08
658	SPICE GRD PAPRIKA	LB	3.04	1 LB	3.04
659	SPICE GRD PEPPER BLACK	CAN	9.78	6 LBS	1.63
660	SPICE GRD PEPPER WHITE	LB	2.45	1 LB	2.45
661	SPICE GRD THYME GROUND	LB	1.88	1 LB	1.88
662	SPICE GRD TACO SEASONING	CAN	1.82	2 LBS	0.91
663	SPICE WH BAY LEAF	LB	2.02	1 LB	2.02
664	SPICE FANCY PARSLEY	CAN	4.25	8 OZS	8.50
665	SALT IODIZED	BAG	4.00	100 LBS	0.04
666	SALT DISPENSER WHITE	CASE	9.83	13 LBS	0.76

Source: Courtesy of Hospitality Financial Consultants, P.O. Box 448, Okemos, MI 48864

FIGURE 7-4 Alternate Ingredient File Sample

MAIN KITCHEN

INVENTORY ITEM		INVENTORY UNIT	ACTUAL USE	DEVIATION	ENDING INVENTORY	PRICE	$ VALUE	% PRICE CHANGE
JUICE, LEMON	12/1 QT	QUART	23	1	11	.97	10.67	
PICKLE CHIPS	6/10 CAN	10 CAN	3	0	6	1.80	10.80	40
OLIVES, BLACK	6/10 CAN	10 CAN	-2	-2	2	3.20	6.40	
OLIVES, STUFFED	4/1 GAL	GAL	3	0	1	6.15	6.15	
TUNA LIGHT	66 OZ. 6/CASE	CAN.	24	9	5	5.25	26.25	22
GELATIN, LEMON	4 1/2 LB. 12/CASE	BOX	13	13	0	2.90	0.00	
GELATIN, LIME	4 1/2 LB. 12/CASE	BOX	0	0	2	2.90	5.80	
GELATIN, ASST RED	4 1/2 LB. 12/CASE	BOX	18	-5	13	3.14	40.82	7.8
GELATIN, ORANGE	4 1/2 LB. 12/CASE	BOX	5	5	2	2.90	5.80	
GELATIN, KNOX UNFLAVORED	10# BAG	LB	3	0	8	.80	6.40	
WALKIN BOX								
CELERY PASCAL		LB	153	30	48	.42	20.16	50

Source: Courtesy of Concept Systems Inc., One Franklin Plaza, Ste. 650, Phila., PA 19102

code numbers and recipe code numbers should not overlap. Likewise, the same four-digit number cannot be used for both. This duplication would lead to confusion and would complicate the data-coding procedures. If veal cutlet had an ingredient file number of 1305 and a recipe number of 1305, it might be impossible to differentiate one from the other. An attempt to change recipe data might inadvertently lead to an ingredient file change.

The safest and most easily understood coding scheme is one in which ingredient numbers and recipe numbers are not allowed to be identical or overlap. Requiring ingredient numbers to be lower than or equal to 1500 and prohibiting recipe code numbers of lower than 2000 assures singular file-numbering schemes. The maximum number of recipes allowed in a recipe file varies with the sophistication of system files and the type of computer hardware selected. Small precost systems usually are limited to 400 recipes, and larger-scale systems can store more than 10,000 recipes. Once a code number is assigned to each recipe, the next step is to code the recipe description. (Note: Although recipe numbers usually are four digits, this does not always have to be the case.)

Recipe description. The *recipe description* primarily consists of the recipe name. In some systems, the description must also contain the recipe portion size, if a data field is not provided for this purpose. The name chosen for a recipe should be identical to the standard recipe's name. Precost recipe files normally provide thirty-five spaces for recording the recipe name. Should portion size information also be included in the recipe name, some abbreviations may be required. Portion sizes may be required in recipe names because they may not serve any purpose in the precost system. The system assumes standarized, controlled portions. The portion-size data adds little to the data processing performed by the system. Since standard recipes are developed for a set number of portions at a predetermined portion size, the system cannot alter this relationship.

Number of portions. Standard recipes are composed of a fixed set of ingredients required to produce a certain *number of portions* at a specific portion size. The number of portions for which a recipe is written is a critical variable in the precost system. To develop recipe costs for both batches and portions requires that the number of portions be used. Because precost applications necessitate expanding ingredient quantities up to a required number of portions, the portions that correlate with ingredient levels must be known.

For example, a recipe for beef stew may be written to provide 100 6-ounce portions. The ingredients required to prepare this batch need to be established. When a precost cycle contains 620 6-ounce portions of beef stew, the system assumes linearity among ingredients and multiplies all ingredients and their costs by a factor of 6.2 (620 ÷ 100). The number of portions for which a recipe is composed is an important factor in subsequent precosting computations. Although it may be an option in some systems, the recipe portion size also deserves attention.

Recipe portion size. The *recipe portion size* may or may not be necessary to complete the requisite header information. Recipe portion sizes may be used to verify the difference between the total quantity of ingredients and their relationship to eventual serving size. This reasoning appears weak when one considers that twenty-five pounds of beef yields less than twenty pounds of edible beef. The necessity for using accurate portion-size data is limited so long as standard recipes have been accurately developed and adequately tested. As mentioned earlier, should portion-size data not be a separate entry, it should be incorporated with the recipe name. The portion size differentiates recipes with the same or similar names.

Consider the foodservice establishment serving three portion sizes of prime rib. Each size must have a separate recipe to enable accurate and separate batch and portions costs. These recipe headers might read—

Recipe Number	Recipe Description	Number of Portions	Portion Size
4111	Prime Rib–Petite Cut	100	6 oz.
4122	Prime Rib–Regular Cut	100	12 oz.
4133	Prime Rib–Super Cut	100	16 oz.

This design produces better information than one recipe for all prime rib cuts would. (Note: In this example, the portion sizes—6, 12, and 16 ounces—would have appeared as part of the recipe description if they had not been requested separately.)

Recipe ingredient information: Code numbers. All ingredients that compose a standard recipe must be listed in the ingredient file. In coding a recipe, each ingredient's code number is recorded in the recipe ingredient section of the recipe file. Some systems limit the number of ingredients that can be recorded. System recipes may vary from recipe card or manual files in that no mixing, production, or cooking instructions may be contained on them. This lack of information often causes confusion in the coding procedure. Recipes written in a step-by-step fashion may have the same ingredient listed in several different places. This repetition is unnecessary with a programmed recipe. Since the computer does not cook or eat, it is concerned only with the total amount of each ingredient required. Each ingredient most likely appears as a single entry.

Ingredient names. Not all systems require input of the ingredient names. Since the unique ingredient code number has already been entered, there is no need to enter the item's name. The precost system files can communicate this information internally. This interfacing of ingredient name via file communication produces a listing of ingredients, by ingredient-file description.

Some vendor systems allow the user to enter a different description of an ingredient for recipe production purposes. For example, item number 0113 may be yellow onions. When used in recipe 6157, Quiche Pie, the onions may need to be chopped. Should a by-product of the precost system be the construction of recipe decks, the user may prefer that in this recipe yellow onions appear as—

0113 Onions, yellow–chopped, finely

For the purpose of precosting, only the ingredient number is needed to access the correct ingredient-file record. Ingredient-name fields in recipes basically provide a description of pre-prep, preparation, or production requirements. These descriptors have no effect on the costing capabilities of a system.

Ingredient quantities. Just as the number of portions is critical to the recipe header information, so, too, are the ingredient quantities essential to the recipe data base information. Without the quantities associated with each recipe ingredient code number, no precosting of batch or portion sizes could be performed. Ingredient quantities can range from a large number of pounds or gallons to a pinch or dash of a particular ingredient.

In order to make the precost possible, the quantities entered for each ingredient must be recognizable to the system. For example, a recipe requiring three slices of the ingredient white bread has no meaning, unless the system has been told (in the ingredient file) the mathematical relationship between one slice and a pound. Because all costing is done on a price-per-pound basis, the precost system, or the user, must convert all ingredient requirements to pounds or fractions thereof. Most systems are furnished with internal conversion tables (to pounds) for standard units of measure. Cups, pints, and liters usually present no problem, whereas a scoop, twist, or "to taste" quantity typically cannot be processed. Some systems contain tables for metric as well as imperial units of measure.

Ingredient yields. An option in only a few precost systems, *ingredient yields* provide significant insight into production/inventory control. Realizing the percentage losses resulting from pre-prep, preparation, cooking, and edible portion considerations might help management understand product movement and discrepancies between ingredient quantities issued and recipe-portion sizes. Ingredient yields are especially important to those precost systems that contain nutrient data files. When a menu must be designed to provide certain nutritional requirements achieved through edible-portion sizes, not based on as-purchased specifications, ingredient yields become especially important. Since most precost applications are cost oriented and not nutritionally oriented, ingredient yield factors typically are not a required input feature.

Production procedures. Although not available in all precost systems, some recipe file packages contain space for the *production procedures required to yield a menu item from a list of ingredients*. Why would a system aimed at cost forecasts and control be concerned with preparation, mixing, and cooking instructions? The reason is that *disposable recipe sheets*, which can be generated from this file, may well increase the informational capabilities and control aspects of the system.

If, for example, it is anticipated that 560 portions of meatloaf are needed, then the precosting of this number of servings is computed internally. The system, working from the coded and filed standard recipe, simply multiplies all ingredients by the correct mathematical factor. Assuming the original recipe was written for 80 portions, then all ingredients would be exploded seven-fold for the precost computation. Printing out the new ingredient requirements, multiplied by seven, is directed at increased production control. If left to multiply the ingredients themselves, kitchen personnel might make costly errors. With the distribution of disposable, expanded recipe sheets, production will likely take place with a greater level of efficiency. Figures 7-5 and 7-6 contain examples of computerized recipe file contents.

FIGURE 7-5 Sample Recipe File Output

```
                STANDARD RECIPE FILE

 FIDF     NAME OF                QUANTITY OF      QUANTITY  INGRED
 NUMBER   INGREDIENT             INGREDIENT       IN LBS    COST

 0417 CHICKEN STEW K14-42  (TURKEY)

 COST PER PORTION:   0.17       NO. OF PORTIONS:  66
 PORTION WGT (OZ):   4.00       RECIPE YIELD:     3.00 GAL


 0076   COOKED DICED TURKEY      6.25 LB          6.25     7.12
 6005   CARROTS COOKED DICED     2.00 LB          2.50     1.60
 2044   FROZEN PEAS              2.00 LB          2.00     0.62
 3101   POTATOES COOKED DICED    3.00 LB          3.00     0.61
 1188   CHICKEN BASE             0.25 LB          0.25     0.59
 2011   MARGARINE                1.00 LB          1.00     0.28
 6018   ONIONS CHOPPED MEDIUM    0.50 LB          0.50     0.16
 1479   PASTRY FLOUR             1.00 LB          1.00     0.09
 1099   SALT                     2.50 TBS         0.08     0.00
 1372   BLACK PEPPER             0.50 TSP         0.00     0.00
 1378   SAGE                     0.25 TSP         0.00     0.00
 0000   WATER FOR BASE           1.25 GAL         0.00     0.00
```

Source: Courtesy of Hospitality Financial Consultants, P.O. Box 448, Okemos, MI 48864

PRECOST SYSTEMS

FIGURE 7-6 Alternate Recipe File Sample

```
                                                        R E C I P E

MAIN KITCHEN
SALAD DEPARTMENT
TUNA SALAD PLATE
RECIPE : 520570


 PORTIONS :   SIZE    :    YIELD      : SERVICE PERIOD  :
----------------------------------------------------------------
:  501.   : 1 PLATE :               : WED, LUNCH       :
----------------------------------------------------------------



 INGREDIENT NAME          :           AMOUNT REQUIRED            :
------------------------------------------------------------------
 LETTUCE                  :   10 HEADS         7 OUNCES          :
******************************************************************
 TUNA SALAD               :   501  3 OUNCE PORTIONS              :
                          :        93 LB    15 OUNCES            :
******************************************************************
 EGGS, MEDIUM  GR A       :   41 DOZEN         9 EACH            :
 TOMATOES  3 TO 1         :   41 LBS          12 OUNCES          :
 SCALLIONS                :    7 LBS          13 OUNCES          :
 PICKLE CHIPS             :    5 -10 CANS      2 EACH            :
 OLIVES, BLACK            :    2 -10 CANS     21 EACH            :
 OLIVES, STUFFED          :    2 GALLONS       1 EACH            :
------------------------------------------------------------------

 M E T H O D  O F  P R E P A R A T I O N
-------------------------------------------
PREPARE 9 INCH PLATE WITH LETTUCE UNDERLINER.  ASSEMBLY:  3 OUNCE
SCOOP OF TUNA SALAD,  1 HARD BOILED EGG CUT IN HALF,  2 SLICES OF
TOMATO,  1 SCALLION,  2 PICKLE CHIPS,  1 BLACK OLIVE AND 1 STUFFED
OLIVE PLACED ON LETTUCE UNDERLINER.
```

Source: Courtesy of Concept Systems Inc., One Franklin Plaza, Ste. 650., Phila., PA 19102

Menu Item File

The *menu item file*, also referred to as the menu item master file (MIMF), contains the planned serving schedules by day and meal period. A foodservice operation that is open for seven days per week and serves three meals per day, each consisting of several entrees, appetizers, and desserts requires more file space than does a five-day-per-week, dinner-only operation. The menu item file may only consist of one option. The file allows the user to enter a proposed menu for some period of time. Although institutional foodservice precost systems can process month-long cyclical menus, small-scale systems may only work with weekly or daily menu offerings.

The only data needed to detail a menu plan are the recipe number and forecasted demand for each recipe item. Since all the recipes are coded with a recipe number (in the recipe file), accessing them by number becomes very simple. The recipe name, or any other descriptor, is not input. The number of servings expected for each menu item on the menu plan fulfills the input requirements. For example:

4570, 350
2175, 216
9872, 127

may be input for a precost system in which number 4570 has 350 forecasted meals, item 2175 has 216 expected takers, and item 9872 has 127 portions required. The ease and simplicity of menu item and portion forecast input is possible because of data coding procedures described earlier in the ingredient and recipe files. Some systems also might employ the menu file for differentiating menu-item offerings from *subassembly recipes* or for developing a data base for future forecasting.

The term *subassembly recipes* describes recipes that use ingredients and procedures but do not result in menu items. For example, the recipe for an egg salad sandwich may only include two ingredients—sliced white bread and egg salad. Assuming that the foodservice operator makes both bread and egg salad in-house, a recipe will be necessary for each item. These recipes may be stored in the recipe file along with the menu item (egg salad sandwich) recipes. The bread and egg salad recipes, however, are called subassembly recipes since their production yields an ingredient to another recipe, not a menu item itself.

Precost systems capable of accommodating subassembly recipes require more file space and need to run on a microcomputer or larger operating system. The use of subassembly recipes can be avoided by operators who elect to cost out the subassembly recipe item and then create a hypothetical ingredient entry in the ingredient file. This method of operation enables egg salad, for example, to appear as an ingredient rather than as a prepared item and accurately reflects its cost. Accurate costs can be derived either by use of an artificial ingredient entry or by a subassembly recipe format. Figure 7-7 depicts the relationship between a subassembly and a menu item recipe.

Although not successfully or fully developed to date, an internal forecasting model for menu item production appears to be a desirable goal for most precost vendors. Some systems may claim that they forecast, or provide data for forecast development, yet few can demonstrate a reliable, working model. Here in the menu item file, this type of data is most useful and

136 PRECOST SYSTEMS

FIGURE 7-7 Relationship of Subassembly Recipes

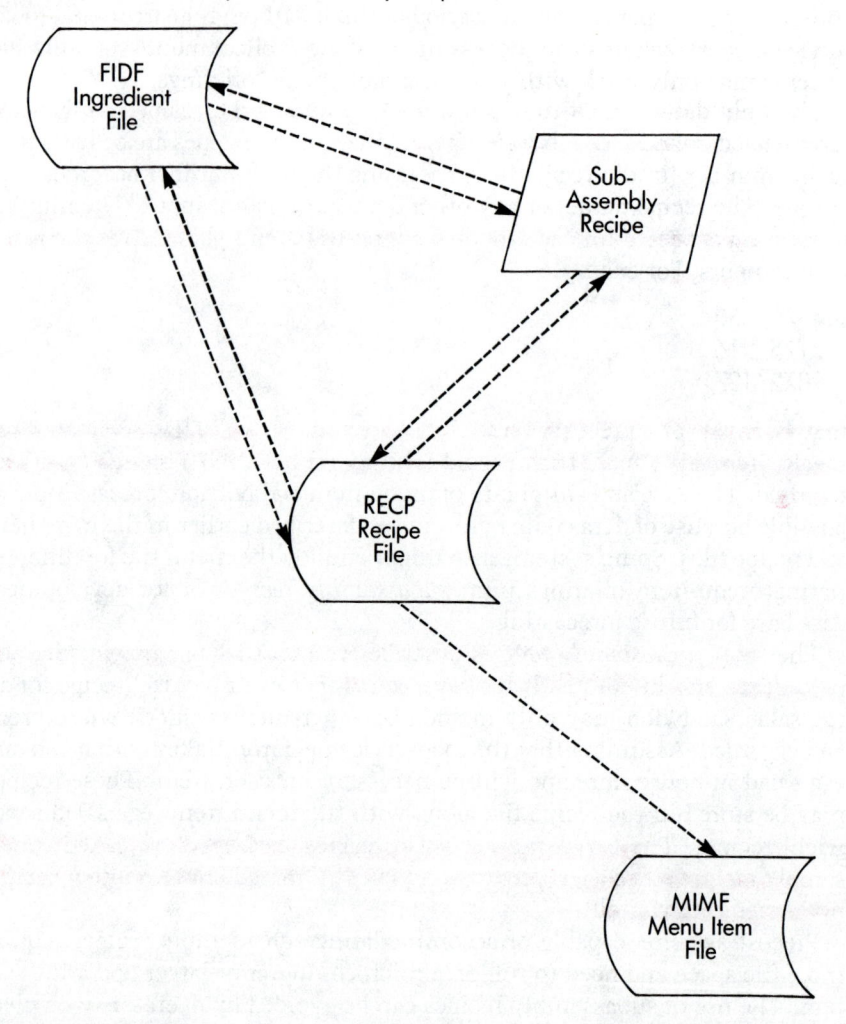

[Diagram showing relationships between FIDF Ingredient File, Sub-Assembly Recipe, RECP Recipe File, and MIMF Menu Item File with dashed arrows connecting them]

should be maintained and used. Perhaps a large part of the problem concerning forecasting models is the nature of the variables encountered. For example, an item like sirloin steak may be extremely popular when served opposite spaghetti, but may become less popular when featured against crab legs. Forecasting the demand for sirloin steak is difficult even when its competing menu item is known. In the future, forecasting models are apt to become much more critical to the foodservice operator interested in reducing wastes and/or stockouts resulting from inadequate forecasting.

The menu item file may control several functions within a precost system. These functions are likely to vary significantly from one vendor package to another. The basic purpose of the menu item file is to afford the food-service operator a space to enter the menu plan and forecasted demand totals for a specific period of time. Figure 7-8 illustrates the role of the menu item file.

FIGURE 7-8 Role of Menu Item File

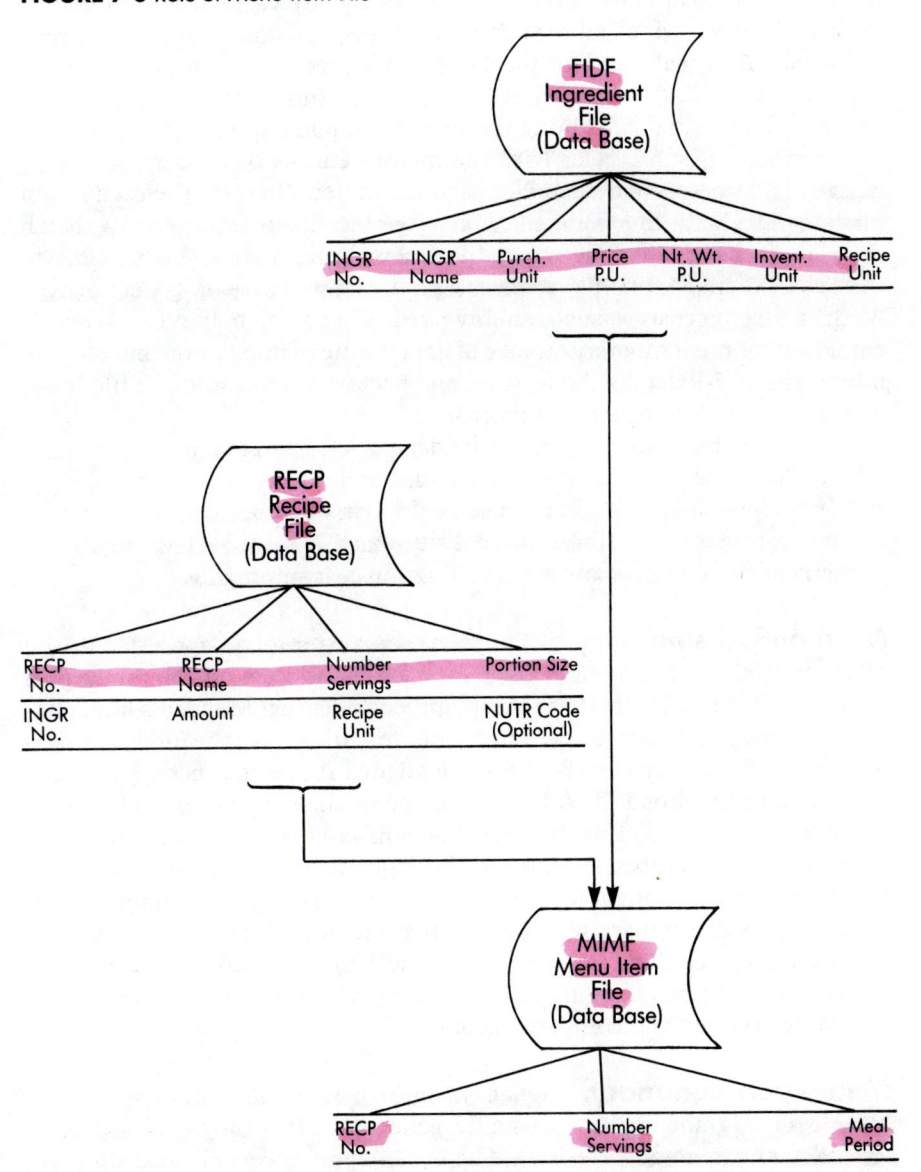

```
                    FIDF
                 Ingredient
                    File
                 (Data Base)

INGR   INGR   Purch.   Price   Nt. Wt.   Invent.   Recipe
No.    Name   Unit     P.U.    P.U.      Unit      Unit


        RECP
       Recipe
        File
     (Data Base)

RECP    RECP      Number        Portion Size
No.     Name      Servings
INGR    Amount    Recipe        NUTR Code
No.               Unit          (Optional)


                    MIMF
                 Menu Item
                    File
                 (Data Base)

RECP              Number                  Meal
No.               Servings                Period
```

138 PRECOST SYSTEMS

Precost File

The *precost file* is primarily a report-generating file capable of interfacing all other files to produce a summary of the menu plan, recipe ingredients, and potential costs (per item, per meal, per day, and per plan). The precost deals with potential costs, since all costs are based on standardized recipes and accurate ingredient descriptions. The precost program creates a precost file and stores data to produce detailed meal-period analyses, ingredient-quantity totals and costs, recipe and food group analyses, and cost summaries across all ingredients, meals, and for the cycle. Since precosting required the most file space to operate and the longest processing time, this file is usually a greater influence in determining the size of computer system required.

The precost file interfaces with the menu item file to pick up the recipe number and forecasted demand for each menu item. In turn, the menu item file integrates with the recipe file to retrieve ingredient requirements, batch size, and recipe name. The recipe file chains back to the ingredient file to collect the ingredient name, cost per pound, and purchase unit descriptions. Because the precost is such an involved procedure, buffer file space is employed for the temporary storage of data during manipulation and computation. Figure 7-9 details the forward and backward integration of file information necessary to generate a precost.

The precost file is a work space that develops formatted reports with real-time data. Reports are dated so that their applicability is known. As costs and/or recipes change, so do precosts. Four types of reports normally found in a precost system are 1) meal period summary, 2) meal cycle summary, 3) portion and meal cost summary, and 4) group cost summaries.

Meal period summary. The meal period summary report details the batch, portion, and ingredient costs for each menu item on the menu plan for a specific meal. To illustrate this point, consider that Monday's lunch has only one item on it, Beef Stew. The menu item file shows the following data on file: 2355, 200. Hence, Beef Stew (assigned recipe number 2355) has a forecasted demand of 200 portions. Located in the recipe file, Beef Stew is found to be composed of twelve ingredients in varying quantities. Since each ingredient code number is found in the ingredient file, cost data and purchase units can be brought forward for reporting. Figure 7-10 contains a sample meal period summary report. Note that Figure 7-10 provides blank data fields for the recording of actual (post-sales) figures onto the report page itself. This provison offers management a sound method by which to maintain more accurate and complete records.

Meal cycle summary. Once all meal period summaries have been completed, a grand report is usually generated. This aggregate report is termed the *meal cycle summary*. The cycle report covers all meals for the

PRECOST SYSTEMS

FIGURE 7-9 Precost File Integration

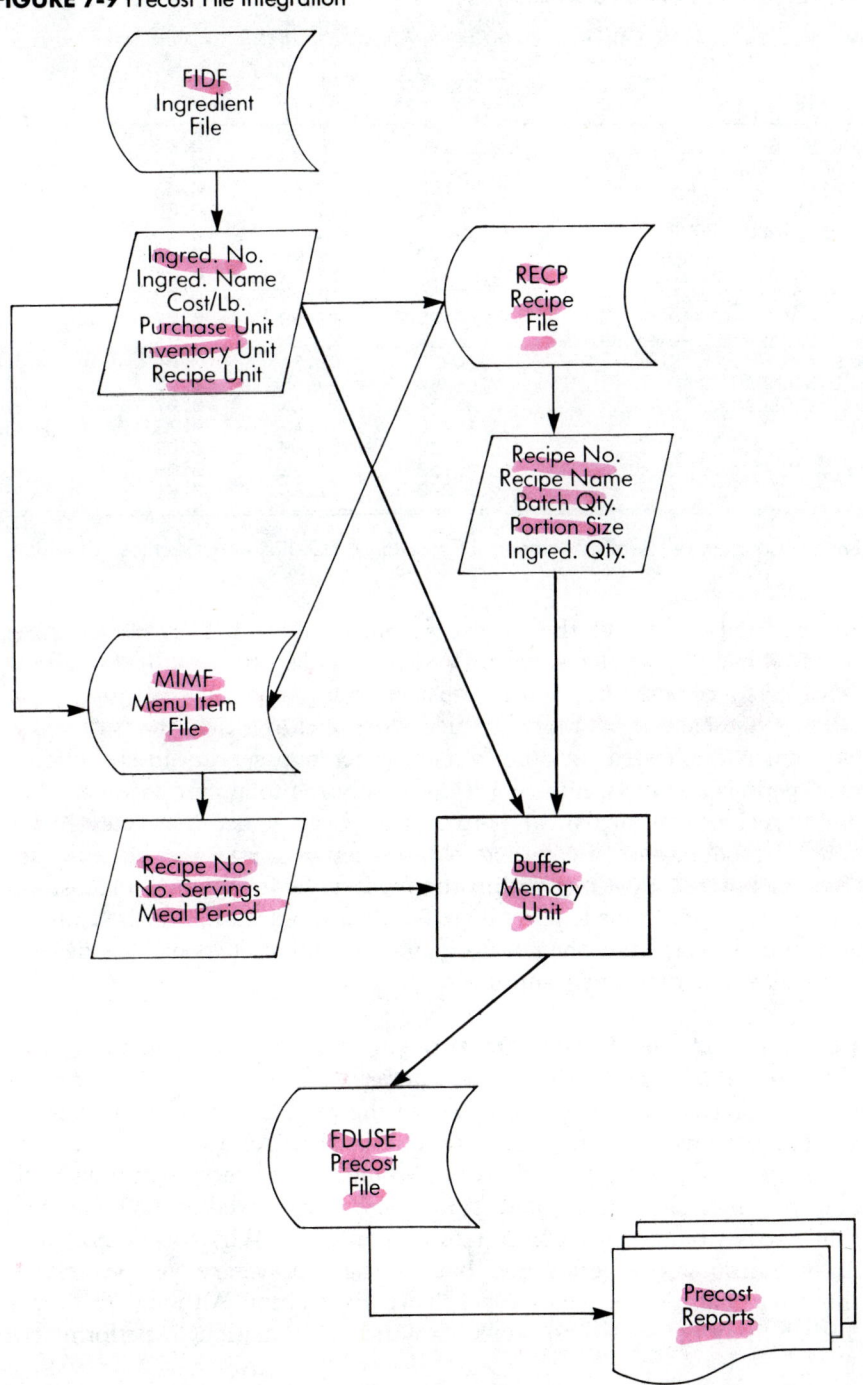

140   PRECOST SYSTEMS

FIGURE 7-10 Meal Period Summary

```
Menu Item List for Tuesday's Lunch.  Count:  Projected = 410   Actual = <     >

 Code    Menu                         Units or    Total    Cost per    Actual
 No.     Item Name                    Servings    Cost     Serving     Servings
 ----------------------------------------------------------------------------
 2034    CANNED PEAS                    200        8.25      0.04      <     >
 2022    COTTAGE CHEESE                 150       24.75      0.17      <     >
 2032    BANANAS                        100        2.81      0.03      <     >
 2026    ICE CREAM                      200       15.63      0.08      <     >
 2325    HOBO VEGETABLE SOUP            250       52.11      0.21      <     >
 2350    CHILI                          200       44.04      0.22      <     >
 2100    BURGER ON BUN                   75       18.79      0.25      <     >
 2120    SEAFOOD PATTIES W/ SAUCE       100       73.34      0.73      <     >
 2300    FRENCH FRIED POTATOES          425       28.98      0.07      <     >
 2305    YELLOW SQUASH W/CH. SAUCE      225       99.68      0.44      <     >
 2315    COLE SLAW                      225        8.24      0.04      <     >
 2311    TOSSED SALAD                   290       44.59      0.15      <     >
 2208    SUNSHINE SALAD                 150       10.31      0.07      <     >
 2007    COFFEE                         200        6.43      0.03      <     >
 2008    TEA                            100        1.68      0.02      <     >
 2009    MILK, SKIM                     150       11.72      0.08      <     >
 2011    MILK, WHOLE                    200       11.88      0.06      <     >
============================================================================
```

Source: Courtesy of Hospitality Financial Consultants, P.O. Box 448, Okemos, MI 48864

entire period over which the precost is being conducted. The report summarizes and lists each recipe number in the menu plan, the number of portions expected to be produced, and the cost of each portion. In addition, it also prints a condensed list of all ingredients required to satisfy the menu plan. No item is duplicated. In other words, if ketchup appears in six different meal periods and in twenty-two recipes, only the total amount of ketchup (for all recipes and meals) is reported. It has been argued that since precost systems produce such a complete report, they can serve as a basis for purchase or issue requisitions within the foodservice framework. Precost systems convert and print lengthy ingredient summaries in purchase units (or issue units) to facilitate the purchase and movement of goods. See Figure 7-11 for a sample meal cycle summary.

Portion and meal cost summary. A *portion and meal cost summary* is a valuable report that most systems offer. Using a simple matrix format, the precost system lists the days of the week across the top, and each meal period down the left-hand margin of the page. An operation that serves a four-week, seven day-per-week cycle would have twenty-eight rows in the matrix. If breakfast, lunch, and dinner were to be served on each day, then this matrix would have a column dimension of six. Why six and not three? Each column carries both a meal period cost and average cost per serving; thus, two columns are needed for each original column. Although this report initially may not appear to provide any new information, it performs two

FIGURE 7-11 Meal Cycle Summary

```
                              WEEKLY PRECOST DOCUMENT
                                  WEEK OF JUNE 8
Meal Summary for Tuesday's Lunch for the week of JUNE 8.

Code   Ingredient                  Number of   Purchase   Total    Price Per   Total
No.    Item Name                   P. Units    Unit       Pounds   Pound       Cost
============================================================================================
660    SPICE GRD PEPPER WHITE      0.104       LB         0.1      2.45        $0.26
665    SALT IODIZED                0.004       BAG        0.4      0.04        $0.01
704    COFFEE                      3.333       LB         3.3      1.90        $6.33
705    BEVERAGE TEA BLACK          0.125       CASE       0.6      2.62        $1.64
804    MARGARINE                   0.166       CASE       5.0      0.33        $1.65
809    CHEESE MONTEREY JACK        0.680       BLOCK      27.2     2.12        $57.70
813    MILK SKIM FORTIFIED         1.172       GAL        46.9     0.25        $11.72
814    MILK WHOLE                  1.563       GAL        62.5     0.19        $11.88
819    COTTAGE CHEESE              5.625       CTN        28.1     0.88        $24.75
854    BANANAS                     18.750      LB         18.8     0.15        $2.81
905    CABBAGE GREEN               45.000      LB         45.0     0.14        $6.30
906    CABBAGE RED                 0.129       CASE       2.1      1.12        $2.32
907    CARROTS BULK                0.165       CASE       8.3      1.06        $8.80
910    LETTUCE HEAD                2.071       CASE       49.7     0.75        $37.29
913    RADISHES CELLO              0.138       CASE       4.1      0.14        $0.58
915    SQUASH SUMMER               3.629       CASE       29.0     1.38        $39.92
957    POTATOES FRENCH FRIES       3.220       CASE       96.6     0.30        $28.98
1009   FISH SURFCAKE               1.143       CASE       40.0     1.68        $67.20
1059   BEEF GROUND                 0.108       LB         21.7     1.30        $28.17
1060   BEEF PATTIES MEDIUM         0.046       LB         13.9     1.11        $15.42
1301   ICE CREAM                   3.125       GAL        25.0     0.63        $15.63
1475   BUNS HAMBURG SESAME 5 INCH  2.083       PKG        6.3      0.54        $3.38
1479   BREAD CRUMBS                4.083       LB         4.1      0.10        $0.41
1500   WATER                       18.983      GAL        151.9    0.00        $0.19
============================================================================================
```

Source: Courtesy of Hospitality Financial Consultants, P.O. Box 448, Okemos, MI 48864

PRECOST SYSTEMS   141

142 PRECOST SYSTEMS

FIGURE 7-12 Portion and Meal Cost Summary

```
Total Costs and Costs per Portion

Meal            Monday         Tuesday        Wednes/         Sunday         Totals:
---------------------------------------------------------------------------------------
Breakfast       0.00 0.00      0.00 0.00      0.00  /         0.00 0.00      0.00 0.00
Lunch           0.00 0.00      463.23 1.13    0.00 /          0.00 0.00      463.23 1.13
Dinner          0.00 0.00      0.00 0.00      0. /  /00       0.00 0.00      0.00 0.00
Totals:         0.00 0.00      463.23 1.13    0/   /00        0.00 0.00      463.23 1.13

The total cost for the week is    $463.23.
```

Source: Courtesy of Hospitality Financial Consultants, P.O. Box 448, Okemos, MI 48864

important functions. First, it allows for all meals, and a summary of all meals, to be analyzed. Second, it offers a new piece of data not generated elsewhere—the average cost per portion. This new data is especially important in the area of accounting. Figure 7-12 contains a sample portion and meal cost summary.

Group cost summaries. Group cost summaries are reports that deal with either a recipe group or ingredient food groups. Should the cost of a menu cycle be unexpectedly high or low, the best method of highlighting these fluctuations is by group analyses. If ingredients are coded according to predetermined number groups, then a food group code segmentation report can be output. If the recipe number is also under the same limitation, it, too, can be reported by the predominant recipe group code number. In either case, the advantages of group reports are that they enable management to gain control over costs within categories and suggest various inflation-fighting recipe changes. Some systems flag any food items whose costs are expected to rise by more than 5 percent. Others key in on recipe groups and arrange cost data from high to low, or vice versa.

Additional Files

At least four additional files are offered by vendors as addenda to basic precost systems. The *nutrient file* contains sixteen nutritional qualities for every food item and/or menu item. The *general ledger* package deals with account receivables and payables. An *inventory file* is based on perpetual inventory and preset order levels. *Payroll* can be expanded to include labor costing of recipes and the printing of payroll checks.

Obviously, all of these applications do not have a direct bearing on the primary focus of a precost—the determination of food costs before the production and service of a menu plan. Figure 7-13 contains a schematic diagram showing a complete system with all possible files included.

FIGURE 7-13 Complete Precost System

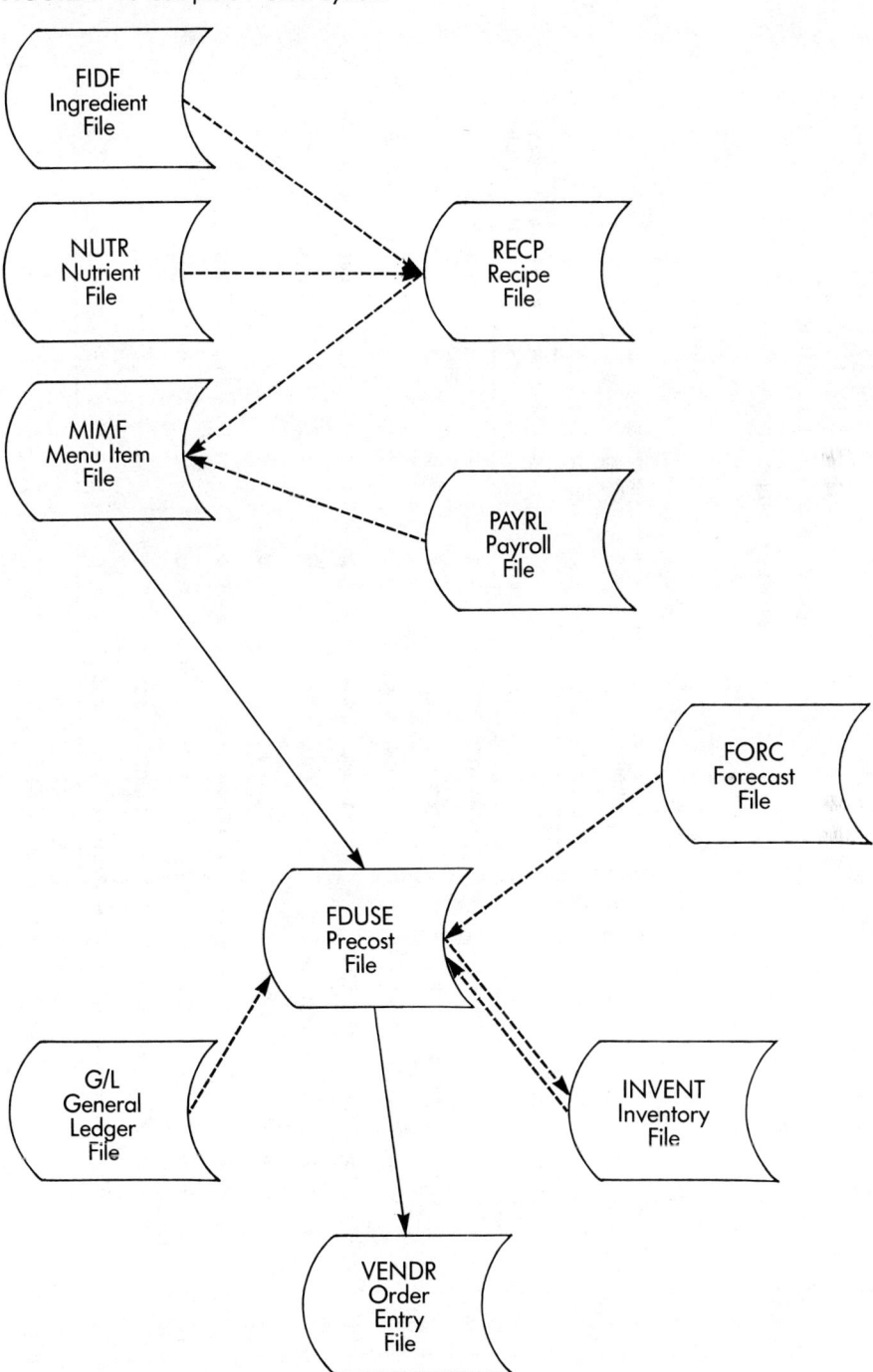

144 PRECOST SYSTEMS

FIGURE 7-14 Sample Vendor Order

```
                              PURCHASE REQUIREMENTS
                                GROCERY ORDER GROUP

                       ORDER DATE    : 05-25 : 05-30 :
                       DELIVERY DATE : 05-28 : 05-31 : (SHORT)/SURPLUS : DATE
ITEM :                             :         :       :         :  QTY : UNITS : SHORT
NUMBER: NAME           : UNIT      :         :       :         :      :       :
 302 : JUICE, LEMON          12/1 QT:  CASE  :   1   :   0     :   8  : QUART :
1060 : PICKLE CHIPS          6/10 CN:  CASE  :   1   :   2     :   3  : 10CAN :
   4 : OLIVES, BLACK         6/10 CN:  CASE  :   1   :   0     :   1  : 10CAN :
  16 : OLIVES, STUFFED       4/1 GAL:  GAL   :   2   :   0     :   0  : GAL   :
 422 : TUNA, LIGHT 6602      6/CASE :  CASE  :   3   :   1     :   2  : CAN   :
1054 : GELATIN, LEMON 4 1/2 LB 12/CASE: BOX  :   5   :   0     :  (5) : BOX   : 05-25
 222 : GELATIN, LIME 4 1/2 LB 12/CASE: BOX   :   0   :   0     :   1  : BOX   :
 224 : GELATIN, RED 4 1/2 LB 12/CASE:  CASE  :   0   :   1     :   3  : BOX   :
 234 : GELATIN, ORANG 4 1/2 LB 12/CASE: BOX  :   0   :   0     :  14  : BOX   :
 651 : GELATIN, KNOX UNFLAVORED 10 BAG: BAG  :   0   :   0     :   4  : LB    :
```

Source: Courtesy of Concept Systems Inc., One Franklin Plaza, Ste. 650., Phila., PA 19102

The availability of general ledger, inventory, and payroll files makes the precost system more of an integrated management package. Integrated management packages are discussed in another chapter of this book. (Note: Figure 7-14 contains a sample vendor grocery order that can be derived through an interaction between the inventory and precost summary files.)

SUMMARY

Precosting is an important management tool aimed at controlling food costs before their production and service. An accurate reflection of costs is a function of the proper use of the ingredient file, the recipe file, the menu item file, and the precost file.

The ingredient file must contain a description and a unique code number for every food item purchased by a foodservice operation. These data are used to formulate a common costing denominator (dollar per pound) to be used throughout the precost system.

The recipe file is designed to hold a description for all recipes likely to be served. The recipe file is interfaced to the ingredient file and uses its dollar-per-pound cost figures to cost out recipes. Recipe costs are determined for each batch (number of servings and portion size) and for each ingredient.

The menu item file provides space for the operator to enter the menu plan and forecasted demand totals for a specific time period.

The precost file, which can interface with all other files, is used to determine preproduction costs (batch and portion). An operator can be informed about cost projections well before the actual service of the meal. Based on these results, the operator can revise the menu plan, modify expected demands, or operate with the current plan. Even though costs are determined based on strict, standardized recipes, not all production personnel follow these recipes to their exact specifications. Standard recipes are essential to achieving successful controls in a foodservice operation. Typical precost module reports include meal period summary, portion and meal cost summary, meal cycle summary, and group cost summaries.

Precost systems can be extended to include one or more of the following files: nutrient data file, general ledger file, inventory file, and payroll files. The latter three files may not enhance a system's precost capabilities or assist in menu planning preparation phases as do nutrient data. All in all, precosting is becoming more important to the foodservice industry as inflation and recession continue to erode the bottom line.

KEY CONCEPTS

The following concepts were introduced in this chapter. Their meanings should be completely understood.

1. *Disposable Recipe Sheet*–a recipe card that has been multiplied upward or downward to reflect accurately ingredient amounts for variable batch sizes; computer output that can be discarded following meal preparation.
2. *General Ledger*–an accounting document used to record, monitor, and control a broad array of financial transactions. Basically a running scorecard of business activity.
3. *Group Cost Summary*–an aggregation of expenses associated with an ingredient food group (e.g., meats, fish, poultry, and dairy products).
4. *Ingredient Code Number*–a unique number assigned to each food item purchased; usually a four-, six-, eight-, or ten-digit number.
5. *Ingredient Description*–a computer file field designed to contain the (generic) name of a food item.
6. *Ingredient File*–the principal file in a precost system required to establish an item's price-per-pound denominator for use throughout the system.
7. *Ingredient Yield*–refers to the potential weight loss of an item during prepreparation, preparation, cooking, or edible portion depletion in recipe production.
8. *Inventory File*–collection of data relating to stock on hand: its value, use, variance, and reorder points.
9. *Meal Cost Summary*–a listing of meal (batch) costs for menu items appearing in a meal plan.
10. *Meal Cycle Summary*–a report detailing meal costs for specific periods in a precost survey.
11. *Menu Item File*–the principal file in a precost system required for input of a meal plan and estimated service requirements.
12. *Menu Plan*–a listing of the recipe items by code number to be offered for service.
13. *Net Weight*–the weight of a food item that is available for use in a recipe; weight after container and packing materials are removed from a purchase unit.
14. *Number of Portions*–yield expected from a standardized recipe with a known portion size.
15. *Nutrient File*–an optional file in a precost system responsible for defining the composition of menu items.
16. *Payroll*–an itemized list of employees, hourly rates, salaries, withholdings, deductions, and like information, for a business enterprise.

PRECOST SYSTEMS

17. *Portion Cost Summary*-A listing of portion costs for menu items appearing in a meal plan.
18. *Precost File*-the principal file in a precost system responsible for integrating the ingredient, recipe, and menu item files to enable a cost analysis.
19. *Precost System*-the determination of potential food costs before the actual production and service of a meal.
20. *Production Procedures*-the steps necessary in prepreparation, preparation, cooking, and serving of a menu item.
21. *Purchase Unit*-a descriptor of the container or package in which a food item is delivered.
22. *Purchase Unit Price*-the dollar amount paid for a purchase unit.
23. *Recipe Code Number*-unique number assigned to each standardized recipe in the recipe file.
24. *Recipe Description*-a computer file field designed to contain the name of a recipe held on file.
25. *Recipe File*-the principal file in a precost system responsible for maintaining the header and ingredient data associated with each recipe.
26. *Recipe Portion Size*-the standard size of a serving of a recipe item.
27. *Standard Recipe*-a tested, proven list of ingredient quantities and procedures that yield a predictable number of portions of a menu item.
28. *Subassembly Recipe*-a recipe that yields an ingredient that serves as input to another recipe; does not produce a menu item.

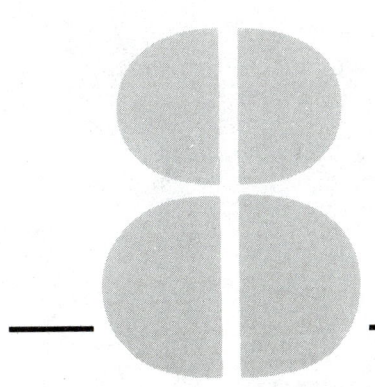

Menu Engineering

Chapter Objectives

1. To introduce a unique method of menu analysis and design
2. To present the mathematical techniques involved in menu engineering
3. To illustrate an application of the menu engineering theory
4. To expand the model from a manual framework to a computerized application
5. To analyze and interpret the menu engineering model

The development of an analytical tool that measures the strength of a foodservice menu is a relatively recent phenomenon. It began with the realization of restaurateurs that food cost percentage points and slow-moving inventories were not the primary indicators of success or failure. Instead, they turned to the concept of gross profit theory and thought of their menu not merely as a list of items for sale, but rather as a powerful marketing tool that could be used to influence purchases and increase profit margins.

Such foodservice experts as Win Schuler, Michael Hurst, and Don Smith have worked to define and refine this concept into a workable model for foodservice management. Because the mechanics of the gross profit theory approach are somewhat tedious and time consuming, many operators agreed in principle with the concept but were unwilling to perform the mathematical procedures required for completeness. In the early 1980s, Don Smith and Michael Kasavana further refined the concept, its terminology, and mathematical procedures into what has now become known as *menu engineering*.* Using related treatments from interrelated disciplines (economics, statistics, finance) has led to the adoption of such phrases as *contribution margin*, *achievement rate*, and *decision matrix*. The development of computer software, capable of quickly and accurately performing all manual processes and reporting extended output, has led to wider interest in the foodservice industry.

The topic of menu engineering is discussed in this chapter in four related parts. Part one deals with an introduction to the concept. Part two is aimed at explaining the mathematical technique itself, and part three presents both manual and computer analysis. Part four is oriented toward managerial strategies as suggested by the analyses and their implementation.

PART ONE: THE CONCEPT

What is the most profitable price to assign to a menu item? What is the potential food cost for a given menu? At what price level and mix of sales does a restaurant maximize its profits? Which current menu items require repricing, replacement, or repositioning on the menu? How can the success of a menu change be evaluated? The answer to these and related questions can be found through the application of "menu engineering."

Although menu engineering at first may appear somewhat complex, it is a tool designed to improve managerial effectiveness in pricing, content, design, and marketing strategies.

---

*See *Menu Engineering* by M. L. Kasavana and Donald I. Smith, Hospitality Publication Inc., P.O. Box 448, Okemos, MI 48864. Published: 1982.

Inflationary Impact

As inflation erodes a restaurant's bottom line, foodservice managers tend to 1) reduce portion size, 2) purchase at lower specifications, 3) eliminate complimentary food items, 4) gravitate toward a la carte service, 5) increase menu prices, 6) reduce labor costs, and 7) tighten operational controls. Although all of these actions are popular survival strategies, they have the potential to affect adversely a consumer's perception of value. A decline in business may result. Perhaps the most effective way to cope with an inflated economy is to develop demand-based, recession-proof menus. The concept of menu engineering is based upon this orientation.

Other solutions to the diminishing profitability problem are to increase: 1) new customer demand (through market segmentation, merchandising, and positioning), 2) old customer demand (through advertising, menu design, and customer service), 3) use of assets (enhance employee productivity and service), and 4) menu-item contribution margins (through improved pricing approaches). These alternatives tend to have a positive effect on perceived value and can lead to a broadened customer base. Menu engineering is perhaps the best means of achieving these ends.

Traditional Menu Pricing

Histroically, the foodservice industry has depended on *cost-multiplier* formulas for the determination of menu prices. Management has been misdirected to the inaccurate conclusion that profits are closely related to percentages. Quite frankly, you cannot bank percentages. Because foodservice management has been conditioned to view profit synonymously with cost of goods percentages, profit margins often are omitted from a menu analysis. Additionally, cost-based multiplier methods, also called *target-pricing schemes*, ignore the most critical principal of marketing, the consumer. A restaurant's clientele and its perception of value should be a primary component of the menu-pricing process.

To illustrate the major weaknesses of a cost percentage-based analysis, consider the hypothetical menu in Table 8-1.

TABLE 8-1 Menu Item Analysis

Menu Items	Item Food Cost	Menu Selling Price	Food Cost	Contribution Margin (Price—Cost)
Chicken	$1.50	$4.50	33%	$3.00
Steak	3.00	7.00	43%	4.00
Lobster	4.50	9.00	50%	4.50

MENU ENGINEERING

In this example, the item with the highest food cost percentage (50 percent), also has the largest contribution margin ($4.50). The contribution margin is found by subtracting the food cost of an item (variable cost) from its selling price. The remaining dollars contributing to pay for overhead (fixed cost) and profit (if any) are called the contribution margin.

If management prefers to sell the item with the highest contribution margin regardless of its food cost percentage, the restaurant may incur its highest food cost percentage. Although this behavior could result in a higher food cost percentage, the restaurant would attain its largest contribution to profit. The contribution margin is important to the pricing decision and when applied together with customer demand (menu mix) it becomes an even more powerful tool.

To demonstrate the critical nature of a *menu mix* on overall costs and margins, consider two menu mixes, A and B in Table 8-2. Each menu contains the same items, with identical standard recipes and the same total number of covers, but sells in varying proportions.

From these data, it is apparent that the menu sales mix producing the highest potential food cost percentage (44.8 percent) also results in the larger *average contribution margin* per item ($4.00). The more management can influence customer demand toward higher contribution margin items (and away from low contribution margin items), the better the resultant bottom line.

What is Menu Engineering?

Menu engineering is a series of processes through which management can evaluate current and future menu pricing, design, and content decisions. The menu engineering approach requires that attention be focused on two critical elements:

1. *Menu Mix (MM)*-an analysis of customer preferences in menu item selection (i.e., customer demand analysis).
2. *Contribution Margin (CM)*-an analysis of the contribution margins (gross profit) of all menu items (i.e., item pricing analysis).

The menu engineering concept requires management to orient itself to the number of dollars that a menu contributes to profit, not merely to monitor cost percentages. A pricing strategy that is based solely on costs and cost markups may be dangerously inaccurate and inadvertently constrain a restaurant's ability to maximize its revenues and profits.

MENU ENGINEERING

TABLE 8-2 Menu Mix Analysis

Menu Mix A

Menu Items	Menu Sales Mix	Food Cost	Dollar Sales	Contribution Margin
Chicken	1000	$1500	$4500	$3000
Steak	400	1200	2800	1600
Lobster	300	1350	2700	1350
TOTAL	1,700	$4,050	$10,000	$5,950

Potential Food Cost = $\frac{\$4,050}{\$10,000}$ = 40.5%

Average Contribution Margin = $\frac{\$5950}{1700}$ = $3.50

Menu Mix B

Menu Items	Menu Sales Mix	Food Cost	Dollar Sales	Contribution Margin
Chicken	300	$450	$1350	$900
Steak	800	2400	5600	3200
Lobster	600	2700	5400	2700
TOTAL	1,700	$5,550	$12,350	$6,800

Potential Food Cost = $\frac{\$5,550}{\$12,350}$ = 44.8%

Average Contribution Margin = $\frac{\$6800}{1700}$ = $4.00

Do not misunderstand! Percentages serve as important managerial controls and provide feedback on operations that cannot be otherwise monitored. Menu engineering involves percentages in an evaluative capacity, but it does not rely on percentages as a basis for a successful pricing effort. Menu engineering ignores the question: "What is a satisfactory food cost percentage?" and asks rather, "Is the restaurant getting a reasonable contribution to profit from its menu mix?"

Every menu projects a potential food cost percentage that management aims to achieve. This potential food cost percentage varies among restaurants and may be difficult to evaluate. For two restaurants serving identical menus in different markets, desired food costs may range from 25 percent to 33 1/3 percent to 50 percent, or more. This fluctuation may be cited as one of the major weaknesses of cost-multiplier pricing techniques. Management that bases prices strictly on costs will be unable to measure total effectiveness of its menu because of the inherent prejudice from which prices are constructed. In other words, a pricing analysis based on cost percentages from which the prices were originally derived is biased and short-sighted. For example, if one desires a 33 1/3 percent potential food cost percentage, multiplying each menu item's cost by a factor of three (100% ÷ 33 1/3%) would be expected to produce a 33 1/3 percent food cost percentage later. This example illustrates a case of achieving a desired outcome by manipulating the data initially.

Cost-multiplier pricing techniques can also artificially force menu items to a price level at which they may become noncompetitive and dysfunctional to the menu mix. Overinflating a menu item's price may drive customers from that item. Ironically, that item probably has the largest contribution margin of any item on the menu. The restaurant's profit will likely decrease, leading to the ultimate removal of a potentially good menu item because of a lack of sufficient demand (sales). Additionally, the unreasonably high menu prices that often result from target-pricing schemes may actually persuade customers to eat out less often, because food at home may appear to be a better value alternative. Competition in the form of the grocery store, not another competing restaurant, often is ignored in the pricing approach.

Menu engineering avoids the shortcomings of cost-multiplier methodolgies by incorporating both a demand-popularity index and a weighted contribution-margin index into its analysis.

PART TWO: THE TECHNIQUE

Menu engineering is a managerial tool for menu analysis and design. It provides a quantitative measurement scheme for evaluating success in menu and related decision areas. The basic menu engineering model can be segmented into twelve component steps.

Steps to Menu Engineering

Menu engineering requires that the foodservice operator be familiar with each menu item's (product) cost, selling price, and number sold (or forecasted sales) for some period of time. As the analysis progresses, a menu item's contribution margin and sales activity is categorized as being relatively high or low. In the final segment of this process, each menu item is classified and evaluated for both its marketing and pricing success. The categorization of items and their eventual assignment to a classification are the result of a series of mathematical and logical procedures. The twelve steps of menu engineering are described below.

Step one. Identify competing menu items. List the names of all competing menu items that appear on the same menu.

Step two. Record the number of items sold (or forecasted). The number of covers of each menu item sold make up the menu mix. These sales data provide important information needed throughout the analysis.

Step three. Compute menu item mix proportions. Each item's sales are divided by the total number of covers sold to yield that item's menu mix percentage.

$$MM\% = \frac{\text{menu item sales}}{\text{total number sold (all items)}}$$

Step four. Categorize menu mix percentages. The menu mix percentages (MM%) are categorized as being either high or low, depending on whether or not they exceed the MM% achievement rate. The achievement rate is determined by multiplying seventy percent (.70) times one divided by the number of competing menu items (1/N). A MM% equal to or exceeding this rate is categorized as being high; otherwise it is considered low.

1. MM% Achievement Rate = (1/N)(.70)
2. High MM% ≥ MM% Achievement Rate
3. Low MM% < MM% Achievement Rate

Step five. List menu item selling prices. The selling prices for all competing items need to be listed. These are simply the published menu prices.

Step six. Determine standard food costs. Menu item standard portion costs are composed of: a) standard recipe costs, b) garnish cost, and/or c) supplemental food cost. For example, consider a 10-oz. steak dinner. This item requires 5/8 of a $3.86 lb. of meat. Its standard recipe cost is found to be $2.30 (5/8 × 3.68). The steak is garnished with onion rings and mushroom caps costing $.28, and comes with dinner roll and butter, salad, and salad dressing costing $.42. This menu item's standard food cost is $3.00 (2.30 + .28 + .42). Not all items have all three cost components, however.

Step seven. Calculate menu item contribution margins. Contribution margins for each item are found by subtracting the item's standard food cost (step six) from the item's menu selling price (step five).

CM = Selling Price − Standard Food cost

MENU ENGINEERING 157

Step eight. Determine the menu contribution margin (CM). The sum of each menu item's CM (step seven) times its respective MM (step two) determines the total menu CM.

Step nine. Compute the item contribution margin proportions. Each item's CM (step seven) is divided by the menu CM (step eight) to yield that menu item's CM% (contribution margin percentage).

$$CM\% = \frac{\text{menu item CM}}{\text{total menu CM}}$$

Step ten. Categorize item contribution margins. The item contribution margins are categorized as being either high or low, depending on whether or not they exceed the average CM achievement rate. This achievement rate is determined by dividing the menu CM (step eight) by the total number of items sold (step two).

1. CM Achievement Rate = Menu CM/Total number of items sold
2. High CM% ≥ CM Achievement Rate
3. Low CM% < CM Achievement Rate

Step eleven. Perform menu item classification. The MM% categories (step four) and the CM categories (step ten) are used to assign menu items into either Dog (Low MM%, Low CM), Puzzle (Low MM%, High CM), Plowhorse (High MM%, Low CM), or Star (High MM%, High CM) classifications. These classifications are not unique to menu engineering but are standard marketing theory terms borrowed for clarity in this model.

Step twelve. Initiate menu item decision making. The decision of whether to retain, reposition, replace, or reprice a menu item can be made intelligently based on the classification of each menu item (step eleven). Although a more detailed decision analysis will be presented elsewhere, a simplified direction includes the following:

Classification	Menu Action*
Star	Retain
Plowhorse	Reprice
Puzzle	Reposition
Dog	Replace

*Note: These actions are greatly simplified for these classifications. They are presented here only as introductory information.

An illustration of the twelve component steps of menu engineering follows. For clarity, a four-item hypothetical menu will be illustrated. Atten-

158 MENU ENGINEERING

tion should be given to the mathematical computations, categories, and classifications processes.

Example of Menu Engineering

Step one. Identify competing menu items. For example, consider a four-item menu consisting of Chicken Dinner, NY Strip Steak, Lobster Tails, and Sirloin Tips.

Step two. Record the number of items sold. During the previous week, sales were:

Menu Item	# Sold
1. Chicken Dinner	420
2. NY Strip Steak	360
3. Lobster Tails	150
4. Sirloin Tips	70
Total items sold	1,000 covers

Step three. Compute menu item mix percentages.

Menu Item	# Sold	% Total
1. Chicken Dinner	420	420/1000 = 42%
2. NY Strip Steak	360	360/1000 = 36%
3. Lobster Tails	150	150/1000 = 15%
4. Sirloin Tips	70	70/1000 = 7%
Total items sold	1,000	Total 100%

Step four. Categorize menu mix percentages. First, determine MM% achievement rate:

$$ACH = \frac{1}{N}(.70) = \frac{1}{4}(.70) = (.25)(.70) = .175 \text{ or } 17.5\%$$

Then categorize MM% according to the achievement rate.

Menu Item	MM%	MM% Test	Category
1. Chicken Dinner	42%	.42 > .175	High
2. NY Strip Steak	36%	.36 > .175	High
3. Lobster Tails	15%	.15 < .175	Low
4. Sirloin Tips	7%	.07 < .175	Low

MENU ENGINEERING

Step five.   List menu item selling prices.

Menu Item	Selling Price
1. Chicken Dinner	$4.50
2. NY Strip Steak	$7.00
3. Lobster Tails	$9.00
4. Sirloin Tips	$5.50

Step six.   Determine standard food costs.

Menu Item	Recipe Cost	Garnish Cost	Supplemental Cost	Standard Food Cost
1. Chicken Dinner	$1.00	.18	.32	$1.50
2. NY Strip Steak	2.30	.28	.42	3.00
3. Lobster Tails	3.50	.49	.51	4.50
4. Sirloin Tips	2.47	.21	.32	3.00

Step seven.   Calculate menu item contribution margins.

Menu Item	Menu Price	Food Cost	CM
1. Chicken Dinner	$4.50	$1.50	$3.00
2. NY Strip Steak	7.00	3.00	4.00
3. Lobster Tails	9.00	4.50	4.50
4. Sirloin Tips	5.50	3.00	2.50

Step eight.   Determine the menu contribution margin (CM).

Menu Item	CM	MM	Item CM
1. Chicken Dinner	$3.00	420	$1,260.
2. NY Strip Steak	4.00	360	1,440
3. Lobster Tails	4.50	150	675.
4. Sirloin Tips	2.50	70	175.

Menu CM = $3,550.

MENU ENGINEERING

Step nine. Compute item contribution margin proportions.

Menu Item	Item CM	CM%
1. Chicken Dinner	$1,260.	1260/3550 = 35%
2. NY Strip Steak	1,440.	1440/3550 = 41%
3. Lobster Tails	675.	675/3550 = 19%
4. Sirloin Tips	175.	175/3550 = 5%
Menu CM =	$3,550.	Total = 100%

Step ten. Categorize contribution margin percentages. First, determine CM achievement rate:

CM_{ach} = $3,550/1000 = $3.55

Then categorize CM according to achievement rate:

Menu Item	CM Test	Category
1. Chicken Dinner	3.00 < 3.55	Low
2. NY Strip Steak	4.00 > 3.55	High
3. Lobster Tails	4.50 > 3.55	High
4. Sirloin Tips	2.50 < 3.55	Low

Step eleven. Perform menu item classification.

Menu Item	MM%	CM	Classification
1. Chicken Dinner	High	Low	Plowhorse
2. NY Strip Steak	High	High	Star
3. Lobster Tails	Low	High	Puzzle
4. Sirloin Tips	Low	Low	Dog

Step twelve. Initiate menu item decision making.

Menu Item	Classification	Simplistic Action*
1. Chicken Dinner	Plowhorse	Reprice
2. NY Strip Steak	Star	Retain
3. Lobster Tails	Puzzle	Reposition
4. Sirloin Tips	Dog	Replace

*Note: Suggested actions here are simplified. Actions are not always this straightforward.

PART THREE: THE ANALYSIS

Menu engineering can be performed either manually or by a computer. Each process requires different types of input information and data-handling procedures. The complete menu engineering analysis exceeds the basic techniques described in part two.

Menu Engineering: Manual Analysis

The manual analysis of a menu requires that several mathematical computations be performed. To simplify this procedure, the use of a worksheet similar to the one illustrated in Figure 8-1 is strongly recommended. Although the form requires that thirteen columns of information be completed, a relatively thorough analysis of the menu can be achieved. Table 8-3 contains an

TABLE 8-3 Explanation of Elements and Codes

Element	Reference	Explanation
(A)	Menu Item	The name of each menu item
(B)	MM	The number of covers (sales) of each item sold
(C)	MM%	The percentage to total menu covers contributed by each item
(D)	MM% Category	The classification of high or low to the MM%
(E)	Menu Price	The menu item's selling price
(F)	Menu Revenues	Total menu revenues equal number of items sold times their selling price (B × E)
(G)	Food Cost	The direct and accompaniment food cost of an item
(H)	Menu Food Cost	The computation of each item's potential food cost (F × B)
(I)	CM	The item's individual contribution margin (E − F)
(J)	Menu CM	The total CM for each item (G × B)
(K)	CM% Category	The classification of high or low to the CM%
(L)	Classification	The assignment of a star, puzzle, plowhorse, or dog label to each item
(M)	Action Taken	The action taken as a result of an item's classification
(N)	Total MM	Sum of all items sold (forecasted)
(O)	Total MM%	A check to ensure (100%) correct mathematics
(P)	Menu Revenues	Total number of sales dollars generated by this menu
(Q)	Menu Food Cost	Total number of food cost dollars incurred by this menu
(R)	Menu CM	Total CM generated by this menu

MENU ENGINEERING

FIGURE 8-1 Manual Worksheet

Sample: MENU ENGINEERING WORKSHEET (MANUAL ANALYSIS)

RESTAURANT: _____ Meal Period: _____ Date: _____

(A) Menu Item	(B) MM	(C) MM%	(D) MM% Category	(E) Menu Price	(F) Total Menu Revenues	(G) Food Cost	(H) Menu Food Cost	(I) CM	(J) Menu CM	(K) CM Category	(L) Classification	(M) Action Taken
Totals:	N	O			P		Q		R			

Potential Food Cost % = $\dfrac{Q}{P}$ Average CM = $\dfrac{R}{N}$

Source: Courtesy of Hospitality Financial Consultants, P.O. Box 448, Okemos, MI 48864

explanation of the elements labeled A through R, and the various codes found in Figure 8-1.

Case problem: The Holly House. Consider the ten-item menu of the Holly House Restaurant for a menu engineering case problem. Table 8-4 contains the name, menu mix, food cost, and price of the selected sample menu items. This item listing satisfies the requirements of Step One (item identification) and Step Two (menu mix) of the twelve-step menu engineering model. Step Three involves computing the menu mix percentages (MM%). Table 8-5 presents these data. Step Four is concerned with a) determination of an MM% Achievement Rate, and b) categorization of items according to the MM% Achievement Rate. Figure 8-2 and Table 8-6 present the mathematical and clerical procedures corresponding to Step Four. Steps Five and Six, dealing with menu prices and food item costs, were addressed in Table 8-4 and therefore require no additional work at this time. Steps

TABLE 8-4 Sample Menu Data: The Holly House Restaurant

Menu Item	Menu Mix (MM)	Food Cost	Menu Price
Lobster Tail	150	$5.31	$12.95
Prime Rib (20 oz.)	60	5.29	11.50
NY Strip Steak	360	4.31	10.50
Top Sirloin Steak	510	3.71	9.50
Shrimp Platter	210	3.49	8.50
Red Snapper	240	2.71	6.95
Prime Rib (12 oz.)	600	3.37	7.50
Chicken Dinner	420	1.54	4.95
Chopped Sirloin	90	2.26	5.50
Tenderloin Tips	360	2.21	5.25

TABLE 8-5 Menu Mix Percentage

Menu Item	Menu Mix	MM%
Lobster Tail	150	5%
Prime Rib (20 oz.)	60	2%
NY Strip Steak	360	12%
Top Sirloin Steak	510	17%
Shrimp Platter	210	7%
Red Snapper	240	8%
Prime Rib (12 oz.)	600	20%
Chicken Dinner	420	12%
Chopped Sirloin	90	3%
Tenderloin Tips	360	12%
Total items sold	3,000	Total 100%

MENU ENGINEERING

FIGURE 8-2 MM% Achievement Rate

$$\text{MM\%}_{\text{ach rate}} = (\frac{1}{N})(70\%) = (\frac{1}{10})(70\%) = 7\%$$

TABLE 8-6 Menu Mix Analysis

Menu Item	Menu Mix %	MM% Test	Classification
Lobster Tail	5%	.05 < .07	Low
Prime Rib (20 oz.)	2%	.02 < .07	Low
NY Strip Steak	12%	.12 > .07	High
Top Sirloin Steak	17%	.17 > .07	High
Shrimp Platter	7%	.07 = .07	High
Red Snapper	8%	.08 > .07	High
Prime Rib (12 oz.)	20%	.20 > .07	High
Chicken Dinner	14%	.14 > .07	High
Chopped Sirloin	3%	.03 < .07	Low
Tenderloin Tips	12%	.12 > .07	High
	100%		

TABLE 8-7 Item Contribution Margins (CM)

Menu Item	Menu Price	Food Cost	CM
Lobster Tail	$12.95	$5.31	7.64
Prime Rib (20 oz.)	11.50	5.29	6.21
NY Strip Steak	10.50	4.31	6.19
Top Sirloin Steak	9.50	3.71	5.79
Shrimp Platter	8.50	3.49	5.01
Red Snapper	6.95	2.71	4.24
Prime Rib (12 oz.)	7.50	3.37	4.13
Chicken Dinner	4.95	1.54	3.41
Chopped Sirloin	5.50	2.26	3.24
Tenderloin Tips	5.25	2.21	3.04

Seven through Ten, however, use the price and cost data handled by the preceding steps.

Table 8-7, Figure 8-3, and Table 8-8 contain the detailed data elements necessary to develop contribution margin category assignments for all menu items. Once all CM and MM% categorization steps have been completed, Step Eleven, which classifies items according to these data, can be performed. Table 8-9 contains the appropriate menu item categorizations for all ten entrees.

FIGURE 8-3 CM Achievement Rate

Compute Menu CM:

Menu CM = (CM)(MM) = $14,065.80

Compute CM Achievement Rate:

$$CM_{ach\ rate} = \frac{Menu\ CM}{Total\ MM} = \frac{\$14,065.80}{3,000} = \$4.69$$

TABLE 8-8 Contribution Margin Analysis

Menu Item	CM	CM Test	Classification
Lobster Tail	$7.64	7.64 > 4.69	High
Prime Rib (20 oz.)	6.21	6.21 > 4.69	High
NY Strip Steak	6.19	6.19 > 4.69	High
Top Sirloin Steak	5.79	5.79 > 4.69	High
Shrimp Platter	5.01	5.01 > 4.69	High
Red Snapper	4.24	4.24 < 4.69	Low
Prime Rib (12 oz.)	4.13	4.13 < 4.69	Low
Chicken Dinner	3.41	3.41 < 4.69	Low
Chopped Sirloin	3.24	3.24 < 4.69	Low
Tenderloin Tips	3.04	3.04 < 4.69	Low

TABLE 8-9 Menu Item Categorization

Menu Item	MM% Class	CM Class	Category
Lobster Tail	Low	High	Puzzle
Prime Rib (20 oz.)	Low	High	Puzzle
NY Strip Steak	High	High	Star
Top Sirloin Steak	High	High	Star
Shrimp Platter	High	High	Star
Red Snapper	High	Low	Plowhorse
Prime Rib (12 oz.)	High	Low	Plowhorse
Chicken Dinner	High	Low	Plowhorse
Chopped Sirloin	Low	Low	Dog
Tenderloin Tips	High	Low	Plowhorse

An alternate manner by which to display item assignments is through the use of a 2 × 2 matrix. The matrix can be constructed so that MM%s are rank ordered, from high to low down the left-hand side of the matrix, and CM values are ranked from low to high across the bottom of the matrix. This yields the basic framework presented in Figure 8-14.

MENU ENGINEERING

FIGURE 8-4 2 × 2 Decision Matrix Framework

	Low CM	High CM
High MM%	High MM% / Low CM — **PLOWHORSE**	High MM% / High CM — **STAR**
Low MM%	Low MM% / Low CM — **DOG**	Low MM% / High CM — **PUZZLE**

TABLE 8-10 Simplistic Action Overview

Menu Item	Classification	Simplistic Action
Lobster Tail	Puzzle	Reposition
Prime Rib (20 oz.)	Puzzle	Reposition
NY Strip Steak	Star	Retain
Top Sirloin Steak	Star	Retain
Shrimp Platter	Puzzle	Reposition
Red Snapper	Plowhorse	Reprice
Prime Rib (12 oz.)	Plowhorse	Reprice
Chicken Dinner	Plowhorse	Reprice
Chopped Sirloin	Dog	Replace
Tenderloin Tips	Plowhorse	Reprice

FIGURE 8-5 Matrix Assignments

PLOWHORSES Prime Rib (12 oz.) Chicken Dinner Tenderloin Tips Red Snapper	**STARS** NY Strip Steak Top Sirloin
DOGS Chopped Sirloin	**PUZZLES** Lobster Tail Prime Rib (20 oz.) Shrimp Platter

The designation of cells as *dogs, puzzles, plowhorses,* and *stars* follows from the characteristics of the cells (as defined in Figure 8-4) and traditional marketing research terminology. Figure 8-5 contains a matrix presentation of this case study, showing the placement of menu items into the proper cell units. The matrix display, although not adding any new information to the analysis, tends to make the findings easier to comprehend.

Although an in-depth discussion of menu actions will not be presented at this point in the chapter, the simplified category actions described earlier may shed light on the eventual value of these analyses. Table 8-10 lists these over-simplified actions beside each menu item. Note that these may not be the corrective actions, nor the only steps needed, to improve on the menu's performance. Menu engineering is concerned with dollars provided through contribution margins, not just with food cost percentage points. The percentages are used to monitor potential food costs for a feasible or actual menu plan.

FIGURE 8-6 The Holly House Worksheet Analysis

MENU ENGINEERING WORKSHEET

Restaurant: __The Holly House__ Date: __July 6__ Meal Period: __Dinner__

(A) Menu Item Name	(B) Number Sold (MM)	(C) Menu Mix %	(D) Item Food Cost	(E) Item Selling Price	(F) Item CM (E−D)	(G) Menu Costs (D×B)	(H) Menu Revenues (E×B)	(L) Menu CM (F×B)	(P) CM Category	(R) MM% Category	(S) Menu Item Classification
LOBS. TAIL	150	5%	5.31	12.95	7.64	796.50	1942.50	1146.00	HIGH	LOW	PUZZLE
P. RIB (20oz)	60	2%	5.29	11.50	6.21	317.40	690.00	372.60	HIGH	LOW	PUZZLE
N.Y. STRIP	360	12%	4.31	10.50	6.19	1651.60	3780.00	2228.40	HIGH	HIGH	STAR
T. SIRLOIN	510	17%	3.71	9.50	5.79	1892.10	4845.00	2952.90	HIGH	HIGH	STAR
SHRIMP PL.	210	7%	3.49	8.50	5.01	732.90	1785.00	1052.10	HIGH	LOW	PUZZLE
RED SNAPPER	240	8%	2.71	6.95	4.24	650.40	1668.00	1017.60	LOW	HIGH	PLOWHORSE
P. RIB (12 oz)	600	20%	3.37	7.50	4.13	2022.00	4500.00	2478.00	LOW	HIGH	PLOWHORSE
CHICKEN DIN.	420	12%	1.54	4.95	3.41	646.80	2079.00	1432.20	LOW	HIGH	PLOWHORSE
CH. SIRLOIN	90	3%	2.26	5.50	3.24	203.40	495.00	291.60	LOW	LOW	DOG
TENDERLOIN TIPS	360	12%	2.21	5.25	3.04	795.60	1890.00	1094.40	LOW	HIGH	PLOWHORSE
						I					
Column Totals:	N 3,000					9,608.70	23,674.50	14,065.80 M			

Additional Computations:

K = I/J
9608.70 / 23,674.50 = .4059

O = M/N
14,065.80 / 3,000 = 4.69

Q = (100%/items)(70%)
(100%/10)(70%) = 7%

Source: Courtesy of Hospitality Financial Consultants, P.O. Box 448, Okemos, MI 48864

TABLE 8-11 Menu Item Food Cost Percent

Menu Item	Food Cost Percent
Lobster Tail	41%
Prime Rib (20 oz.)	46
NY Strip Steak	41
Top Sirloin Steak	39
Shrimp Platter	41
Red Snapper	39
Prime Rib (12 oz.)	45
Chicken Dinner	31
Chopped Sirloin	41
Tenderloin Tips	42

In the Holly House case, for example, this menu had items with varying individual food cost percentages. These percentages are computed in Table 8-11. Based on the MM% for this sample, this operation will have a potential (or target) food cost percentage of 40.6%. Refer to Figure 8-6 for a recap of all computations using a slightly modified worksheet than one introduced in Figure 8-1. The use of a single-page form can greatly simplify the analysis and summarize all the requisite intermediate data.

Menu Engineering: Computerized Analysis

Because of the computer's ability to perform mathematical computations at high speed (nanoseconds) and with extreme accuracy, menu engineering has become a prime candidate for automation. Computer software designed specifically to handle menu engineering applications was developed and tested in the early 1980s by Kasavana and Smith. The computing capabilities of a computer make it ideal for the twelve-step model described earlier, but more importantly, allow for further, detailed analysis than would be feasible otherwise. The computer can carry out a market basket study, an item analysis graph, and a menu engineering summary. This information is all in addition to the basic item analysis, menu mix analysis, and the item analysis square (matrix) that can be produced manually.

The *market basket analysis* allows the user to code each menu item into a dominant food grouping. The computer, containing a food market basket file, can forecast price changes for the dominant-coded group and perhaps suggest price changes in lieu of forcasted price levels. For example, beef may cost $1.70/lb. to purchase today. The market basket data, compiled from national consumer product indices, may indicate a future price of $1.95/lb. This 14.7 percent price increase may be sufficient to suggest a change in menu price because of an anticipated cost of goods. This part of the model is innovative and requires significant modification to render it applicable to foodservice management.

FIGURE 8-7 Computer Worksheet

Sample: MENU ENGINEERING INPUT SHEET (COMPUTER ANALYSIS)

Restaurant: _____ Meal Period: _____ Date: _____

(A) Menu Item	(B) Direct Food Cost	(C) Accompaniment Cost	(D) Menu Price	(E) MM	(F) Food Group Code

Source: Courtesy of Hospitality Financial Consultants, P.O. Box 448, Okemos, MI 48864

TABLE 8-12 Explanation of Elements and Codes

Element	Reference	Explanation
(A)	Menu Item	The name of each menu item
(B)	Direct Food Cost	The direct portion cost of the item
(C)	Accompaniment Cost	The garnish cost of an item (if any)
(D)	Menu Price	The menu item's selling price
(E)	MM	The number of covers (sales) of each item sold
(F)	Food Group Code	The predominant food group code (optional)

The item analysis graph offers a tremendous improvement over manual data processing output. The graph not only continues to classify menu items into the four-cell model (dogs, puzzles, stars, and plowhorses), but it also displays their relative ranks and plots them according to both MM% and CM achievement rates. Therefore, it is possible to discriminate within any one quadrant to determine the proper action that management should take to enhance the profit of its menu. The menu engineering summary primarily displays the menu totals for revenues, food cost, and contribution margin (referred to as marginal profit), while producing the potential food cost percentage, average contribution margin, and the *Hurst menu score*. The Hurst menu score is a popular menu summary index that is equivalent to the average contribution margin.

The application of a computer-based menu engineering program greatly simplifies the user's data collection and coding procedures. Figure 8-7 contains the computerized menu engineering worksheet. This six-element form should be compared with the eighteen-element form (Figure 8-1) suggested for the manual analysis. The six input elements of this form are explained in Table 8-12.

Case problem: The Holly House. Using the same problem as illustrated for the manual example earlier, it is possible to complete a computer data input form similar to the one in Figure 8-8. Computer data fields normally have input specifications. Because the menu item name field was designed to handle only up to fifteen characters, the name "Top Sirloin Steak" was abbreviated to "T Sirloin Steak." The food group code numbers were selected from among the following ten codes:

0—depicts Pasta items
1—depicts Beef items
2—depicts Poultry items
3—depicts Dairy items
4—depicts Fish items

172 MENU ENGINEERING

FIGURE 8-8 Completed Computer Worksheet

MENU ENGINEERING INPUT SHEET

Restaurant: _The Holly House_ Meal Period: _Dinner_ Date: _07/06/85_

(A) Menu Item	(B) Direct Food Cost	(C) Accompaniment Cost	(D) Menu Price	(E) MM	(F) Food Group Code
Lobster Tail	4.00	1.31	12.95	150	7
Prime Rib (12 oz.)	4.79	.50	11.50	60	1
NY Strip Steak	4.00	.31	10.50	360	1
T Sirloin Steak	3.21	.50	9.50	510	1
Shrimp Platter	3.09	.40	8.50	210	7
Red Snapper	2.21	.50	6.95	240	4
Prime Rib (12 oz.)	2.87	.50	7.50	600	1
Chicken Dinner	1.04	.50	4.95	420	2
Chopped Sirloin	1.71	.55	5.50	90	1
Tenderloin Tips	1.71	.50	5.25	360	1

Source: Courtesy of Hospitality Financial Consultants, P.O. Box 448, Okemos, MI 48864

MENU ENGINEERING   173

5—depicts Salad Bar items
6—depicts Pork items
7—depicts Shellfish items
8—depicts Other Meat items
9—depicts a Specialty item

These codes are all presented during initial contact between the user and the menu engineering program execution.

Figure 8-9 is an actual printout in which the user entered (typed in) the restaurant name, number of entrees to be analyzed, and the specific data elements (taken from the worksheet) for each of the ten items. At this time, all user operations, with the exception of selecting an analysis option, are completed. Figure 8-10 contains the response the computer automatically makes once all menu items have been entered into the system. The user then selects an option from the seven offered. Option seven, requesting a complete analysis (including options 1–6), was chosen for this example. From

FIGURE 8-9 Interactive Data Input

```
WHAT IS THE NAME OF YOUR RESTAURANT?? MENU ENGINEERING CASE

HOW MANY MENU ENTREES ARE THERE TO BE ANALYZED??  10

ENTER THE NAME OF EACH MENU ITEM, FOLLOWED BY A COMMA, THEN
THE ITEM'S DIRECT FOOD (PORTION) COST, INCLUDE DECIMAL POINT BUT OMIT DOLLAR
SIGN, THEN A COMMA, FOLLOWED BY THE ITEM'S ACCOMPANIMENT (GARNISH) COST, IF
NONE ENTER A ZERO, THEN A COMMA, THEN THE ITEM'S MENU SELLING PRICE , THEN A COMMA
FOLLOWED BY THE AVERAGE NUMBER OF COVERS SOLD PER WEEK FOR THIS ITEM, THEN
A COMMA, FOLLOWED BY THIS ITEM'S DOMINANT FOOD GROUP CODE NUMBER (NOTE:
0-DEPICTS PASTA, 1-DEPICTS BEEF, 2-DEPICTS POULTRY, 3-DEPICTS DAIRY, 4-DEPICTS
FISH, 5-DEPICTS SALAD BAR, 6- DEPICTS PORK, 7-DEPICTS SHELLFISH, 8-DEPICTS
OTHER MEATS, AND 9-DEPICTS A SPECIALTY ITEM). FOR EXAMPLE:

    EXAMPLE- LOBSTER NEWBURG,3.45,1.75,12.95,55,7

HENCE, THIS ITEM COSTS $3.45, ITS GARNISH COSTS $1.75, IT SELLS FOR $12.95,
55 OF THIS ITEM WERE SOLD LAST WEEK, AND ITS FOOD GROUP IS DESIGNATED BY A 7.

ITEM # 1  =>LOBSTER TAIL,4.00,1.31,12.95,150,7
ITEM # 2  =>PRIME RIB 20 OZ,4.79,.50,11.50,60,1
ITEM # 3  =>NY STRIP STEAK,4.00,.31,10.50,360,1
ITEM # 4  =>T SIRLOIN STEAK,3.21,.50,9.50,510,1
ITEM # 5  =>SHRIMP PLATTER,3.09,.40,8.50,210,7
ITEM # 6  =>RED SNAPPER,2.21,.50,6.95,240,4
ITEM # 7  =>PRIME RIB 12 OZ,2.87,.50,7.50,600,1
ITEM # 8  =>CHICKEN DINNER,1.04,.50,4.95,420,2
ITEM # 9  =>CHOPPED SIRLOIN,1.71,.55,5.50,90,1
ITEM #10  =>TENDERLOIN TIPS,1.71,.50,5.25,360,1
```

Source: Courtesy of Hospitality Financial Consultants, P.O. Box 448, Okemos, MI 48864

this point on, the computer carries out necessary mathematical and logical procedures to satisfy the request for a complete menu engineering analysis. Table 8-13 and Figure 8-10 present the flow of output produced in a computer-based system.

Table 8-13 displays an item analysis for the Holly House data. Each item is presented with its selling price, direct cost, supplemental cost, total item cost, contribution margin, and total item demand. This portion of the complete analysis basically reiterates the input data (as a check on accurate entry) while computing total item costs (direct plus supplemental food cost) and item contribution margins (item sale price less total item cost).

Table 8-13 Item Analysis

ITEM ANALYSIS

ENTREE NAME	ITEM SALE PRICE	DIRECT FOOD COST	SUPPL. FOOD COST	TOTAL ITEM COST	ITEM CONTR. MARGIN	TOTAL ITEM DEMAND
LOBSTER TAIL	12.95	4.00	1.31	5.31	7.64	150
PRIME RIB 20 OZ	11.50	4.79	0.50	5.29	6.21	60
NY STRIP STEAK	10.50	4.00	0.31	4.31	6.19	360
T SIRLOIN STEAK	9.50	3.21	0.50	3.71	5.79	510
SHRIMP PLATTER	8.50	3.09	0.40	3.49	5.01	210
RED SNAPPER	6.95	2.21	0.50	2.71	4.24	240
PRIME RIB 12 OZ	7.50	2.87	0.50	3.37	4.13	600
CHICKEN DINNER	4.95	1.04	0.50	1.54	3.41	420
CHOPPED SIRLOIN	5.50	1.71	0.55	2.26	3.24	90
TENDERLOIN TIPS	5.25	1.71	0.50	2.21	3.04	360

Source: Courtesy of Hospitality Financial Consultants, P.O. Box 448, Okemos, MI 48864

FIGURE 8-10 Interactive Option Selection

```
*************************************************************************
                    MENU ANALYSIS FOR:    MENU ENGINEERING CASE
                                JULY 29, 1984
*************************************************************************

     1.  ITEM ANALYSIS
     2.  MENU MIX ANALYSIS
     3.  MENU ENGINEERING SUMMARY
     4.  MARKET BASKET ANALYSIS
     5.  ITEM ANALYSIS SQUARE
     6.  ITEM ANALYSIS GRAPH
     7.  COMPLETE ANALYSIS

CHOOSE ONE OF THE ABOVE OPTIONS? 7
```

Source: Courtesy of Hospitality Financial Consultants, P.O. Box 448, Okemos, MI 48864

MENU ENGINEERING

TABLE 8-14 Menu Mix Analysis

MENU MIX ANALYSIS

ENTREE NAME	%MENU COST	% MM SHARE	GROUP RANK	% CM SHARE	CONTR. MARGIN	GROUP RANK	MENU CLASS
LOBSTER TAIL	8.29	5.00	LOW	8.15	7.64	HIGH	?PUZZLE?
PRIME RIB 20 OZ	3.30	2.00	LOW	2.65	6.21	HIGH	?PUZZLE?
NY STRIP STEAK	16.15	12.00	HIGH	15.84	6.19	HIGH	**STAR**
T SIRLOIN STEAK	19.69	17.00	HIGH	20.99	5.79	HIGH	**STAR**
SHRIMP PLATTER	7.63	7.00	LOW	7.48	5.01	HIGH	?PUZZLE?
RED SNAPPER	6.77	8.00	HIGH	7.23	4.24	LOW	PLOWHORSE
PRIME RIB 12 OZ	21.04	20.00	HIGH	17.62	4.13	LOW	PLOWHORSE
CHICKEN DINNER	6.73	14.00	HIGH	10.18	3.41	LOW	PLOWHORSE
CHOPPED SIRLOIN	2.12	3.00	LOW	2.07	3.24	LOW	<< DOG >>
TENDERLOIN TIPS	8.28	12.00	HIGH	7.78	3.04	LOW	PLOWHORSE

Source: Courtesy of Hospitality Financial Consultants, P.O. Box 448, Okemos, MI 48864

The computer next prints Table 8-14, the menu mix analysis. This menu mix analysis presents the results of significant quantitative processes. The menu cost percentages are found by dividing the number of items sold times the cost per item, by the sum of the number of items sold times their respective prices. The percentage of menu mix (MM) share and contribution margin (CM) share are determined similarly. The main difference between the menu analysis and the preceding item analysis is that the menu mix uses the number sold or demanded as a weighting factor for proportionality indexing. The group ranks for both the MM and CM values have been assigned using the same decision rules as those in the manual model. In other words, an MM value is high if it is equal to or greater than $1/N$ times .7, and a CM value is high if it is greater than or equal to the menu's average contribution margin.

The final column in Table 8-14 is the menu class assignment. Identical to the manual model, the computer classifies an item as a dog, star, puzzle, or plowhorse depending on its MM and CM group rankings. The menu mix analysis segment of the complete analysis contains valuable information that in and of itself exceeds the entire output of the twelve-step manual approach.

The menu engineering summary in Figure 8-11 aggregates the menu mix analysis into more traditional units of measure. The total sales level (number sold times the respective item price) and the potential food cost (number sold times the respective item cost) figures are used to generate the potential food cost percentage for this menu. As mentioned earlier, while not relying on food cost percentages to reflect adequately menu profitability and/or

FIGURE 8-11 Menu Engineering Summary

```
                     MENU ENGINEERING SUMMARY
-----------------------------------------------------------------


THIS MENU MIX HAS A TOTAL SALES LEVEL OF $ 23674.5

THIS MENU MIX HAS A POTENTIAL FOOD COST OF $ 9608.7

THIS MENU MIX HAS A POTENTIAL FOOD COST % OF 40.5867

THIS MENU MIX HAS A TOTAL DEMAND FACTOR OF 3000

THIS MENU MIX HAS A MENU MARGINAL PROFIT OF $ 14065.8

THIS MENU MIX HAS A HURST MENU SCORE OF 4.6886

THIS MENU MIX HAS AN AVERAGE CONTRIBUTION MARGIN OF $ 4.6886
```

Source: Courtesy of Hospitality Financial Consultants, P.O. Box 448, Okemos, MI 48864

marketability, menu engineering does advocate the use of cost percentages for achieving internal controls over purchasing, production, and service.

The potential food cost percentage, being a weighted average of item demands, does establish a targeted level of efficiency and productivity. The total demand factor indicated in the summary table is simply a summation of the individual item demands for the menu. The marginal profit figure is the overall menu contribution margin. To avoid confusion in terminology, the phrase *marginal profit* is used in place of the contribution margin when reference is made to the entire menu plan. The final two output variables, the Hurst menu score and the average contribution margin, are identical. Because many operators are familiar with the Hurst scheme, it appears appropriate to reinforce its applicability, in light of contribution margin theory. This menu engineering summary displays information not available elsewhere in the analysis.

Market basket analyses are important to operations that prepare a large number of items over a relatively long menu cycle. The market basket concept is intended to be an extension of the consumer price index for the foodservice industry. The current and future prices per pound of dominant recipe ingredients are used to suggest repricing, or other appropriate action, for specific menu items. Although this segment of the complete analysis is expected to be significantly refined and sophisticated, unless the menu engineering module is interfaced with a precost system, true percent changes and cost evaluations are extremely difficult.

Table 8-15 contains a simplified market basket analysis for the Holly House data. Note that all beef, shellfish, fish, and poultry items in this sam-

TABLE 8-15 Market Basket Analysis

```
                      MARKET BASKET ANALYSIS

                       MENU ENGINEERING CASE
     ENTREE       PREDOMINANT     PRESENT    FORECASTED    PERCENT
      NAME        FOOD  GROUP     COST/LB     COST/LB      CHANGE

LOBSTER TAIL      SHELLFISH        1.23        1.41         14.63
PRIME RIB 20 OZ   BEEF             1.70        1.95         14.71
NY STRIP STEAK    BEEF             1.70        1.95         14.71
T SIRLOIN STEAK   BEEF             1.70        1.95         14.71
SHRIMP PLATTER    SHELLFISH        1.23        1.41         14.63
RED SNAPPER       FISH             0.79        0.83          5.06
PRIME RIB 12 OZ   BEEF             1.70        1.95         14.71
CHICKEN DINNER    POULTRY          0.95        1.04          9.47
CHOPPED SIRLOIN   BEEF             1.70        1.95         14.71
TENDERLOIN TIPS   BEEF             1.70        1.95         14.71
```

Source: Courtesy of Hospitality Financial Consultants, P.O. Box 448, Okemos, MI 48864

ple have identical percent changes. This probably will not be the case when portion sizes, ingredient quantities, and item purchase specifications are incorporated into the study.

The item square that follows the market basket output is an important alternate visual presentation of the menu classifications found in the menu mix analysis segment. Figure 8-12 is intended to relate more clearly competing menu items along CM and MM dimensions. The same matrix cell inclusion rules were applied here as in the manual approach.

The most significant result gained from computerized menu engineering analysis is found in Figure 8-13. The graphic output generated in this subrou-

FIGURE 8-12 Item Analysis Square (Matrix)

```
************************************************************************
*                              *                                        *
*      PLOWHORSE               *       STAR                             *
*      ---------               *       ----                             *
*      RED SNAPPER             *       NY STRIP STEAK                   *
*      PRIME RIB 12 OZ         *       T SIRLOIN STEAK                  *
*      CHICKEN DINNER          *                                        *
*      TENDERLOIN TIPS         *                                        *
*                              *                                        *
************************************************************************
*                              *                                        *
*      DOG                     *       PUZZLE                           *
*      ---                     *       ------                           *
*      CHOPPED SIRLOIN         *       LOBSTER TAIL                     *
*                              *       PRIME RIB 20 OZ                  *
*                              *       SHRIMP PLATTER                   *
*                              *                                        *
************************************************************************
```

Source: Courtesy of Hospitality Financial Consultants, P.O. Box 448, Okemos, MI 48864

178 MENU ENGINEERING

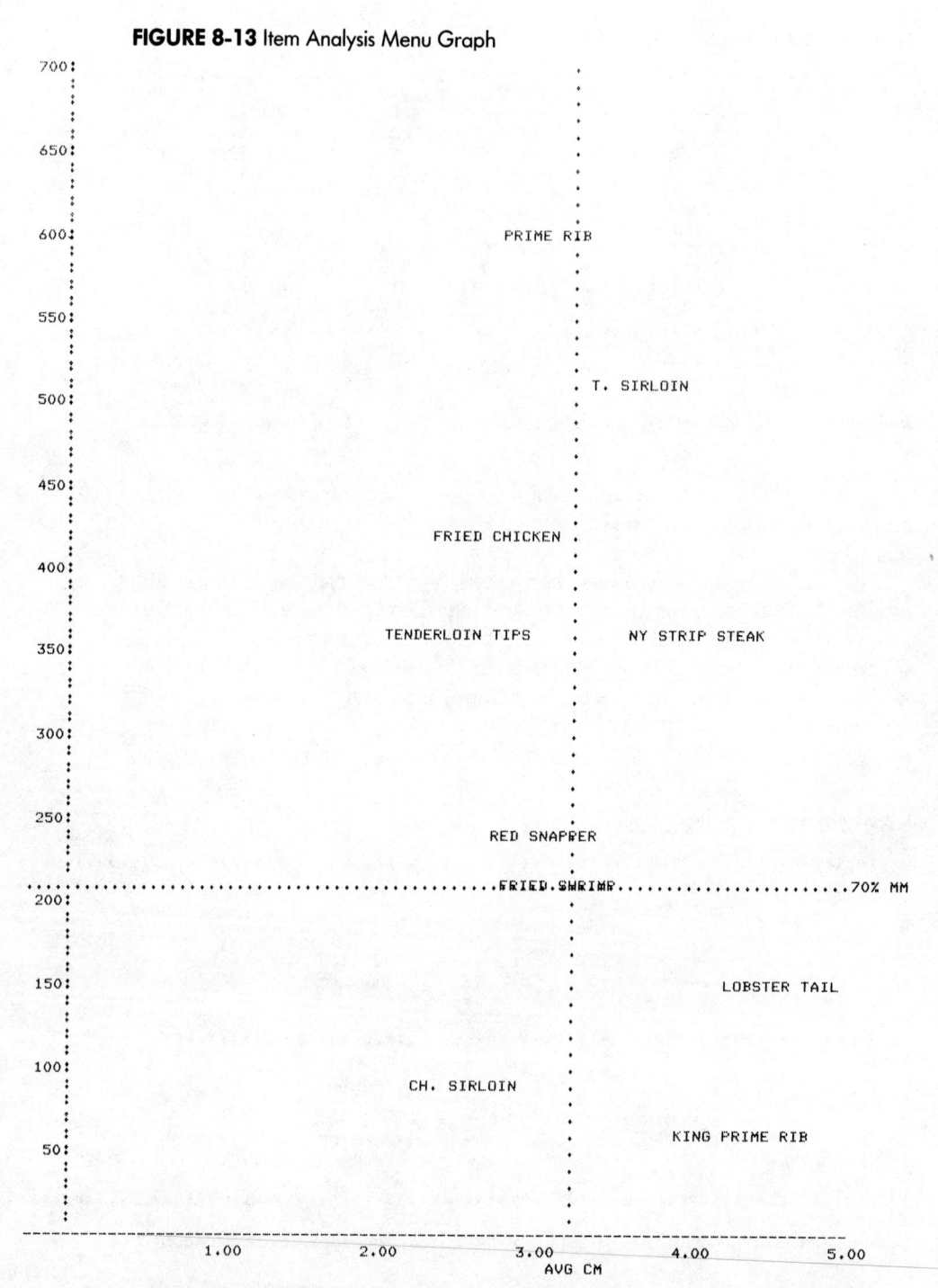

FIGURE 8-13 Item Analysis Menu Graph

```
700:
    :
    :
    :
650:
    :
    :
    :
600:                                       PRIME RIB
    :
    :
    :
550:
    :
    :
    :
500:                                     . T. SIRLOIN
    :
    :
    :
450:
    :
    :                               FRIED CHICKEN .
    :
400:
    :
    :
    :
350:                     TENDERLOIN TIPS    .    NY STRIP STEAK
    :
    :
    :
300:
    :
    :
    :
250:
    :                                RED SNAPPER
    :
    :
200:············································FRIED·SHRIMP························································70% MM
    :
    :
    :
150:                                                  LOBSTER TAIL
    :
    :
    :
100:
    :                           CH. SIRLOIN
    :
    :
 50:                                              KING PRIME RIB
    :
    :
    :
    ─────────────────────────────────────────────────────────────
              1.00      2.00      3.00      4.00      5.00
                                 AVG CM
```

Source: Courtesy of Hospitality Financial Consultants, P.O. Box 448, Okemos, MI 48864

tine of the analysis plots an item's location within a quadrant based on its MM percentage and CM achievement rates. The dotted lines are located at the appropriate achievement rate levels; the horizontal line corresponds to the 70% MM rate, and the vertical line corresponds to the average CM rate.

The advantage of this plotting over the two-by-two matrix display is that the relative positions of menu items (in regard to each other) can be known. For example, the plowhorse category had four items assigned to it. These items are Red Snapper, Prime Rib—12 ounce, Chicken Dinner, and Tenderloin Tips. Without any further differentiation, all these items would be assumed to be equivalent and would suggest the same corrective managerial action (repricing). It becomes apparent that they do not all contribute the same amount to the restaurant's profit or menu sales. Alternate decision strategies may be required. The Prime Rib is just shy of being grouped as a star. The Red Snapper barely escaped the dog classification. Note the similar positions of the Chicken Dinner and the Tenderloin Tips. This *menu graph* presents a unique tool for analyzing competing items and selecting the best decision strategies for their enhanced contribution to profit.

PART FOUR: DECISION MAKING

Menu Item Classification

Earlier, some general decision actions were presented for each menu item classification. The following discussion of menu item classifications is intended to assist the reader in understanding how to perform a satisfactory menu revision. (Note: Individual restaurants and circumstances require individual attention.)

Stars are the most popular and profitable items on the menu. These items, usually a restaurant's *signature* items, can carry a disproportionate share of the *burden of margin* and profit. This high CM allows marketers to offer lower priced demand items (plowhorses, for example) on the same menu. When an item is classified as a star, it is recommended that 1) rigid specifications for quality, quantity, and presentation be maintained, 2) high-visibility menu locations be employed, and 3) range of price elasticity be determined. "Super Star" items (highest margin stars) are obviously less price-sensitive than any other items on the menu. The less price-sensitive an item, the more likely it is to carry a greater share of the restaurant's increasing cost of overhead.

Plowhorses are relatively popular items that yield a lower contribution margin (than the menu's average CM). These items are often referred to as *demand generators* as they fail to carry their burden-of-margin and can be used to attract the price-sensitive buyer. These items present an opportunity to create significant price promotions. With plowhorse items 1) care must be taken when increasing their selling price (because of consumer/price responsiveness behavior), 2) lower menu profile positions are appropriate, 3) combining this item with a low-cost product improves CM position, 4) imperceptible portion reductions should be considered, and 5) demand should be shifted to other, more profitable items, through merchandising programs and menu positioning.

Puzzles yield a high CM but experience only limited success in popularity. Solution strategies for puzzle items tend to be more complex than other classifications. Some possible decision strategies are to 1) eliminate the item, especially if it is a slow seller; 2) decrease the item's selling price (care must be taken not to detract from the demand for higher CM items); 3) reposition the item on the menu; 4) limit the total number of puzzles on a menu as they affect overall customer demand levels; and/or 5) rename the item to influence its popularity.

For example, one Chicago restaurant slightly modified the recipe for one of its puzzle items and changed its name from Coq au vin to Chicken a la Whiskey. The demand for this item increased significantly primarily because of the name change.

Dogs, the unwanted menu items (from the perspectives of both the consumer and management), are troublesome because they generate relatively few sales and low contribution margins. Fortunately, the corrective action for dogs is more straightforward than for the other classifications—take dog items *off the menu!* If it is necessary to maintain the same number of menu items, then replace a dog with an item that offers a greater demand level and/or profit potential.

Special Cases

One reason for maintaining an unpopular menu item can be referred to as the *minority veto syndrome.* The phrase *minority veto* describes those individuals responsible for negating a large volume of sales at a particular restaurant because it no longer carries an item preferred by that person (or persons). The delineation of this concept is credited to Mr. Richard Bruner of the MSU University Club, E. Lansing, MI. This person, therefore, is capable of negatively influencing demand. A feasible solution to this problem is to reprice the item so that it yields a larger CM than the menu's average, thereby moving it out of the dog classification. Another solution is to take the "not on the menu" approach, whereby the restaurant carries the item in inventory (assuming a reasonable shelf life), but not on its menu. The special guests (minority veto controllers) are informed that this item is available to them, but only on special request. This tactic not only is a strong public relations vehicle, but it also allows the restaurateur to increase the item's CM through an upscaled price.

In addition to these recommendations, the decision-making process for revising a menu item may be clouded by its relationship as a *by-product* to a plowhorse or star item. For example, a menu item such as tenderloin tips may appear on the menu only because it is prepared from leftover, excess steak. The fact that the steak item exists creates the availability of this by-product item. Menu items that are by-products are difficult subjects for menu analysis, since several marginal costs (inventory, labor, and preparation) may be minimal in the item's overall cost scheme. Hence, in the case of a by-product, there may be additional factors of low cost or availability that keep this item on the menu. The test of a by-product is to ask the question, "How will the discontinuance of this item affect any item in inventory?" If the elimination of a menu item creates a surplus of unused by-product, a new menu item opportunity exists.

A menu item that is served in a variety of portion sizes is referred to as a *multiple portion product*. As examples, consider steak by the ounce, lobster by the tail, and various cuts of prime rib. In the latter, two or more size cuts clearly can be used to illustrate this complementary menu item situation. In some restaurants, the smaller-size cut may be a demand generator, but not a significant CM contributor (a plowhorse), while the larger-size cut complements this item by being strong in both sales and CM. Together, these items contribute heavily to the menu mix and the restaurant's overall profit. The test of a complementary relationship is to ask: "If a menu item were discontinued, would the item still need to be prepared for service elsewhere on the menu?" In other words, even though one cut of prime rib may be considered for deletion, the other cut would still need to be prepared. Hence, the complementary item is not an independent item. The menu decisions surrounding complementary items may be handled best by studying the related products jointly.

New Menu Item Development

New menu item development should be considered carefully and pretested (as specials) before being added to a menu. When adding new menu items, one should attempt to build from existing products or by-product items currently held in inventory. This practice reduces additional inventory burdens. Other important considerations are:

1. What are the item's requirements for skill and labor intensity? (the lower, the less disruptive)
2. What is the item's popularity potential? (the greater, the better)
3. Can this item not be adequately prepared at home? (uniqueness is important)
4. Is the item relatively stable in cost and availability? (stability is desirable)

5. Does this item make a good presentation? (level of perceived value)
6. Will the item net a high contribution margin? (the higher, the better)

Consider, for example, the following low-meat intensity products: Mexican foods, pastas, eggs, poultry, and vegetable entrees. There are two reasons to add new menu items:

1. *To increase demand*—Add menu item with high degree of popularity to increase frequency or broaden the market. For example, a high popularity item with a broad market appeal is a salad bar, which has been effective in building demand for both table service and fast-food enterprises. A second example is the signature item. These items also increase restaurant demand, but for a different reason; the item simply cannot be obtained elsewhere.
2. *To increase contribution margin*—Add items that have high CM, particularly if they do not require adding additional items to inventory. A signature item as discussed can create greater market share, prestige, and visibility, but at a higher than average CM.

Success in marketing is primarily evaluated by an ability to increase customer demand and/or contribution margins.

How to Make Price Changes

Planning is critical to price changes. Because anticipating increases in cost of goods, labor, and other expenses is often difficult, flexibility in pricing is an important element of survival. The following suggestions detail price flexibility techniques. This list is not assumed to be exhaustive, however.

1. *Take small increases as soon as possible.* When anticipating a need for a price increase, many restaurateurs believe in taking the necessary increase as soon as possible. In general, it is more desirable to take two smaller increases rather than one large increase when dealing with a price-sensitive market. This significant pricing approach is not dysfunctional to perceived value.
2. *Call as little attention to the increase as possible.* Changing menu format when making major price revisions is not advisable.
    a. *Reorder menus.* Do not scratch out old menu prices. Replace the old menus with new repriced ones. Make arrangements for a printer to maintain a supply of the restaurant's current menu in inventory. This supply would be complete, except for the printing of prices. The restaurateur calls the printer with the latest price changes. The printer, in turn, makes the necessary printing plate changes and runs the newly

priced menus through the press. This relatively inexpensive procedure does require some prior planning.

    b. *Date menus.* When reprinting menus, one should always date the menu to avoid menu confusion. A date code can be used to insure internal control and private reference.

3. *Incorporate menu recommendations for inflation-proof pricing.* Again, flexibility is the key.

    a. *The blackboard.* Restaurateurs with limited menus and casual concepts may find blackboard menus very effective. They are practical, low cost, and easy to change. They provide the utmost in flexibility.

    b. *The hand-written menu.* Menu lithography creates a personalized appeal and allows for in-house menu changes. A large supply of unpriced menus are produced at one time, all in a script style lettering. This stored inventory of unpriced menus allows management to add prices by hand, in the same print style used on the menu. This practice does not require that the menu be rerun by the printer. This low-cost method for changing prices maintains graphic continuity, all done in-house, by the restaurant's staff.

    c. *The give-away menu.* Restaurants targeting tourist-type markets can print souvenir menus on inexpensive newsprint. These menus can be used as mailers. This type of menu requires constant reordering and can be repriced frequently.

    d. *Priceless entrees.* When prestige menu items defy price forecasting because of frequent price increases, it may be best not to print their price at all. Some comment on the menu is usually necessary to explain the reason for a priceless entree and should suggest that the server be asked to quote the day's price. A significant gain in price flexibility can be achieved.

4. *Take advantage of timing.* When possible, it is recommended that price increases be made during a period when the market is sensitive to the overall rise in retail prices (key to the consumer's price index). Customer acceptance is at greater than normal levels during these times. Also, the higher the guest visit frequency, the more likely guests will be familiar with the price structure. Therefore, try to limit major price increases to low-volume periods.

5. *Implement discount pricing.* Promotional pricing or temporary price cutting can be effective in increasing business during low-volume periods. For example, one table service chain lowered the price of one of its most popular items three days a week (Monday, Tuesday, and Wednesday). The price lowering was advertised outside the restaurant and promoted on the menu. This very successful discounting tactic worked well in building business during slow times.

Note: Price cutting used as a strategy rather than a temporary tactic is a serious and potentially dangerous marketing action. This action usually is designed to increase an enterprise's market share at the expense of a competitor's, who usually responds with similar actions. Another objective of discounting is to create new business or regain previously lost business. Discounting is often ineffective because it is implemented during economic downturns (bad timing), or as a result of increased competitive penetration. Without well-planned advertising and financial staying power, discounting only exacerbates a struggling operator's problems.

Price cuts by industry leaders that dominate a large share of the market (McDonald's, Burger King, Pizza Hut) will find these price cuts matched by their competitors, especially if these cuts seriously affect demand. This discounting by the followers may literally lead to bankruptcy because of their different cost structures.

6. *Develop a "monopoly" restaurant*. When a restaurant achieves the status of a monopoly (positioned in the market's mind as unique and unparalleled) in the clutter of competition, price sensitivity is more likely to be lower. This trend applies especially to restaurants that tend to be personally oriented rather than price dominated in their marketing positioning.

7. *Implement odd pricing*. The general pricing rule is: An operator should know the market well. When an item's price is increased, demand is less affected for odd pricing, as long as the new price remains within the menu price points. Consumers more readily accept an increase to $5.95 than a jump to $6.00. This fact has been shown to be a significant concern and should be taken into consideration in a pricing strategy.

SUMMARY

Menu engineering is designed to measure the marketing power of a menu through its menu mix and contribution margin. Menu engineering does not focus on food cost percentage points as an end, but rather as a control factor in the overall foodservice scheme. Menu engineering, which extends gross profit theory into the realm of higher order analysis and microeconomics, can be viewed in four related parts: the concept, the model, the analysis, and the corrective strategies.

The concept of menu engineering is oriented toward defining which items on the current menu require repricing, repositioning, retention, and replacement. Menu engineering is also a best-test method for measuring the success of a menu change by establishing a profitability index as a benchmark against which all future menus can be evaluated. Although menu engineering may at first appear somewhat complex, it is an uncomplicated tool designed to improve effectiveness in menu pricing, content design, and marketing strategies.

In an attempt to ward off the inflationary impact, menu engineering enables foodservice operators to fight back by recession-proofing their menus. Historically, the foodservice industry has been dependent on cost-multiplier formulas for the determination of menu prices. This orientation has misdirected management to believe that profits are closely related to cost percentages. This simply is not the case. In fact, prices built only on costs ignore the most important business constituent—the consumer. In essence, an objective of the menu engineering model is to orient management to its higher contribution margin items as a means toward bottom-line enhancement. Hence, menu engineering is a series of processes that emphasize menu mix and contribution margin analysis as opposed to using only food cost percentage indices.

The basic menu engineering mathematical model can be segmented into twelve component steps. An operator who is familiar with each menu item's product cost, selling price, and number sold can categorize items into relatively high and low levels of achievement. This categorization leads to eventual classification of items by both marketing (sales) and pricing success.

Briefly, the twelve steps are to: 1) identify competing menu items, 2) reorder the number of items sold, 3) compute menu item mix proportions, 4) categorize menu mix percentages, 5) list menu item selling prices, 6) determine standard food costs, 7) calculate menu item contribution margins, 8) determine the menu CM, 9) compute the item CM proportions, 10) categorize item CMs, 11) perform menu item classification, and 12) initiate menu item decision making. The simplified decision strategies introduced in this section include repricing, retaining, replacing, and repositioning. But remember that these item decisions cannot be applied this easily in reality. They require additional insights, expertise, and intuition that can best be gained through experience.

This analysis can be performed either manually or by a computer. The manual procedure, which is time consuming, does not produce as complete or as precise an output as an automated approach. The complete menu engineering model features a decision matrix and a strategy graph. Computer solutions also contain a market basket analysis highlighting future trends in food item costs. The computer model for menu engineering, referred to as MENENG, was developed by Smith and Kasavana for use in all types of foodservice operations (clubs, restaurants, and institutions). The inherent computing capabilities have led to many simplifications in data-handling procedures (for the user). The computer-generated graph that classifies all menu items according to both MM% and CM achievement rates is helpful in the determination of decision strategies. In general, the computer analysis produces more valuable information than does the twelve-step manual process it replaces, and does so in a matter of minutes. To use menu engineering analysis, the model should be interfaced to a precost system. This interfacing provides on-line forecasted CM levels enabling before-the-fact adjustments in menu plans.

KEY CONCEPTS

The following concepts were introduced in this chapter. Their meanings should be completely understood.

1. *Achievement Rate*–a mathematical decision rule designed to segment relatively high from low menu items in the menu engineering model.
2. *Average Contribution Margin*–the menu contribution margin divided by the number of items sold.
3. *Burden of Margin*–an economic concept describing the need for the more popular items to cover the inability of less popular items to achieve the average CM requirements of the menu (required CM pricing).
4. *By-Product*–a term used to denote the relationship between a primary menu item and its subsidiary products.
5. *Contribution Margin (CM)*–the number of dollars available to pay fixed expenses and result in profit; determined by subtracting an item's direct cost from its selling price.
6. *Cost-Multiplier*–an approach to pricing that requires the increase of product cost by some targeted proportionality factor.
7. *Decision Matrix*–a technique designed to present menu engineering data in an easy-to-comprehend format.
8. *Demand Generator*–an item placed on the menu as a loss leader that tends to produce additional item sales (e.g., plowhorse item).
9. *Dog*–term used to describe a menu item with a relatively low level of popularity (MM%) and a low contribution margin (CM).
10. *Gross Profit*—see *Contribution Margin.*
11. *Hurst Menu Score*–another name for a menu's average contribution margin.
12. *Market Basket Analysis*–similar to the Consumer Price Index (CPI), but specific to the foodservice vendor futures market.
13. *Menu Engineering*–a quantitative approach to menu analysis; based on demand, marketing indices, pricing, and contribution margin factors.
14. *Menu Graph*–an illustrative presentation of menu engineering data depicting the relative location of all items to the menu's average contribution margin and the menu mix achievement rate.
15. *Menu Mix*–also called the sales mix; a measurement of the relative sales produced by competing items on the same menu.
16. *Minority Veto Syndrome*–describes the potential domination of a group of customers by one individual.

17. *Multiple Portion Product*–a menu item that is available in more than one size serving on a menu (e.g., small and large cuts of prime rib).
18. *Plowhorse*–term used to describe a menu item with a relatively high level of popularity (MM%), but a low contribution margin (CM).
19. *Puzzle*–the term used to describe a menu item with a relatively high level of contribution margin (CM) but a low level of popularity (MM%).
20. *Signature Item*–a restaurant's featured, house specialty item.
21. *Star*–term used to describe a menu item with a relatively high level of popularity (MM%) and a high level of contribution margin (CM).
22. *Target Pricing*–see *Cost-Multiplier.*

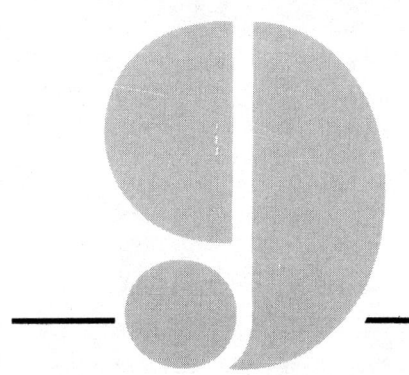

Back Office Systems

Chapter Objectives

1. To introduce the foodservice general accounting application segment of an FIS
2. To present the major subcomponents of a back office system package
3. To analyze a variety of approaches taken by vendors in the foodservice system marketplace
4. To identify sophisticated system technology capable of assisting in order entry, telecommunication, and multiunit management

Instead of focusing on cash-register oriented systems, many foodservice computer companies have concentrated their efforts on the *back office* area. Although not as obvious as the service and cashiering functions, the accounting and inventory control techniques used in a restaurant can prove to be equally important. Back office systems assist in providing increased customer counts, enhanced employee motivation, tighter cash flow monitoring, improved operational efficiencies, and significant cost savings. Such areas as 1) inventory control, 2) payroll, 3) general ledger accounting, 4) sales and revenue analysis, 5) production cost control, and 6) financial statement preparation are essential to effective managerial decision making and key expense factoring. In addition, recent technological advances have produced the necessary hardware and software that make order entry systems and multiunit reporting schemes a reality. The application of host and satellite component units, coupled with telecommunications, will lead to significant savings in various segments of the foodservice industry.

INVENTORY CONTROL

An effective *inventory control* process allows management to stock a sufficient level of product for a minimal capital outlay. In other words, overstocking and/or stockouts are unlikely, and only the most necessary dollars are tied up in inventory. Correctly equating purchases to production is not an easily defined mathematical relationship to identify or to achieve operationally. Stock that does not correlate well with its recipe use will always exist. Waste, spoilage, and pilferage are variables that deserve attention in the inventory model. All inventoriable items have a *reorder point* assigned to them regardless of whether it is predetermined or otherwise computed. The purpose of a reorder point is to initiate a *purchase order*, which, in turn, leads to product replenishment. The maximum amount of any product to be carried in inventory is usually identified over time, and the number of units required to attain a *par level* is the quantity typically ordered.

Inventory Measures

Because automated systems tend to track sales and then reflect those transactions on goods in inventory, they represent a *perpetual* (running balance) *inventory.* For example, if a preset key is carrying a cheeseburger descriptor, its price and related inventory ingredients can be programmed into the key. When this preset is depressed, one hamburger patty, one slice of cheese, one burger bun, and one unit of condiment are subtracted from the inventory on hand figures. This procedure will enable the foodservice operator to investigate inventory movements and exercise tighter controls over stock replenishments. Figure 9-1 is a simplified illustration of this preset perpetual inventory application. Because of the theoretical nature of a perpetual inventory and its inability to reflect other use or product movements, a *physical inventory* is routinely (weekly) taken to prove the perpetual inventory levels.

Discrepancies between these two balances must be reconciled to determine the cause. The physical inventory is used to correct the perpetual inventory to an actual stock-on-hand status. Since food costs generally represent 40 percent of each foodservice dollar (on average), an ability to chart product movement, cost changes, and various adjustments can be critical to an operation's success. Despite its importance, inventory modeling is the least uniform application area across FIS configurations. To be more specific, even though most managers control their inventory on an *issue unit* basis, precost systems focus on *purchase unit* and cash register systems depend on *recipe unit* to operate.

Does each of these units connote the same information to the manager? The answer, unfortunately, is no. A food item such as canned peach halves is purchased by the case, issued in #10 cans, and used in a recipe by count (by peach half). The relationship between an issue unit and a purchase unit, although not an established one, may remain fairly constant, especially if

FIGURE 9-1 Perpetual Inventory Via Preset Key

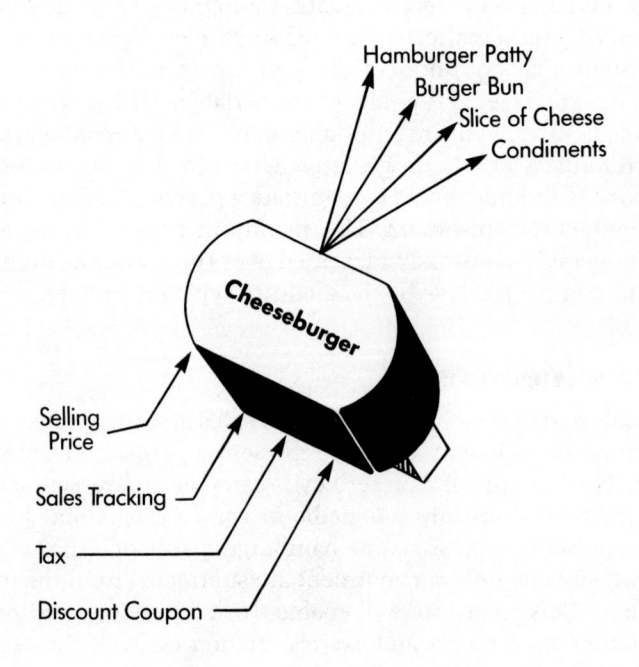

the items were purchased from the same vendor. In this example of canned goods, a case was assumed to be composed of six #10 cans. This may or may not always be the makeup of a case lot. The relationship between a recipe unit and any other unit, however, is usually even more inconsistent than the purchase-issue unit situation. In other words, there are not always sixty-one peach halves in each #10 can. There may be fifty-three one time, sixty-seven the next, and forty-eight the next. Certain assumptions of unit associations are inherent in many foodservice systems, and the user should be familiar with these designs. Without a knowledge of these principles, the transition from ingredients purchased to menu items sold is only a rough approximation, at best.

The Inventory Dilemma

Accountants are interested in *inventory extension* that produces a dollar value of goods on hand. The purchase price is multiplied times each purchase unit and a total inventory value derived. Typically, this is not as important to the restaurateur as is the number of issue units on hand. Without a sufficient quantity of ingredients, menu items are impossible to produce and sales are lost. Obviously, the production supervisor is interested in the yield of the inventory issue unit so that it can be translated into servicable recipe portions.

The inventory problem gets even more complex when these different interests in stocked items are discussed from a processing viewpoint. Cash register systems handle inventory by recipe or count units, and this practice requires the restaurant to reorient itself to its purchased products. All standarized recipes may need to be converted to reflect a recipe unit, rather than simply a weight or more common description.

For example, a meatball sandwich might contain 4 ounces of beef whereas a lasagne dinner portion might only contain 2 ounces. Should the operator define a recipe unit for beef as a 2-ounce portion, then the recipe for the meatball sandwich would read: 2 recipe units of beef, not 4 ounces. To carry this further, all goods that are purchased and received may have to be entered similarly into the system to establish correct inventory supply levels. When purchasing 40 pounds of beef, one may have to input this procurement as 320 recipe units. This change creates an awkward situation for production personnel and a cumbersome procedure for data input. The obvious reason for using these methods is to aid the system in perpetual inventory computation. Most operators refuse to accept this approach, because it forces them to fit their business to the computer rather than the reverse.

The operator who monitors issue units must be able to take a physical inventory, or update an inventory file, without all the bother of tedious con-

FIGURE 9-2 Purchase, Issue, and Recipe Unit Definition

Purchase Unit (description)	Case
Net Wt. of Purchase Unit (pounds)	34.0
Issue Unit (count-description)	6-#10 cans
Recipe Unit (count-description)	52-halves

FIGURE 9-3 Beef Ingredient Definition

Purchase Unit	Pkg.
Net Wt. Purchase Unit	5.00
Issue Unit	1-pound
Recipe Unit	16-ounce

versions. A precost system might provide this luxury. Not all precost systems handle the inventory dilemma in the same way. The more sophisticated systems provide three data input specification fields usually in their ingredient file creation mode.

Figure 9-2 contains an example of a format for purchase unit, issue unit, and recipe unit definition for the canned peach half example referred to earlier. This approach provides the system with the information necessary to convert among all units. Perhaps the beef for the meatball sandwich that was described as containing 4 ounces could be purchased in 5-pound packages, issued by the pound, and used by the ounce. Its definition fields might appear similar to the data found in Figure 9-3.

A batch recipe leading to the preparation of 50 meatball sandwiches would call for 200 (ounces) recipe units, be translated into 16.7 (pounds) issue units for requisitioning, and be converted to 3.3 (packages) purchase units for purchase order purposes. The rounding off of numbers, inherent in any mathematical routine, must be addressed. Most systems always round up to the next integer. Hence, the inventory dilemma can be resolved so long as the system's design acknowledges this problem and allows for multiunit conversion tabling. Figure 9-4 contains an example of a register-produced inventory report. Figure 9-5 contains a precost system sample. Compare and contrast their differences. These concepts are discussed elsewhere in this chapter.

PAYROLL

Another major back office area of concern is the payroll department. Because the foodservice industry is highly labor intensive, control over the payroll function is critical. Payroll costs usually represent 35 percent of each food-

BACK OFFICE SYSTEMS 195

FIGURE 9-4 Sample Cash Register Inventory Report

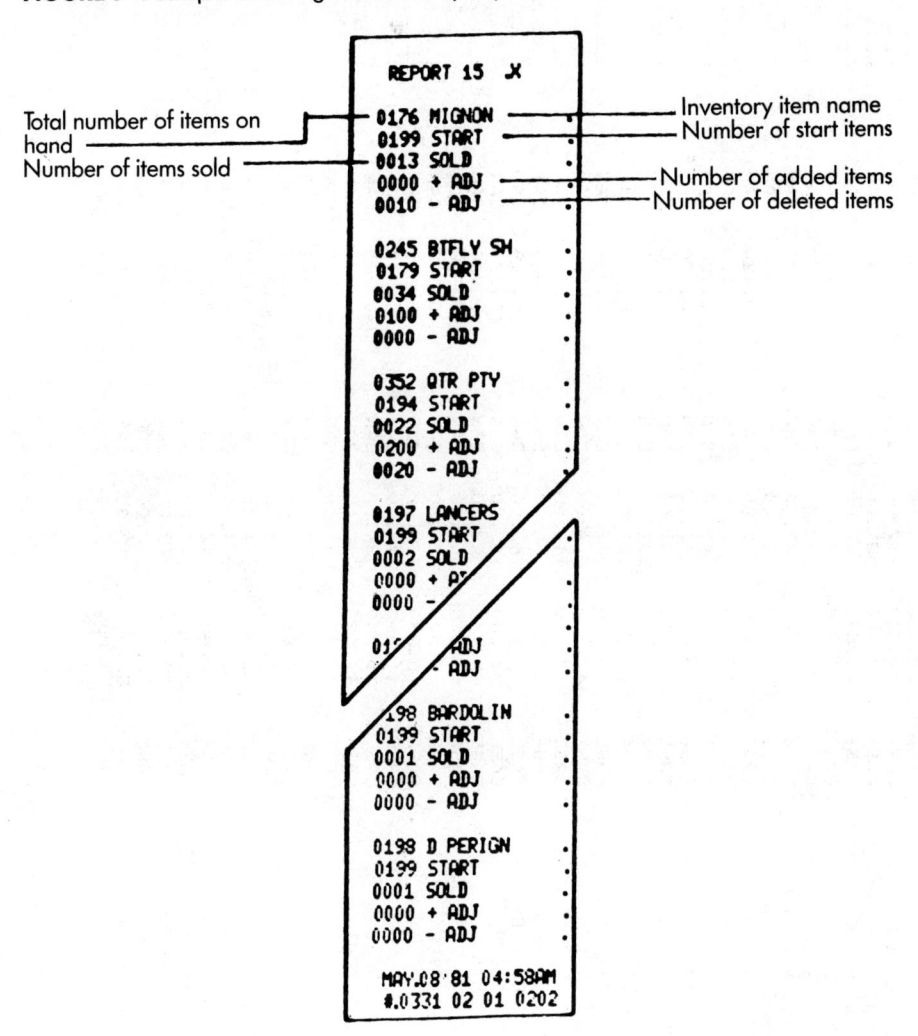

```
                          REPORT 15  X
                                                        ┌── Inventory item name
Total number of items on ┌── 0176 MIGNON ────────────┤
hand                     │    0199 START ────────────── Number of start items
Number of items sold ────┤    0013 SOLD
                         └── 0000 + ADJ ─────────────── Number of added items
                              0010 - ADJ ─────────────── Number of deleted items

                              0245 BTFLY SH
                              0179 START
                              0034 SOLD
                              0100 + ADJ
                              0000 - ADJ

                              0352 QTR PTY
                              0194 START
                              0022 SOLD
                              0200 + ADJ
                              0020 - ADJ

                              0197 LANCERS
                              0199 START
                              0002 SOLD
                              0000 + A
                              0000 -
                              01      ADJ
                                    - ADJ

                              198 BARDOLIN
                              0199 START
                              0001 SOLD
                              0000 + ADJ
                              0000 - ADJ

                              0198 D PERIGN
                              0199 START
                              0001 SOLD
                              0000 + ADJ
                              0000 - ADJ

                              MAY.08 81 04:58AM
                              #.0331 02 01 0202
```

Source: Courtesy of MICROS Systems, Inc.

196 BACK OFFICE SYSTEMS

FIGURE 9-5 Sample Precost System Inventory Module

INGRED	SEQ No	INGREDIENT NAME - ALL ITEMS	UNIT	PRICE	NET WT	RECIPE	COST/LB	INV UNIT	ON-HAND
100001	1	FR CAN CHERRY MARASHINO	GAL	32.000	32.00	CHERRY	1.000	GALLON	<------>
100002	2	FR CANNED CITRUS SALAD	CASE	22.320	36.00	CAN	0.620	CAN	<------>
100003	3	FR CANNED FRUIT COCKTAIL	CASE	20.160	42.00	CAN	0.480	CAN	<------>
100004	4	FR CANNED GRAPES SEEDLESS	CASE	19.320	42.00	CAN	0.460	CAN	<------>
100005	5	FR CANNED GRAPEFRUIT SEG	CASE	17.600	32.00	CAN	0.550	CAN	<------>
100006	6	FR CANNED MANDARIN ORANGE	CASE	21.840	42.00	CAN	0.520	CAN	<------>
100007	7	FR CANNED PEACH SLICED	CASE	17.220	42.00	CAN	0.410	CAN	<------>
100008	8	FR CANNED PEAR HALVES	CASE	20.160	42.00	CAN	0.480	CAN	<------>
100009	9	FR CANNED PINEAPPLE CRUSHED	CASE	18.060	42.00	CAN	0.430	CAN	<------>
100010	10	FR CANNED PINEAPPLE SLICES	CASE	17.640	42.00	CAN	0.420	CAN	<------>
100011	11	FR CANNED PINEAPPLE TIDBIT	CASE	17.640	42.00	CAN	0.420	CAN	<------>
100012	12	FR CANNED BLUEBERRIES	CASE	11.340	42.00	CAN	0.270	CAN	<------>
200051	51	VEGETABLE BEAN CUT GREEN	CASE	9.240	42.00	CAN	0.220	CAN	<------>
200052	52	VEGETABLE BEAN REFRIED	CASE	16.380	42.00	CAN	0.390	CAN	<------>
200053	53	VEGETABLE BEET SHOESTRING	CASE	11.760	42.00	CAN	0.280	CAN	<------>
200054	54	VEGETABLE CARROTS DICED	CASE	8.400	42.00	CAN	0.200	CAN	<------>
200055	55	VEGETABLE CORN CREAM	CASE	10.080	42.00	CAN	0.240	CAN	<------>
200056	56	VEGETABLE CORN WHOLE KERNAL	CASE	9.660	42.00	CAN	0.230	CAN	<------>
200057	57	VEGETABLE MUSHROOM PIECES	CASE	41.520	24.00	CAN	1.730	CAN	<------>
200058	58	VEG CANNED PEAS	CASE	9.240	42.00	CAN	0.220	CAN	<------>
200059	59	VEG CANNED POTATO SLICED	CASE	11.520	36.00	CAN	0.320	CAN	<------>
200060	60	VEG CANNED TOM. PUREE DICE	CASE	10.920	42.00	CAN	0.260	CAN	<------>
200061	61	VEG CANNED TOMATO PIECES	CASE	11.340	42.00	CAN	0.270	CAN	<------>
200062	62	VEG DRIED ONIONS MAGIC	CASE	16.740	9.00	CAN	1.860	CAN	<------>
200063	63	VEG DRIED PEPPERS	CASE	19.200	60.00	CAN	0.320	CAN	<------>
200064	64	VEG DRIED CONVERTED RICE	CASE	7.500	25.00	CAN	0.300	CAN	<------>
200065	65	VEG BEANS KIDNEY	CASE	8.830	25.00	CAN	0.353	CAN	<------>
300101	101	JUICE APPLE	CASE	11.560	34.00	CAN	0.340	CAN	<------>
300102	102	JUICE ORANGE	CASE	10.200	34.00	CAN	0.300	CAN	<------>
400103	103	JELLIES PRESERVE APRICOT	CASE	44.520	42.00	JAR	1.060	JAR	<------>
300103	104	JUICE CRANBERRY	CASE	12.480	32.00	CAN	0.390	CAN	<------>
300104	105	JUICE GRAPE	CASE	21.280	19.00	CAN	1.120	CAN	<------>
300105	106	JUICE GRAPEFRUIT	CASE	9.860	34.00	CAN	0.290	CAN	<------>
300106	107	JUICE PINEAPPLE	CASE	11.560	34.00	CAN	0.340	CAN	<------>
300107	108	JUICE TOMATO REGULAR	CASE	8.500	34.00	CAN	0.250	CAN	<------>
300108	109	JUICE V8	CASE	11.220	34.00	CAN	0.330	CAN	<------>
400151	151	JELLIES PURE GRAPE	CASE	21.000	42.00	JAR	0.500	JAR	<------>
400152	152	JELLIES APPLE STRAWBERRY	CASE	18.480	42.00	JAR	0.440	JAR	<------>
400154	154	JELLIES PRESERVE RED RASPB	CASE	33.600	42.00	JAR	0.800	JAR	<------>
400155	155	JELLIES PRESERVE STRAWBERRY	CASE	32.340	42.00	JAR	0.770	JAR	<------>
400156	156	JELLIES PRESERVE APPLE	CASE	32.000	50.00	JAR	0.640	JAR	<------>
400157	157	JELLIES ASSORTED	CASE	4.000	10.00	JAR	0.400	JAR	<------>
500201	201	SOUP BEEF BARLEY	CASE	18.480	24.00	CAN	0.770	CAN	<------>

Source: Courtesy of Hospitality Financial Consultants, P.O. Box 448, Okemos, MI 48864

service dollar and deserve special attention in the total FIS configuration. Not only is the labor intensity of the industry an important factor, but coupled with the high degree of employee turnover and strict government regulations, this area also is one of the most logical for automation. All in one day, an employee may work as a host for one hour, be moved to the kitchen for two hours, wash dishes for one hour, and then tend bar for three hours. Assuming each job is associated with a different pay scale and that many employees work on a similar swing shift, the payroll clerk would have a difficult time calculating the proper wages, deductions, and tip credits. With an automated system, this process is greatly simplified. Payroll accounting is one area that has been given a large amount of attention in recent years and will continue to be actively pursued by system specialists.

Cash register systems can be equipped with sign-in and sign-out keys that allow employees to log hours through the register. The traditional time clock to record *time in attendance* is not needed. Sophisticated time clock-based systems are beginning to emerge and compile comprehensive payroll summary reports. Figure 9-6 contains a compiled summary report. Not only does a system retain data from the current period, but it also compares recent trackings with historical periods. Also, specific deductions, personnel data, and work histories can be carried in a payroll file.

Payroll systems can also be interfaced to a line printer capable of printing and signing (signature stamping) payroll checks. System-produced checks are not a new idea. Producing them in-house is! Formerly, restaurateurs might have contracted with service bureaus for payroll determination and record keeping as well as check printing. These no longer have to be off-the-premises procedures. Additional features of a payroll system that make it especially attractive to the foodservice area are its ability to handle employee meals and departmental reports, correlate sales to labor expenditures, schedule employee hours, and keep overtime/sick pay records.

GENERAL LEDGER ACCOUNTING

General ledger accounting usually spans such broad areas as accounts receivable, accounts payable, budgeting, bank reconciliation, and check audit reporting. The accounting component of the FIS package closely resembles its counterpart in unrelated industries. Major similarities exist in the accounts receivable and payable sector, since invoices need to be processed, errors detected, vendor transactions recorded, and receivables aged. Although most foodservice operators may not operate according to their projected budgetary expenditures, automated systems are exceptionally adept at generating *dynamic* (multiple sales level) *budgets*. Some systems might

FIGURE 9-6 Sample Payroll Report

PAYROLL SUMMARY
AUGUST 19XX

EMP NO.	NAME	GRS PAY	MONTH FED TX	FICA	SDI	GRS PAY	QUARTER FED TX	FICA	SDI	GRS PAY	YEAR FED TX	FICA	SDI
1	JOE HARRIS	1250.00	275.00	0.00	0.00	2500.00	550.00	0.00	0.00	11303.64	1958.00	0.00	0.00
2	MARY JONES	650.00	84.50	39.52	6.50	1300.00	169.00	79.04	13.00	5398.50	658.00	324.58	53.39
3	LYNDA LARSON	0.00	0.00	0.00	0.00	0.00	0.00	0.00	0.00	577.48	75.10	35.11	5.77
4	KAREN NELSON	750.00	97.50	45.60	7.50	1500.00	195.00	91.20	15.00	6640.60	863.20	403.74	66.40
5	JOAN OLSEN	1000.00	230.10	60.80	10.00	2000.00	460.20	121.60	20.00	8878.00	1513.20	539.78	88.78
6	JANE B. SMITH	650.00	84.50	39.52	6.50	1300.00	169.40	79.04	13.00	5739.25	746.70	348.94	57.39
7	MARK AMES	900.00	162.00	54.72	9.00	1800.00	324.00	109.44	18.00	8100.00	1372.80	492.48	81.00
8	JAMES CARLSON	850.00	127.50	51.68	8.50	1700.00	255.00	103.36	17.00	7650.00	1147.50	465.12	76.50
9	JAMES E. WILLIAMS	600.00	49.10	36.48	6.00	1200.00	98.20	72.96	12.00	5100.00	576.30	310.08	51.00
10	ARRINGTON ARMSTRONG	1250.00	227.50	76.00	12.50	2500.00	455.00	152.00	25.00	11368.40	1758.54	691.19	113.68
11	FRED MOSS	525.00	47.30	31.92	5.25	1050.00	94.60	63.84	10.50	4318.72	498.60	262.57	43.19
12	JERRI FEDERSEN	750.00	120.70	45.60	7.50	1500.00	241.40	91.20	15.00	6552.19	921.38	398.37	65.52
	TOTALS	9175.00	1505.90	481.84	79.25	18350.00	3011.80	963.68	158.50	81564.78	12089.32	4271.96	702.62

	NAME	HOURS MNT QRT	YTD	WEEKS M Q	Y	STATE TAX MNT QRT	YTD	CITY TAX MNT QRT	YTD	OTHER INCOME MNT QRT	YTD
1	JOE HARRIS	176 360	1112	0 0	0	27.50 55.00	93.80	0.00 0.00	0.00	0.00 0.00	0.00
2	MARY JONES	176 360	1112	0 0	0	8.45 14.90	66.10	0.00 0.00	0.00	0.00 0.00	0.00
3	LYNDA LARSON	0 0	176	0 0	0	0.00 0.00	7.50	0.00 0.00	0.00	0.00 0.00	0.00
4	KAREN NELSON	176 360	1112	0 0	0	9.75 19.50	86.25	0.00 0.00	0.00	0.00 0.00	0.00
5	JOAN OLSEN	176 360	1112	0 0	0	23.00 46.00	151.30	0.00 0.00	0.00	0.00 0.00	0.00
6	JANE B. SMITH	176 360	1112	0 0	0	7.40 14.80	71.60	0.00 0.00	0.00	0.00 0.00	0.00
7	MARK AMES	184 368	1120	0 0	0	16.20 32.40	137.50	0.00 0.00	0.00	0.00 0.00	0.00
8	JAMES CARLSON	176 360	1112	0 0	0	12.75 25.50	114.75	0.00 0.00	0.00	0.00 0.00	0.00
9	JAMES E. WILLIAMS	176 360	1112	0 0	0	4.90 9.80	57.60	0.00 0.00	0.00	0.00 0.00	0.00
10	ARRINGTON ARMSTRONG	183 367	1119	0 0	0	22.75 45.50	175.85	0.00 0.00	0.00	0.00 0.00	0.00
11	FRED MOSS	176 360	1112	0 0	0	4.75 9.50	50.05	0.00 0.00	0.00	0.00 0.00	0.00
12	JERRI FEDERSEN	176 360	1112	0 0	0	12.00 24.00	36.00	0.00 0.00	0.00	0.00 0.00	0.00
	TOTALS	1951, 3975,	12423,	0		149.45 298.90	1048.30		0.00		0.00

	NAME	ADDRESS	CITY, STATE, ZIP	SOC SEC NO.	HR RL DP	HIRED MT-DY-YR	TRMNT MT-DY-YR	TIPS QRT YTD	+/- FICA SDI	YTD FICA SDI
1	JOE HARRIS	3725 JASPER	ANYTOWN, U.S.A.	627093358	1 2 0	6-01-75		0.00 0.00	0.00 0.00	0.00 0.00
2	MARY JONES	12345 E. 15TH STREET	ANYTOWN, U.S.A.	481741523	1 0 0	10-17-76		0.00 0.00	1.60 0.00	0.00 0.01
3	LYNDA LARSON	5932 CHERRY STREET	ANYTOWN, U.S.A.	352745123	2 0 0	3-01-76	1-31-XX	0.00 0.00	0.17 -0.00	0.00 -0.01
4	KAREN NELSON	8492 JONES ROAD	ANYTOWN, U.S.A.	538416213	2 0 0	1-01-75		0.00 0.00	1.98 -0.00	0.00 -0.01
5	JOAN OLSEN	9933 S. EDEN PLACE	ANYTOWN, U.S.A.	521748900	2 0 1	7-18-76		0.00 0.00	2.66 0.00	0.00 0.00
6	JANE B. SMITH	1254 SOUTH G STREET	ANYTOWN, U.S.A.	532137581	2 0 1	7-18-76		0.00 0.00	1.72 -0.00	0.00 0.00
7	MARK AMES	3231 SMITH AVE.	ANYTOWN, U.S.A.	477322120	2 0 1	6-15-75		0.00 0.00	2.43 0.00	0.00 0.00
8	JAMES CARLSON	389 E. SIERRA PARKWAY	ANYTOWN, U.S.A.	339396211	2 0 3	8-19-75		0.00 0.00	2.30 0.00	0.00 0.00
9	JAMES E. WILLIAMS	2520 E. FIRST	ANYTOWN, U.S.A.	532131907	2 0 0	5-20-75		0.00 0.00	1.53 0.00	0.00 0.00
10	ARRINGTON ARMSTRONG	4329 BULLION DRIVE	ANYTOWN, U.S.A.	421367949	2 0 4	7-01-76		0.00 0.00	3.40 -0.00	0.00 0.00
11	FRED MOSS	1026 BATTERY AVE.	ANYTOWN, U.S.A.	328067924	2 0 0	12-16-77		0.00 0.00	1.29 0.00	0.00 0.00
12	JERRI FEDERSEN	37 COIL CANYON DRIVE	ANYTOWN, U.S.A.	478430008	1 0 1	4-07-77		0.00 0.00	1.96 0.00	0.00 0.00
								0.00 0.00	21.04	-0.01

Source: Courtesy of E•Z KEEP SYSTEMS DIVISION, Edwin K. Williams & Co. 5324 Ekwill Street, Santa Barbara, CA 93111

even provide a program that allows management to simulate a business cycle and subsequently generate an associated budget. In many FIS systems, the accounting module is constructed according to the Uniform System of Accounts. This strong feature forces operators to adhere to a standardized chart of accounts and yields statistics that can be evaluated across the foodservice industry. Unless operations are charted similarly, they are difficult to compare and/or analyze. The Uniform System offers numerous advantages not only to the back office, but also to the entire establishment. Expense disbursements also can be monitored through the general ledger package. The ability to settle invoices in a manner consistent with managerial policies (taking payment discount terms) and to audit the check-writing function are important features in any accounting module. The FIS general ledger component is essential, but it may not be unique to foodservice management.

SALES AND REVENUE ANALYSIS

Sales and revenues are not the same thing. Generally, sales refers to the number of units sold whereas revenues describe the dollars represented by the units sold. Although sales analyses focus on front-of-the-house activities, they must be regarded as an integral back office application. Sales data can be transmitted to the back office automatically through remote POS terminals, or they can be manually entered off sales documents produced in the dining area. The former approach describes an integrated FIS system. The latter requires a rekeying of register data into the back office package. Systems can chart sales by meal period, server, outlet, settlement, discount, hour, or day. All of this information can be collapsed into a comprehensible analysis of sales activities and the generation of electronic sales journals. From this data base, the average check, menu mix, contribution margin, and operating profit can also be derived. Probably no more important data for the foodservice operator exists than that contained in this module. An outgrowth of a sales and revenue analysis is a cash flow study.

A major weakness of any foodservice system is its inability fo forecast future sales accurately. This presents difficulty to the operator trying to schedule cash, product, and personnel requirements. To date, no one forecasting model quantifies all associated foodservice variables to yield a highly reliable estimation of sales. Figure 9-7 contains a facsimile of a computer-generated Daily Net Gross Sales report. Note that the columns are identified by either a P.P. (per person) or a $ (dollar) symbol and that a projection is compared with an actual transaction column. An explanation of variance between the projected and actual appears at the bottom of the report.

200 BACK OFFICE SYSTEMS

FIGURE 9-7 Sample Daily Net Gross Report

```
14:17:29
DAILY NET GROSS  -  DINNER  -  SATURDAY   -    5/08/82
MGR: THOMAS BRUSSOW
```

	#CUSTS 325 PROJECTED		334 ACTUAL		
	STANDARD	STANDARD	ACTUAL		
	P.P. $	P.P. $	P.P. $	OVER / UNDER

NET SALES   6196.17

SALES
	P.P.	$	P.P.	$	P.P.	$	OVER/UNDER
ENTREE	10.97	3565.25	10.97	3663.98	12.10	4041.50	377.52
APPETIZER	0.53	172.25	0.53	177.02	0.74	247.65	70.63
DIN ADD-ONS	0.15	48.75	0.15	50.10	0.14	46.00	4.10
DESSERT	0.24	78.00	0.24	80.16	0.16	53.45	26.71
COFF/TEA/MLK	0.15	48.75	0.15	50.10	0.16	52.00	1.90
FINE WINE	1.12	364.00	1.12	374.08	0.74	247.20	126.88
COCKTAILS	3.50	1137.50	3.50	1169.00	3.50	1170.65	1.65
AFT DIN DRK	0.00	0.00	0.00	0.00	0.40	132.00	132.00
PROMO BAR	0.00	0.00	0.00	0.00	0.00	1.25	1.25
MODIFIERS	0.00	0.00	0.00	0.00	0.00	0.00	
SALES TAX		171.08		175.81		234.28	
DISCOUNTS						-29.81	
ADJUSTMENTS						0.00	
TOTAL	17.19	5585.58	17.19	5740.25	18.55	6196.17	455.92

GROSS   (STD GROSS)

	P.P.	$	P.P.	$	P.P.	$	OVER/UNDER
ENTREE	6.47	2102.75	6.47	2160.98	6.99	2334.19	173.21
APPETIZER	0.38	123.50	0.38	126.92	0.51	171.75	44.83
DIN ADD-ONS	0.08	26.00	0.08	26.72	0.07	22.84	3.88
DESSERT	0.17	55.25	0.17	56.78	0.11	37.86	18.92
COFF/TEA/MLK	0.12	39.00	0.12	40.08	0.11	36.84	3.24
FINE WINE	0.56	182.00	0.56	187.04	0.37	123.60	63.44
COCKTAILS	2.34	760.50	2.34	781.56	2.60	868.54	86.98
AFT DIN DRK	0.00	0.00	0.00	0.00	0.29	96.58	96.58
PROMO BAR	0.00	0.00	0.00	0.00	0.00	0.78	0.78
MODIFIERS	0.00	0.00	0.00	0.00	0.00	0.00	
SALES TAX		171.08		175.81		234.28	
DISCOUNTS						-29.81	
ADJUSTMENTS						0.00	
TOTAL	10.65	3460.08	10.65	3555.89	11.67	3897.45	341.56
		61.90%		61.90%		62.90%	

	STANDARD		STANDARD		ACTUAL			
	HRS	$	HRS	$	HRS	$	OVER / UNDER	
LABOR								
COOK-UNKNOWN	0.00	0.00	0.00	0.00	8.63	47.94	47.94	
COOK - DINNER	30.75	206.03	30.75	206.03	22.88	140.37		65.66
DISHWSHR	17.50	71.23	17.50	71.23	17.08	63.57		7.66
BUSBOY	15.50	44.95	15.50	44.95	23.73	73.02	28.07	
BARTENDER-DIN	18.00	77.40	18.00	77.40	16.56	75.87		1.53
WAITER	77.00	171.72	77.00	171.72	86.97	194.23	22.51	
COCKTAIL	6.00	22.32	6.00	22.32	0.00	0.00		22.32
WINE SOM'L'R	9.50	25.65	9.50	25.65	10.21	46.83	21.18	
HOST/HOSTESS	9.50	41.14	9.50	41.14	5.33	20.73		20.41
RESERVATIONS	6.00	28.26	6.00	28.26	6.00	23.33		4.93
COAT CHECK'G	7.00	15.61	7.00	15.61	0.00	0.00		15.61
MAINTENANCE	0.00	0.00	0.00	0.00	2.50	11.11	11.11	
MGR-SHIFT	0.00	98.00	0.00	98.00	20.25	160.48	62.48	
MGR-GENERAL	0.00	61.78	0.00	61.78	0.00	61.77		0.01
TOTAL	196.75	864.09	196.75	864.09	220.14	919.25	55.16	
		15.47%		15.05%		14.83%		
		2.66PP		2.59PP		2.75PP		

OVERHEAD

A.	10.80%	603.24	10.80%	619.95	10.80%	669.19
B.	0.68PP	221.00	0.68PP	227.12	0.68P	227.12
TOTAL		824.24		847.07		896.31

NET GROSS

	1771.75	1844.73	2081.89
	5.45PP	5.52PP	6.23PP

VARIANCE FROM PROJECTED TO ACTUAL

DUE TO N CUSTS	72.98	GAIN
DUE TO SALES	341.56	GAIN
DUE TO LABOR	55.16	LOSS
DUE TO OVERHEAD	49.24	LOSS
TOTAL VARIANCE	310.14	GAIN

BACK OFFICE SYSTEMS

FINANCIAL STATEMENTS

Regardless of the type of FIS, the eventual output is a series of financial reports. Figure 9-8 depicts an explanation of a broad-based foodservice system and its interrelation to key personnel. Note certain information extends beyond these spheres. In Figure 9-9, it becomes even more obvious that financial statement preparation plays a central role in the overall system's success. All system components tend to interface to the financial reporting module, rendering it the essential data base for analysis. The two most typical financial reports that management is likely to require are the income statement and balance sheet. The income statement contains revenue and expense data and includes an index of profit. The balance sheet presents a photograph of the firm's financial health at a specific time. Together they provide a comprehensive overview of the restaurant's financial health. Oper-

FIGURE 9-8 Sample Foodservice Information Systems Overview

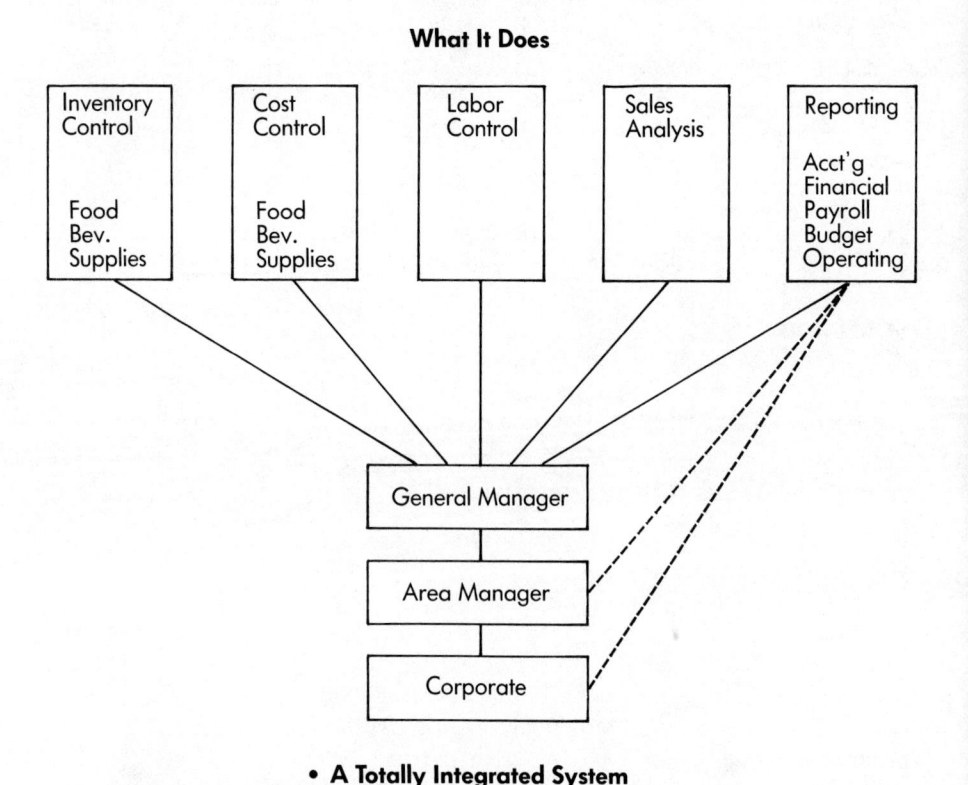

What It Does

- A Totally Integrated System

Source: Courtesy of Uveon Computer Systems, Inc.

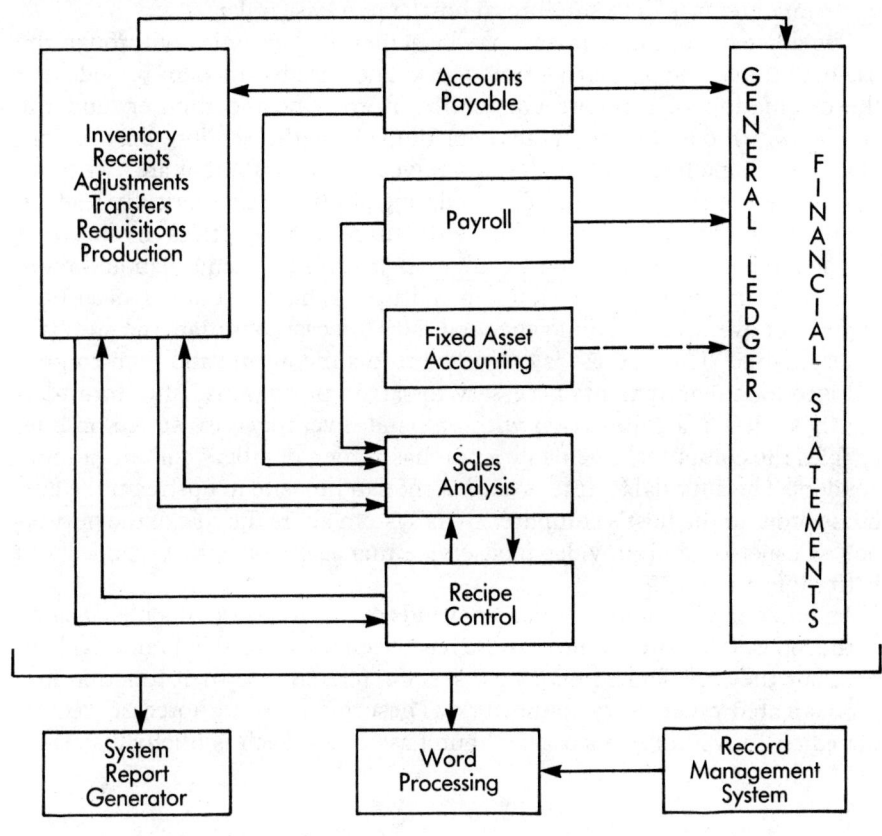

FIGURE 9-9 Sample Foodservice Information System Configuration

Source: TOM/LCS, Seattle, Washington

ators must be careful to understand the composition of each financial statement, its strengths and weaknesses, and the methods of derivation employed within a systems context.

ORDER ENTRY TECHNOLOGY

The state of the art for integrated FIS applications is evolving into sophisticated *order entry systems*, designed to provide on-line communications between foodservice operators and their purveyors. This linkage is a direct result of *telecommunications* technology that interfaces a large, host computer at the food vendor's office with a series of independent, satellite mini- or microcomputers at various restaurant sites. At scheduled times, the vendor's current price list is downstreamed (sent from the host to the satellite via phone lines) to the operator's computer, which, in turn, eventually upstreams (returns from satellite to host) a purchase order.

The downstreaming of prices may be achieved electronically through the use of *autodial* and *autoanswer modems*. The autodial modem provides for the origination of a phone connection from a host computer, and the autoanswer modem actually answers the call at the satellite destination. Once the phone line is secured, the receiver "reads" data that are "written" into the host's memory unit. This updating of prices automatically leads to the replacement of historical prices with current market prices. By knowing up-to-date costs, the restaurant can better control its menu plan and more effectively monitor its financial expenditures. The restaurateur need only approve or override a system-generated sales forecast to initiate the purchase order module. The forecast is converted into a menu mix and then computed into food requirements necessary to satisfy projections. After formulating these needs, a comparison with on-hand inventory, also stored on-line, enables the computer to generate a purchase order, or orders, for one or more vendors. The autodial feature is used at the satellite site to upstream the purchase order to the host's computer. This system alters the role of the purveyor's salesperson and provides foodservice management with expanded and better information.

An order entry system normally depends on six in-house modules located at the foodservice site. Some of these have been introduced in previous chapters, but they are defined here with specific reference to their function in a sophisticated order entry framework. These modules are forecast, recipe, ingredient, inventory, precost, and purchase order. Each is briefly discussed below.

Forecast Module

The *forecast module* is essential to the generation of reliable food stores needed to satisfy a specific meal plan. Although many institutional foodservice units might adhere to a four-week cyclical menu, often their food purchasing schedule is one or more times per week. Commercial restaurants usually follow this multiple order frequency pattern as a result of inaccurate planning or the belief that smaller orders tie up less cash and storage space. Whatever the reason, the forecast period should correlate well with the purchase order schedule to provide a closer fit. Managers who try to forecast for a month but purchase items every three days may be creating more paperwork and problems than necessary. For example, a one-week forecast used to produce a one-week purchase order appears to make more sense.

How is a reasonable forecast derived? Computer systems typically do not provide forecasting models for foodservice management. Traditionally someone within the operation is counted on to "guess-timate" the number of covers expected to be consumed during some period of time. In order to automate this function, it is necessary to understand how the mysterious forecast was made by the restaurant's staff. Once this process is approximated mathematically, the computer can be programmed to produce similar forecasts. The foodservice manager should always be able to override any system-generated forecast, but must do this in a timely manner, as all subsequent in-house functions cannot begin until a reasonable forecast is logged into the computer. Often managers know of special events or circumstances that alter the system forecast, and they need to override the computer's analysis. Once the prediction of a menu mix is complete, the recipe module is invoked.

Recipe Module

The *recipe module* contains the file of standardized recipes that correspond to the menu items found in the forecast plan. Each menu item and its projected number of servings is exploded into its component parts (ingredients) for costing and purchase order purposes. It is assumed that the standard recipe deck is accurate and that the persons involved in item preparation are adhering closely to the recipe specifications. These assumptions are critical. Any system's output will be only as good as its input. The recipe module is

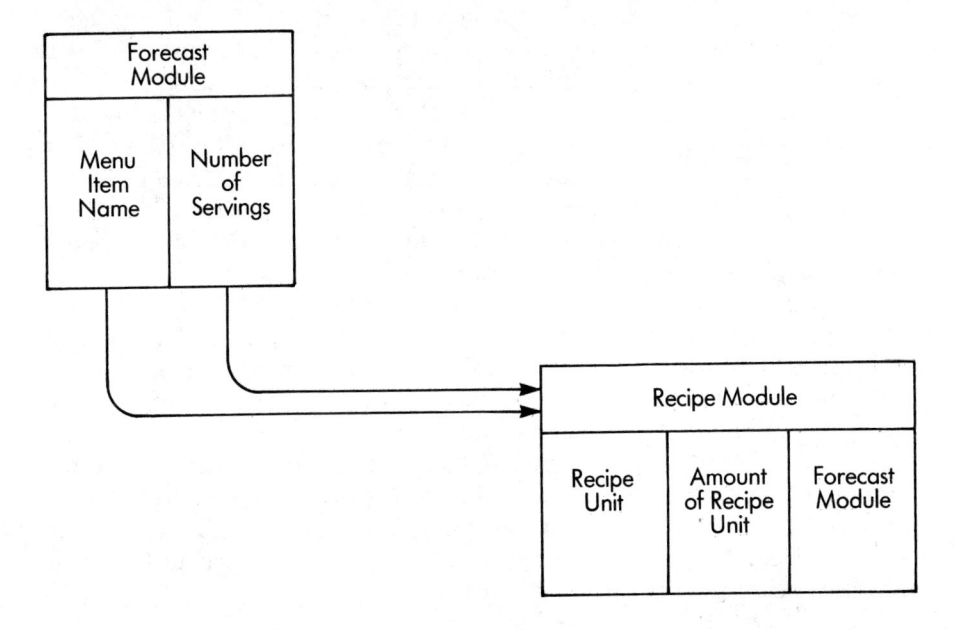

FIGURE 9-10 Relationship Between Forecast and Recipe Modules

essential to the order entry scheme since it breaks down each menu item into its ingredient parts. (Note: Because the recipes contain only recipe unit data for each ingredient, the system must eventually convert recipe units to issue units in order to evaluate on-hand inventory quantities.) Figure 9-10 depicts the relationship between the forecast and recipe modules.

Ingredient Module

A major responsibility of the order entry system is handled by the *ingredient module*. This module receives the updated price list from the vendor's computer and also converts the recipe units to issue units and ultimately, purchase units. The updated prices make intelligent menu plan decisions possible and provide an opportunity for foodservice management to study recipe and menu mix changes at will. The conversion of recipe to issue unit to purchase unit is critical to the formulation of a purchase order. Once the forecast is represented by its component recipes and these, in turn, are exploded into their ingredient parts, the ingredient file's prices and conversions enable the system to move on to the inventory module.

Inventory Module

Although a perpetual inventory can be charted in an automated system, weekly physical inventories are usually used to verify the quantities residing in the *inventory module*. Each ingredient has an inventory level associated with it, and these levels almost always are recorded as issue units. As mentioned earlier, the ingredient module must contain the conversion table necessary to change recipe explosions (in recipe units) to issue units for the purpose of determining order quantities. The several means for determining order quantities and the absolute mathematical differences between what is in stock and what is needed may not satisfy most operators.

Hence, various *algorithms* (computer formulas) can be designed to determine a safe order quantity. For example, the mathematical difference (12) between the number of cans of corn on hand (25) and the number needed (37) may not satisfy a par stock system's reorder requirements. Management may desire to bring this item's stock to 45 cases whenever it is ordered. Some items may have to be coded as par stock, others on a need-only basis, and some items may be on a need-plus-10 percent buffer schedule. In any case, there are many ways to define order quantities. It is important that the system handle each ingredient individually. The inventory module has as its output the number of issue units needed for a given period. Through an online interface, this needs list is converted to purchase unit quantities. This conversion occurs in the purchase order module.

Precost Module

The precost module in an order entry system works identically to the in-house techniques discussed in chapter seven. Assuming that a system forecast and an ingredient and recipe file are established, the computer proceeds to develop a food usage report for a given cycle. This needs listing is then compared to on-hand stock (found in the inventory module) to yield a purchase order. The precost module details batch costs, portion costs, and average portion costs per meal period by day and by week. Additional report formats (food groups and vendor groups) are also available.

Purchase Order Module

The required list of inventory to be purchased is transmitted to the purchase order module. The purchase order module is constructed so that it interfaces with the ingredient file where the issue units can be converted to purchase units for order entry purposes. At this point, the foodservice operator receives the prescribed needs list developed internally by the system. Once the operator has had an opportunity to edit and approve a specific purchase order, it is available for communication to a vendor. The vendor's host system connects to the user's terminal via modem technology for the upstreaming function. The vendor receives the operator's order and begins a standardized delivery routine.

SUMMARY

Back office systems are extremely important to a foodservice operation, even though they are not as obvious as cash register-based systems. Back office packages help provide increased operational controls and efficiencies through a variety of techniques such as 1) inventory control, 2) payroll, 3) general ledger accounting, 4) sales and revenue analysis, 5) production cost control, and 6) financial statement preparation. Additional application areas involve vendor order entry schemes and designs for multiunit reporting networks.

Inventory control hinges on an operation's ability to purchase adequate stocks and to use efficiently all that is bought. All inventoriable items have a reorder point assigned to them. This stocking level may or may not be predetermined. In any case, the reorder point initiates a purchase order. The purchase order, of course, is designed to provide sufficient production replenishment. Since food costs represent close to 40 percent of every foodservice dollar, an ability to chart product movement, cost changes, and the like can be critical to a restaurant's success. Perpetual and physical inventories are performed to tighten overall operational controls.

Despite its importance, inventory modeling is not standardized across the foodservice industry. The identification and charting of recipe, issue, and purchase units can be quite a complex managerial task. Often, the restaurateur needs to assume constant relationships among these varying units. The movement of purchased goods into prepared menu items is simplified. The inventory unit dilemma tends to be just that.

Payroll and payroll accounting are critical to effective management. Payroll costs usually are the single largest nonfood expenditure for a foodservice establishment. A reliable, dedicated system application performs an invaluable service. Similarly, general ledger acounting also can be a major problem for foodservice operators who are either "uninterested" or "too busy" to adhere to company policies regarding the disposition of receivables and/or payables. Additionally, systems can be very helpful in budgeting. Computers enable the development of dynamic budgets versus static budgets. These documents, if constructed according to the Uniform System of Accounts, play a vital role in determining the restaurant's financial success.

Sales and revenue analysis, financial statement preparation, and order entry techniques are relatively new system software packages available in the marketplace. Since purveyor order entry systems are the wave of the future, firms may be wise to experiment with them now.

KEY CONCEPTS

The following concepts were introduced in this chapter. Their meanings should be completely understood.

1. *Algorithm*-term used to describe a solution set (formula) accomplished through a computer system.
2. *Autoanswer Modem*-a hardware device located at the receiving site of a telecommunications network; answers a call without user intervention.
3. *Autodial Modem*-a hardware device located at the sender's site of telecommunications network; initiates a call without user intervention.
4. *Back Office*-that part of the restaurant with which the guest does not come into direct contact.
5. *Dynamic Budget*—a method of planning in which expenditures are forecasted for varying levels of sales.
6. *Forecast Module*-a software package designed to predict dyanmic levels of variables (e.g., sales, costs, waiting time) based on measures of historical data.
7. *Ingredient Module*-a software package designed to enable the capturing, storage, and maintenance of foodservice ingredients (both food and nonfood).

8. *Inventory Control*–the concept of maintaining a sufficient stock level for a minimal capital outlay.
9. *Inventory Extension*–a means of establishing monetary value of stock on hand; the sum of the multiplication of inventory units times their respective costs.
10. *Inventory Module*–a software package designed to enable the capturing, storage, tracking, and maintenance of foodservice ingredient valuation and use.
11. *Issue Unit*–inventory unit preferred by a foodservice operator for tracking stock movements.
12. *Order Entry System*–a technique in which an item or a complete purchase order is sent to a production center or purveyor to initiate a purchase transaction.
13. *Par Level*–a predetermined maximum inventory stock level; at the reorder point, a specific quantity is ordered to attain the par level.
14. *Physical Inventory*–an actual count of stock gained from inspection and analysis of inventory on hand.
15. *Purchase Order*–a written document that describes items being purchased from a purveyor.
16. *Purchase Unit*–inventory unit normally tracked by a precost inventory system.
17. *Recipe Module*–a software package designed to enable the capturing, storage, and maintenance of foodservice menu items.
18. *Recipe Unit*–inventory unit normally tracked by a cash register inventory system.
19. *Reorder Point*–a predetermined minimum inventory stock level; when reached, the item is replenished (reordered).
20. *Telecommunications*–the use of telephone calling and switching devices to transport computer signals from one device to another.
21. *Time in Attendance*–a measurement of how long an employee was at the workplace.

10

Beverage Control Systems

Chapter Objectives

1. To introduce the concept of automated beverage dispensing and control systems

2. To identify the required component parts of a beverage control system

3. To present alternative beverage system configurations and their application capabilities

4. To highlight both the advantages and disadvantages of a computerized beverage system

5. To suggest cost-benefit considerations in system selection, design, and implementation

The advent and use of sophisticated beverage dispensing and control systems is a recent development in foodservice practices. Just as cash register systems have evolved from a transaction orientation, through a report orientation, to a marketing orientation, so, too, have beverage control systems. The major difference between these evolutionary cycles is the amount of time that elapsed from start to present. Cash registers have been developing for more than three decades; beverage systems have only existed for about ten years.

Only within the past decade have computer capabilities been brought to bear on dispensing system technology. The use of computers to dispense, track, price, and monitor operational factors (such as inventory and cash) has become readily available to bar and restaurant operators. The American Business Computers company summarizes the scope of computer bars when they state, "In less than three seconds, the drink is poured, priced, taxed, and totaled and assigned numbers for server, station, and transaction. This information is automatically printed on the guest check and retained for accounting." Industry vendors further claim that beverage control systems insure a more uniform quality and quantity drink at enhanced levels of productivity and control.

Beverage control systems are composed of five major subsystem component parts: 1) order entry, 2) delivery, 3) dispensing, 4) tracking, and 5) support equipment. The amount of fluid that flows in the system is a function of timing, pressure, and valve calibration. Although most systems are capable of outputting from 1 to 3 ounces per second, with a 1/1000th of an ounce portion-size accuracy, not all systems use the identical components or control units. For this reason, the area of beverage control systems is difficult to comprehend initially. For example, a drink can be requested by pressing a button on a dispensing gun, keyboard, tower faucet, or cash register unit. Do each of these activation switches involve the same procedures within the system? Which one is better and for which application areas? The answers to these questions can be found in this chapter.

An unlimited number of equipment configurations can be designed for a beverage control system. The most common characteristics of an operating system involve the construction, location, and number of delivery and dispensing networks required. This parameter is critical to system selection and operational success. Vendors claim that operators who can support an automated beverage system may experience a 20 to 40 percent labor cost savings and an increase in gross revenues of from 15 to 18 percent and be able to cost justify their system expenditure within twenty-four months of purchase. These claims, combined with promised reductions in spillage, waste, and pricing errors, make an attractive package for any foodservice operation.

Why have only a relatively small percentage of operators adopted these schemes? Although there may be many reasons, the primary factors appear to be 1) fear of automated systems in general, 2) misconceptions about the intermixing of ingredients, 3) lack of familiarity with gaseous pressure devices, 4) psychological considerations within the mixology process, and 5) a failure to acknowledge inherent controls within a beverage system. Although the solution to these problem areas will take time and education, it is anticipated that a large segment of the beverage industry will incorporate automated control systems within the next decade.

SYSTEM COMPONENTS

Beverage systems must be designed to enhance production and service capabilities while expanding accounting information and controls. Perhaps not as obvious, but equally important, dispensing units must be easy to clean (sanitize) and not allow liquids to intermix in the delivery network. In order to insure that these objectives are met, beverage control systems generally use some or all of the following component parts. (Note that not all parts operate identically in all systems; many modifications and alterations exist.)

1. Order Entry Device
    a. remote keyboard
    b. selection button
2. Delivery Network
    a. cooling system
    b. pressure regulators
    c. dispensable liquids
    d. storage areas
3. Dispensing Units
    a. control unit
    b. timing device
4. Tracking Device
    a. cash drawer
    b. reporting unit
5. Support Equipment Options
    a. journal printer
    b. sensing devices
    c. interfaces

Figure 10-1 contains a simple schematic representation of the logical flow of activities within a beverage control system.

FIGURE 10-1 Beverage Control System Activity Flow

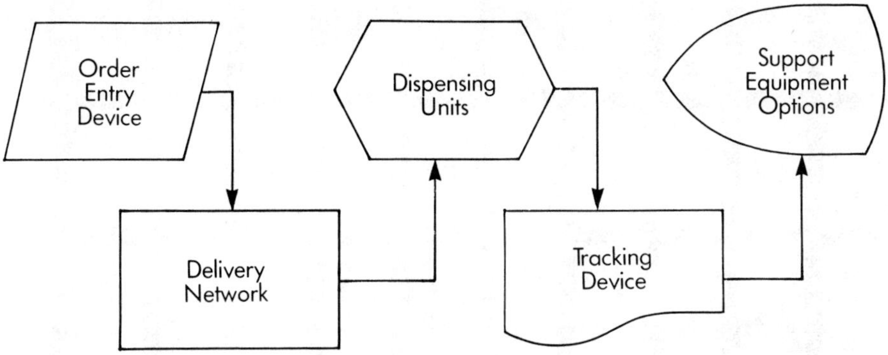

Order Entry Device

Order entry devices range from a push button on a dispensing gun, to a key on an electronic cash register, to a micromotion cell on a point-of-sale device. The primary function of an order entry device is to initiate the activities involved in producing, pricing, and recording the selected beverage. This initiation can be accomplished through a variety of ways. The most popular order entry device is a preset button located on a dispensing unit. When the correct selection button is activated, the delivery network assumes control of the system and continues the activity flow. In beverage systems that contain *keyboard units, keyboard masks,* or similar hardware with preset keys (or price look-ups), the same shift in control takes place. On keyboard units like button selection units, each key is a single drink key. See Figures 10-2 and 10-3 for keyboard samples. Note that the keyboard mask contains the correct serving glass as well as a wide drink selection.

The main differences between initiation of a drink selection on a dispensing unit as opposed to a keyboard device are efficiency, selection, and control alternatives. Although the point of dispensing appears to be the most efficient place from which to request a beverage, the drink selections available at a dispensing unit usually are ten or less. An operation that frequently sells more than ten different products may be wise to initiate some drinks at the dispenser and the remainder through a keyboard device. From a control perspective, the keyboard provides tighter monitoring of activities through centralized order entry and allows for preregistering (prechecking) of drinks. The keyboard is especially effective because the keyboard device requires the insertion of a guest check in order to operate. The use of a dispensing device

216 BEVERAGE CONTROL SYSTEMS

FIGURE 10-2 Sample Keyboard Configuration

GIN	BOURBON	VODKA	WHISKEY	SCOTCH			BEER PITCHER	SANGRIA PITCHER	TAX DATE
MARTINI	BOURBON MANHATTAN	VODKA MARTINI	WHISKEY MANHATTAN	ROB ROY	CHIVAS	VO	BEER STEIN	SANGRIA GLASS	VOID
DRY MARTINI	DRY BOURBON MANHATTAN	DRY VODKA MARTINI	DRY WHISKEY MANHATTAN	DRY ROB ROY	JB	JIM BEAM	BEER PILSNER	WINE CARAFE	QUANTITY
TOM COLLINS	BOURBON SOUR	VODKA SOUR	WHISKEY SOUR	SCOTCH SOUR	CUTTY	OLD GRANDAD	BEER PREMIUM 1 BOTTLE	WINE ½ CARAFE	SUB TOTAL
GIN COCKTAIL	OLD FASHIONED	VODKA COCKTAIL	WHISKEY COCKTAIL	SCOTCH COCKTAIL	DEWARS	JACK DANIELS	BEER PREMIUM 2 BOTTLE	WINE GLASS	FOOD
PREMIUM GIN	PREMIUM WHISKEY	RYE	BRANDY	PREMIUM SCOTCH	CLEAR		BEER GLASS	WINE BOTTLE	CIGAR
PREMIUM MARTINI	PREMIUM MANHATTAN	RYE MANHATTAN	BRANDY MANHATTAN	PREMIUM ROB ROY	ERROR CORRECT	BARTENDER #	NEW CHECK CUSTOMER	MISC	CREDIT CARD TENDERED
DRY PREMIUM MARTINI	DRY PREMIUM MANHATTAN	DRY RYE MANHATTAN	DRY BRANDY MANHATTAN	DRY PREMIUM ROB ROY	7	8	9	ADD CHECK	CHARGE TENDERED
RUM	PREMIUM SOUR	RYE SOUR	BRANDY SOUR	PREMIUM SCOTCH SOUR	4	5	6	TIPS	CASH TENDERED
BACARDI	PREMIUM COCKTAIL	RYE COCKTAIL	BRANDY OLD FASHIONED	CANCEL TRANSACT	1	2	3	TOTAL	NO SALE
					0		SERVICE TOTAL		

Source: Courtesy of NCR Corporation

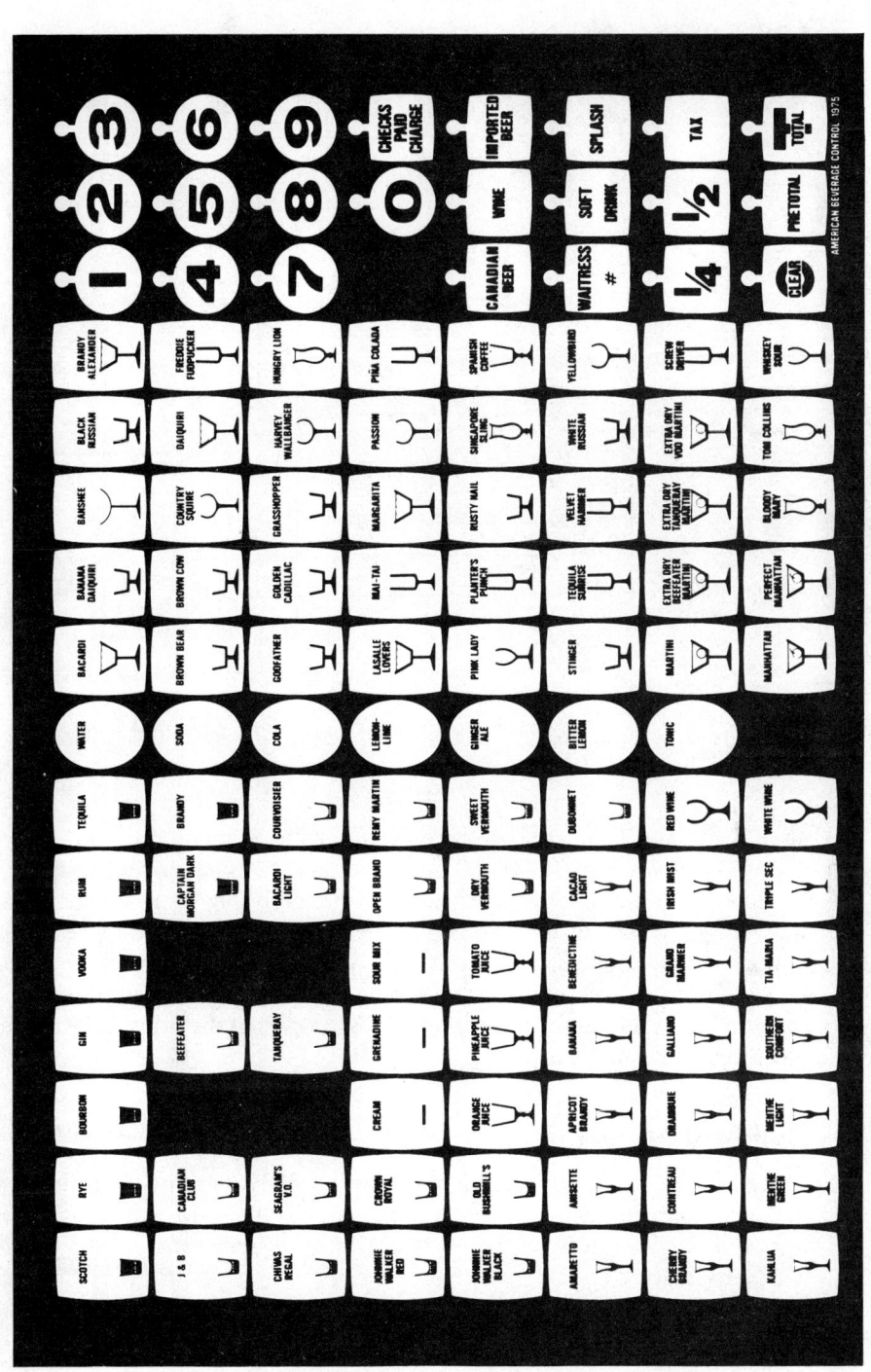

BEVERAGE CONTROL SYSTEMS 217

FIGURE 10-3 Sample Keyboard Mask

Source: Courtesy of American Business Computers

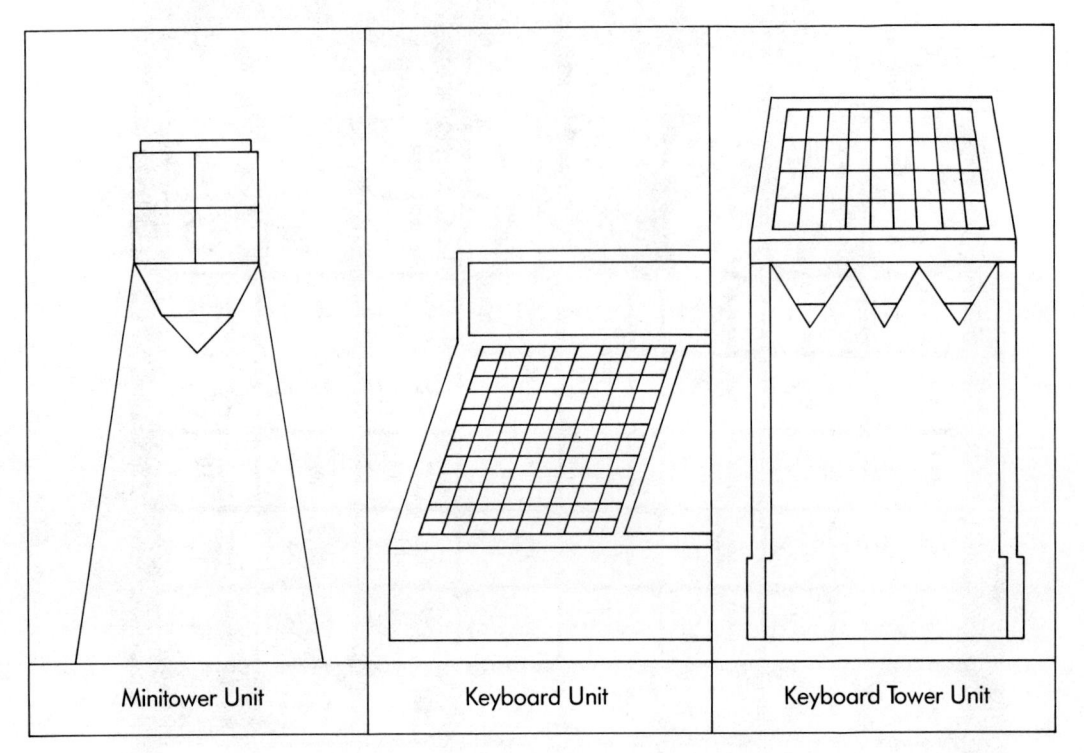

FIGURE 10-4 Sample Order Entry Devices

| Minitower Unit | Keyboard Unit | Keyboard Tower Unit |

as both an order taker and a delivery unit may bring about a cost reduction in system acquisition.

Three order entry configurations are depicted in Figure 10-4. The minitower unit consists of a dispensing faucet and three portion-size selector options (and a cancellation button). The keyboard terminal is composed of a large selection of preset drink keys, and the keyboard tower unit combines the best qualities (wide selection at the dispenser) of the other two units and has three dispensing faucets.

Delivery Network

The beverage control system depends on its delivery network to transport the drink ingredients from their storage units to the dispensing heads. To do this, the delivery network must be a *closed system* capable of regulating both temperature and pressure conditions at various locations and stages of delivery. To accomplish temperature conditions for dispensable liquids, beverage systems normally use cooling systems. Common systems include cold plates, cold boxes, and/or cold rooms.

Although it may be relatively clear that some beverages must be served below 40°F, at 40°F, or above 40°F to be acceptable, the different forces placed on liquids to transport them is not so obvious. Most dispensing systems use four types of pressure to deliver the necessary ingredients to a dispensing unit: gravity, compressed air, carbon dioxide, and nitrogen (or nitrous oxide). The pressure source selected to move a particular ingredient is a function of its effect on taste and wholesomeness. If carbon dioxide were to be attached to a wine dispenser, for example, the wine would become carbonated and spoiled. Similarly, if compressed air were hooked up to a postmix soft drink dispenser, the resultant product would not have any carbonation. The regulation of the proper gas to the correct product is essential to a quality delivery network. In addition to transporting the dispensable liquids through the delivery network, gases are also instrumental in affecting a product's *timing* (mixture), portion size, and head or foaming. Table 10-1 contains an index of the appropriate pressure systems and their applications to various dispensable liquids.

Not all systems can dipense all liquid ingredients required in a beverage operation. Five categories of dispensable liquids can be adequately transported through a delivery and dispensing network: liquor, wine, beer, *postmix drinks*, and perishables. Each of these products may require a different temperature, pressure, and/or storage area. For this reason, they are discussed individually as follows.

TABLE 10-1 Dispensable Pressure Systems

Dispensable Liquid	Pressure System(s)	Controlled Application(s)
1. Liquor	Gravity and compressed air	Removal from bottles, transportation, timing, and portion size
2. Wine	Nitrogen or nitrous oxide	Transportation, timing, and portion size
3. Beer	Compressed air	Transportation, timing, portion size, and head control
4. Postmixes	CO_2 Regulator	Carbonation, transportation, timing, portion size, and foam control
5. Perishables	Compressed air	Transportation, timing, and portion size

BEVERAGE CONTROL SYSTEMS

Liquor. Almost any brand of liquor and accompanying liquid ingredients can be stored, transported, and dispensed at an automated bar. Portion sizes of liquor can be calibrated to range from one-half to three and one-half ounces and can be maintained with amazing accuracy. Some systems allow for drinks to have varying liquor volumes as an option, such as the different liquor volumes in a martini, a dry martini, and an extra dry martini. A *calibration* of the liquor portion size can be set so that each desired variation can be dispensed by the beverage system.

Large computer bar systems can store more than sixty different brands of liquor and can offer more than twelve hundred drink selections. Because of the sophistication of the system, the training of bartenders is simplified. The system recalls the drink recipe and dispenses the necessary ingredients. The bartender's role is limited to completing the production process, serving the drink, and collecting money for the transaction.

Liquor-dispensing systems can be portable (small scale) or permanent (large scale). In either case, the system has many control features aimed at

FIGURE 10-5 Stacked Row Liquor Storage Rack

Source: Courtesy of ABC Computer Bar

FIGURE 10-6 Underbar Liquor Storage Rack

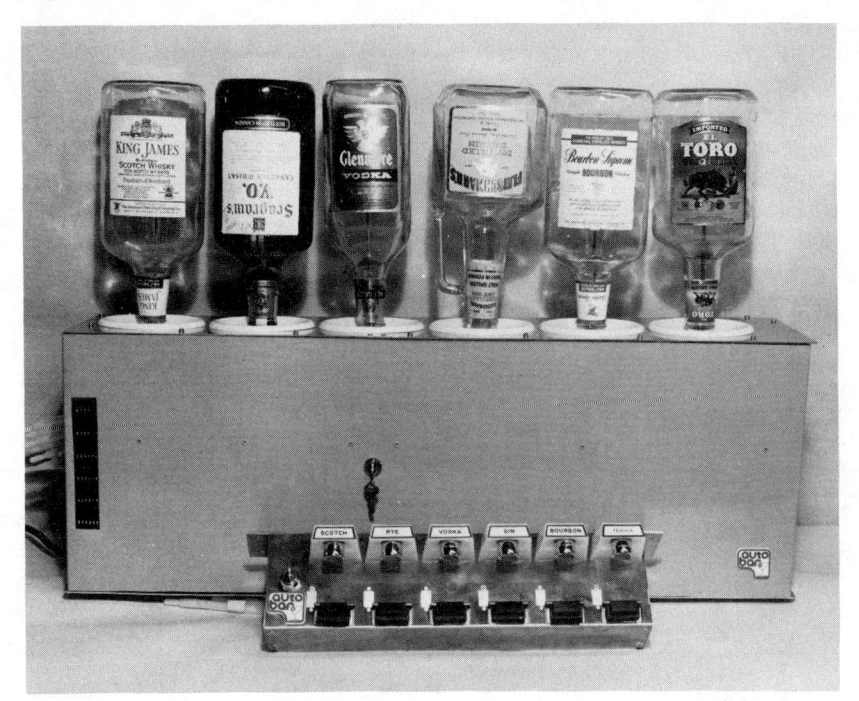

Source: Courtesy of AutoBar Systems Corporation

tracking sales, performing audit functions, monitoring inventory levels, and maintaining product quality. The control unit on a liquor dispensing system is responsible for carrying out these functions. The stored product is gravity-fed to the delivery pumps and flows through to the dispensing unit. The regulation of product (timing), rate of flow (pressure), and recording of transactions (documentation) is under the guidance of the control unit. The control unit is the nucleus of the system.

Liquor systems can have a variety of dispensing units attached to them and use preset keyboards, selection buttons, and keyboard masks for operation. In addition to these options, liquor systems can be interfaced to other register-based systems, or in the case of a hotel, can be directly connnected to the guest accounting module. Liquor-dispensing systems have a wide range of capabilities and are expected to revolutionize the beverage management industry.

Liquor storage racks insure a separation of ingredients. To protect against intermixing, each liquor has its own feeding head and delivery line to the dispenser unit. Liquor storage racks can be of a stacked row design (see Figure 10-5) or of a variation of this row design. Figure 10-6 presents an under-

BEVERAGE CONTROL SYSTEMS

bar storage rack for comparison. In both cases each liquor bottle is set into its delivery line. Because half-gallon bottles are acceptable to the storage racks, savings in product cost and inventory restocking are normally stated as system gains. Large storage racks can hold in excess of sixty brands of liquor in more than 110 rack slots, allowing fast-moving items to occupy three or more spots. Smaller underbar storage racks may accommodate only six bottles, but they are half-gallon in size. Because gravity feeding permits all the liquid to drain from each bottle without any external pressure at the source, the product's taste and consistency are preserved. Also, the absence of any moving parts at this point further minimizes the amount of potential system maintenance that may be required.

Racks can be located up to 300 feet from the dispensing unit or as close as under the bar. Most vendors claim that one large storage rack can handle up to four dispensing stations. A schematic diagram of one feasible configuration is presented in Figure 10-7. Liquor storage racks can be purchased with sensing devices that communicate empty bottle messages to a drink selection keyboard.

FIGURE 10-7 Integrated Liquor System Configuration

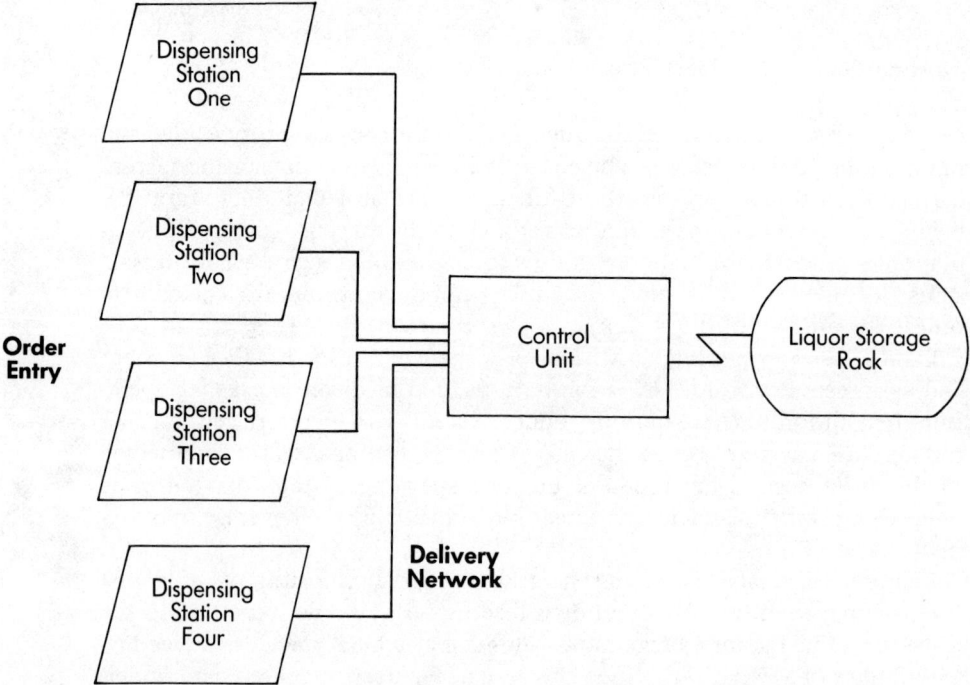

Wine. Wine can be dispensed at a rate of up to three ounces per second and in three control portion sizes: liter, half-liter, and by the glass. For a long time, wine dispensing presented a perplexing problem to the automated beverage system manufacturers. The problem centered on finding a gas that would assist with the transportation of the wine without changing any of its qualities. Vendors found that nitrogen provided a suitable solution to this problem. In a liquor system, compressed air is the medium, whereas in a wine dispenser, nitrogen or nitrous oxide is preferred.

A wine-dispensing system usually contains a red wine, a rose, and a white wine. Those wines that are best served chilled are cooled while passing over a cold plate or through a cold box on their path to the dispensing unit. A wine served at room temperature, on the other hand, is routed around the cold plate and directly to the dispenser. Because of the economics of wine systems, normally only house wines, placed in five- to ten-gallon tanks are fed through a dispensing system. Individual bottled wine sales are still maintained but are entered into the cash register on a separate wine key or set of keys. The beverage operator can track all types of wine sales and achieve better overall levels of control.

Wine can be stored in five- to ten-gallon tanks located in a storage area 300 feet from the dispenser. Wine dispensing is much less complicated than liquor dispensing, since the storage tanks are connected to a nitrogen regulator that transports wine through to the dispensing unit. The path to the dispenser can run through a temperature modification unit, or it can be moved directly to the dispensing head. Wine dispensing can be directly interfaced to a liquor system, though it uses a different pressure system for delivery. Whether wine is dispensed independently or as a branch in a comprehensive liquor control system, the ability to move the product quickly and accurately is a major gain to an operator.

Beer. Because of the nature of draft beer, its dispensing normally requires a separate, independent system. Although cash register terminals can interface with beer systems, beer systems often are complete with their own transaction device, counting unit, and dispensing valve/faucet. Because the pressure requirements, portion sizes (glass, mug, or pitcher), and storage areas for beer are different than for other liquids, the design for a free-standing beer system is further supported.

Equally important to a quality draft product is the presence of a uniform head. To meet this need, beer system vendors equip their systems with *head control adjustment* features. Head control adjustment units allow the beverage manager to select a perfect head size ranging from one-half to two full ounces. This adjustmeent feature allows the bar to present a constantly uniform product and provides a higher yield per keg.

FIGURE 10-8 Minitower Beer Dispensing Unit

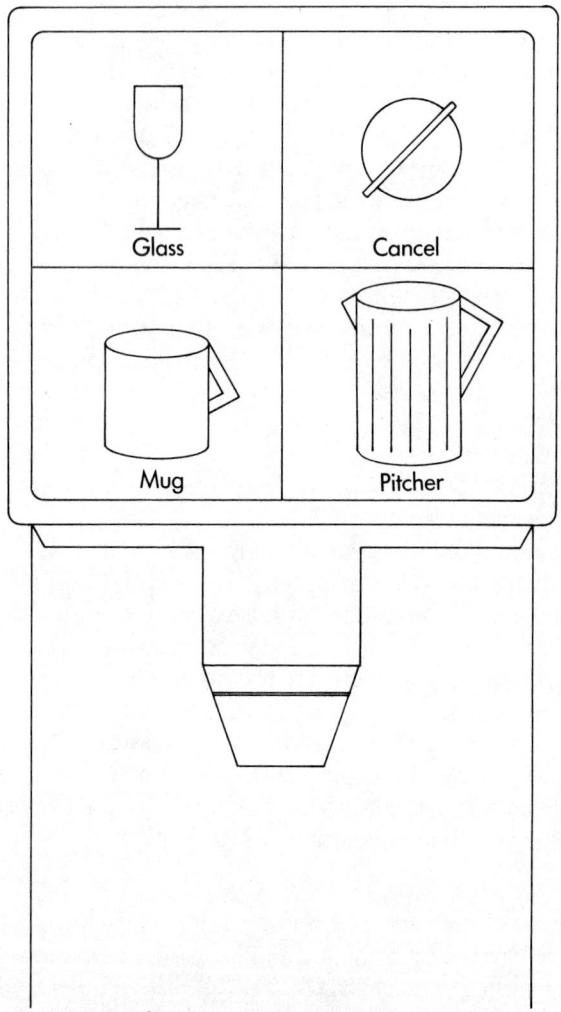

Source: Based Upon Easy Bar Fast Draft System

Another important feature of beer-dispensing units is their portion size control adjustment capabilities. Two different dispensers are available on beer systems. One is the minitower dispenser on which three or more portion size options can be selected. The selection grid may also carry an order-cancel button. See Figure 10-8 for an example of this unit.

The second option is a modified beer faucet unit. The typical tap lever is converted to a portion-controlled switch by the addition of a cable attachment connected to an automated control unit. Each tap is now set to serve

FIGURE 10-9 Modified Beer Faucet Unit

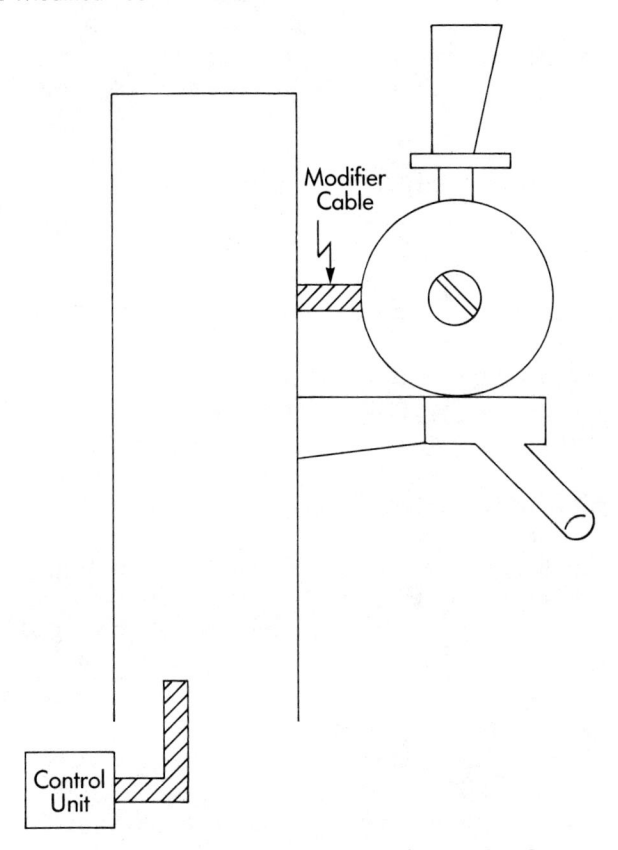

Source: Based Upon Beermatic System by AutoBar Systems

only one portion size for each pull of the tap lever. Hence, a bar serving three different portion sizes would need to connect three different taps to one control unit. See Figure 10-9 for an example of this design. In addition to tighter portion and head control, beer systems also contain drink counter units that report how many of each portion size were removed from inventory. The installation of a beer-dispensing system is not usually as complex as that of a liquor control system.

Beer to be dispensed is kept in a cold room (walk-in) or a cold box located within 150–200 feet of the dispensing unit. Beer is stored in half or full kegs that are typically placed one floor below the bar area. The flow of beer is facilitated by the attachment of an air regulator unit to the stored keg. Filtered compressed air is used to move the liquid without altering its taste. Some beer systems feature *automatic keg switching* and allow up to six kegs to be tapped simultaneously. The use of automatic keg switching means less attention to changing kegs and more attention to operations. Auto-switching systems are designed so that only the keg that is currently in use has pressure applied to it, and therefore no additional pressurizing equipment is necessary.

Postmix syrup and water. Postmix syrup and carbonated water dispensing were the pioneering systems for the beverage industry. Soft drinks can be dispensed through a gun, tower, or a faucet without any loss in quality. Most postmix dispensing systems contain eight fluid lines, of which six contain syrup and two contain refrigerated carbonated water lines (for mixing).

The most common problems for dispensing systems involve serving the product cold (below 40°F), formulating the proper mix (ratio of syrup to water), and moving the product at extremely high flow rates (without foaming). Manufacturers have been able to solve most of these problems through the implementation of a *closed refrigeration system* and the use of *syrup flow regulators.*

Postmixes are an important part of liquor-dispensing systems because of the popularity of mixed drinks. Soft drinks can be dispensed with alcohol by several means. One option is to place the soft drink in a glass separately, requiring a separate postmix dispenser. Another option is to activate both the liquor and soda flow simultaneously. A more advanced dispensing mode involves presetting a drink key, or button, which, when activated, will automatically output both flows. In any case, postmix units are critical to a total beverage system.

Postmix soda syrups and carbonated water must be located within 150 to 200 feet of their dispensing unit. All syrups are stored in metal five-gallon tanks that are connected to CO_2 cylinders. The movement of syrup through the lines and to the dispensing unit is accomplished through a closed refrigeration network. Water, which normally comes from a city supply, is filtered and passed through a carbonator. The water is then cooled via a cold plate, ice chest, or mechanical refrigeration unit. Most postmix lines allow for non-carbonated water to be carried as a viable beverage option. Water is moved from supply to service along with the syrup and carbonated water flows.

Figure 10-10 illustrates a simple postmix and water-dispensing system. Note that the carbon dioxide cylinder has two gauges attached to it. One gauge indicates the amount of CO_2 remaining in the tank; the other indicates its output pressure.

Perishables. Some systems incorporate highly perishable items. Perishable items such as cream, juices, and drink mixes can be used in the system just as any other fluid. The major problem with perishables is maintaining a

FIGURE 10-10 Postmix Syrup and Water System

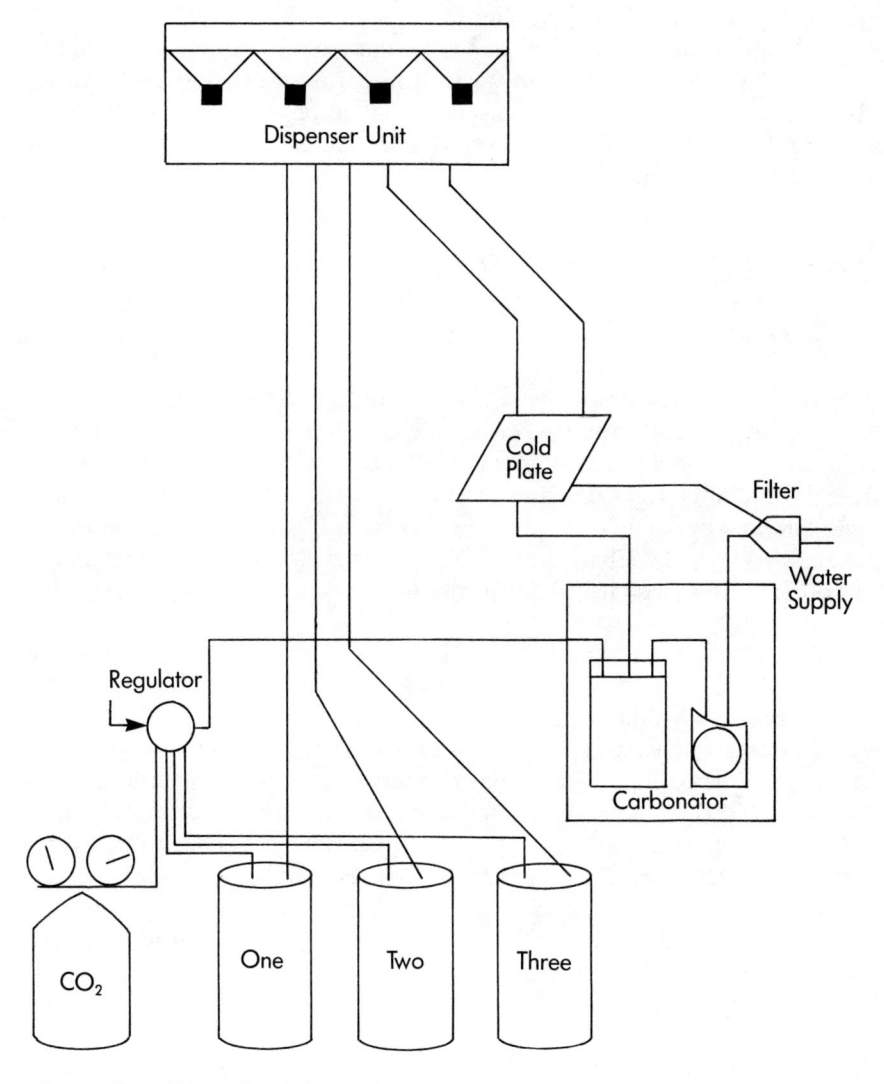

Source: Based Upon Bar-O-Matic Systems

rotated, fresh stock and a very clean container and line. Normal maintenance usually requires that all perishable lines be flushed daily and all dispensing valves be cleaned thoroughly each week.

The perishables are fed through their distribution lines via compressed air. Vendors calibrate perishable dispensers based on the pulp, powder, and consistency of the specific brand used by the bar operation. A change in brands necessitates a change in this calibration.

Perishables must be stored in air-tight containers to extend their shelf life and to enable them to be transported through the dispensing lines. All perishable lines must be kept very clean or else no product will be allowed to flow through. Perishables are normally maintained in a cold box kept just below the service bar.

Dispensing Units

Although many vendor systems can be configured with a variety of dispensers, the most common selection of options includes the five following types.

1. *Touchbar Faucet Unit* (TFU). Touchbar dispensers can be located under the bar, behind the bar, on an ice machine, or on a pedestal stand. They are not very popular components of a computer-based system because they do not offer the versatility, flexibility, and expandability that other units do. Touchbar faucets usually are preset for one specific liquid output per push and are usually dedicated to one beverage each. A double shot of bourbon requires two pushes on the bar lever.

2. *Hose and Gun Unit* (HGU). The hose and gun dispenser has dominated the electronic bar marketplace for many years. The control buttons on the gun handle can be connected to liquors, carbonated beverages, water, and/or wine tanks. The press of a button produces a premeasured flow of the desired liquid. Hose and gun units first became popular because of their high level of consistency and a mobility, yet they still enabled a bartender to finish off a drink with some creativity and flair. As bar control systems have become more sophisticated, with the number of available liquors exceeding the gun selection by almost ten times, managers are starting to move away from these units. Some bars compromise and either add more gun units and/or add a different unit option to increase their control over the distribution of a larger number of alcoholic beverages.

3. *Console Faucet Unit* (CFU). Console faucet units are similar to touchbar faucet units in that they can be located in almost any part of the bar area. They differ, however, in their ability to handle various beverages in a variety of portion sizes. By using the buttons located above the faucet units, a bartender can trigger four different portion sizes from the same faucet unit. Additional options include a double hose faucet unit capable of moving a large quantity of liquid in a smaller amount of time. In any case, the console faucet unit can be located up to 150 feet from its source and can produce a variety of measured output.

4. *Minitower Pedestal Unit* (MPU). In an attempt to capture the major advantages of both the gun and faucet units, the minitower was developed. The minitower has the button selection of a gun unit and the portion-size capabilities of the faucet unit with increased operational control. In order for a drink to be dispensed, the minitower requires that a button on the dispenser be pressed and that a glass be inserted under the unit. The minitower has become especially popular for items that need no additional ingredients before service. Such items as wine, beer, and call liquors are typically used in the minitower. This unit can be located on a wall, an ice machine, or on a pedestal at the bar. The minitower unit is also referred to as a portion control tower unit.

5. *Bundled Tower Unit* (BTU). The most sophisticated and flexible dispensing unit is clearly the bundled tube tower unit. The dispensing head may contain more than 110 beverage lines and a glass-sensing unit. A drink must be registered on another piece of equipment since the bundled tower is designed only to dispense liquids, not handle transactions. Each liquor contains its own line to the tower, and a variety of pressurized systems can be incorporated to enhance liquid flows. Wine, for example requires nitrogen to aid its flow. Soda requires CO_2 to assist in its movement.

All ingredients required for a specific drink are simultaneously dispensed by this unit. This unit is different from the other types in which ingredients are placed in the glass in sequence. To complete the bartending service, the server merely shakes or garnishes the requisite glassware or mix. The dispensing tower can be located up to 300 feet away from its supply rack. This unit tends to be the most expensive and has the widest display of capabilities.

In general, all dispensing units can be locked and have a cancel-drink option to abort a drink erroneously entered, before its service. Additionally, dispensers can be calibrated to dispense between one-half (.5) and three and one-half (3.5) ounces of liquor at one time and up to pitchers and liters for other beverages. Hence, portion sizes can be customized to almost any operation-desired size. Knowing that portions can also vary (a dry martini, an extra dry martini, etc.) enables a good bar manager to mix more than 1,000 different drinks from a limited selection of ingredients.

Tracking Devices

A beverage control system normally contains a control unit, a register device, and a reporting system. The *control unit* is responsible for directing all the system resources. It is the control unit that translates and communicates a request from an order entry terminal through to the delivery network and on to the dispensing unit so that a drink can be served. Control units can be simply a series of electronic relays, a microprocessing device, a microcomputer, or a minicomputer. Whichever hardware is used, this unit is primarily responsible for regulating all essential mechanisms within a beverage system.

Control units usually are located very close to the beverage storage units. For a liquor system, the control unit is usually mounted right on the liquor rack. The reasons for this remote location are increased security and efficiency. In order to maintain system continuity, the control unit must not be disturbed. Should a bartender spill an item on this unit, or bump into the unit, the reliability of the system might be compromised. The control unit needs to communicate effectively with the delivery network, and locating it close to the supply enhances a system's speed in processing and ability to dispense. The control unit is a critical system component deserving special attention and consideration in the design and layout of a system.

Individual brand, drink, portion size, sales, tax, server, and service location can be tracked and recorded via a terminal device, cash register, centralized totalizer, or counter unit. Although most systems record and process all drink transactions at the time of entry, some do not record the activity until a guest check is eventually closed out. The most complete control procedure begins with prechecking (requiring the entry of a check into the register before an order is accepted), continues through guest-check settlement, and concludes with cashier balancing (reconciliation or settlement). The totalizer or counter unit generates sales data for analysis based on drink sales mix and length of service period. The totalizer also generates employee sales analysis based on ticket (guest check) auditing and sales volume productivity. *Register devices* are essential for effective guest settlement and serve as a data base for the production of comprehensive operational and financial reports. Some systems contain various price mode options that can be selected to alter all or some prices. The three most common price modes available are regular price, happy hour price, and entertainment price. This feature allows bars to collect different amounts for the same or slightly modified drinks.

The *reporting system* presents management with various types of information essential to effective beverage system operations. There are numerous forms of sales mix reports that detail the number of each drink sold and the revenues represented by those sales. Inventory usage reports, similar to the one illustrated in Figure 10-11, relate sales to inventory. Server reports detail each person's sales productivity and accountability for guest checks.

Although the list of system reports is numerous, any data entered into the system (including time and attendance in some cases) can be used to produce a needed report. One traditional problem with register-based system reports has been the format of their printing. Until recently, reports were

FIGURE 10-11 Example of an Inventory Usage Report

BAR INVENTORY REPORT		OUNCES SOLD	BRAND CODE #
		Date June 29, 1975	
	Report No.	Z 54	
Offline Ct./Trans. #/No Sale Ct./Reset Ct./Program Ct.		19 29 5 76 46	
1E. BAR SCOTCH	1E	Z 172 .02 401	1E
2E. PREMIUM SCOTCH 1	2E	Z 131 .07 402	2E
3E. PREMIUM SCOTCH 2	3E	Z 136 .06 403	3E
4E. PREMIUM SCOTCH 3	4E	Z 205 .03 404	4E
5E. SPECIAL STOCK	5E	Z 98 .04 405	5E
6E. BAR BOURBON	6E	Z 28 .04 406	6E
7E. PREMIUM BOURBON 1	7E	Z 47 .03 407	7E
8E. PREMIUM BOURBON 2	8E	Z 57 .06 408	8E
9E. PREMIUM BOURBON 3	9E	Z 42 .05 409	9E
10E. BAR WHISKEY	10E	Z 39 .04 410	10E
11E. PREMIUM WHISKEY 1	11E	Z 68 .05 411	11E
12E. PREMIUM WHISKEY 2	12E	Z 46 .06 412	12E
13E. BAR GIN	13E	Z 209 .03 413	13E
14E. PREMIUM GIN 1	14E	Z 95 .05 414	14E
15E. BAR VODKA	15E	Z 230 .07 415	15E
16E. PREMIUM 1	16E	Z 139 .05 416	16E
17E. BAR RUM	17E	Z 76 .06 417	17E
18E. PREMIUM RUM 1	18E	Z 32 .03 418	18E
19E. TOTAL OUNCES SOLD	19E	Z 1850	19E
Consecutive No./Date/Terminal No.		618 6/24/75	204

Source: Courtesy of NCR Corporation

printed on a small-format printing unit, and managers had to rely on rolls of cash register tape for printing reports. These documents, cumbersome to handle, limited management's ability to receive a large quantity of comprehensible information and made it difficult to file and retrieve information from these reports. Modern beverage systems have significantly upgraded their reporting capabilities and are moving toward complete information systems.

Support Equipment Options

Beverage control systems are being expanded to encompass a larger dimension of bar operations. Although many new pieces of support equipment are being tested, at least three warrant attention. The first is a *journal printer*. The journal printer is used to produce comprehensive reports from the system's data storage base. Providing for a large format printing, the journal printer can be programmed to produce detailed accounting and financial reports. A second support feature is the use of *sensing devices*. At least three different types of sensing devices are available on most sophisticated systems. These devices are glass sensor, guest-check sensor, and an empty-bottle sensor. Each is briefly described as follows.

1. *Glass Sensor*–electrical mechanism located in a dispensing tower that will not allow the flow of any liquid until a glass is positioned below its lines.
2. *Guest-Check Sensor*–in the presale phase of a transaction, a guest check must be placed in the register for a drink to be dispensed; in the postsale phase, a guest check must be inserted in the register to complete a settlement.
3. *Empty Bottle Sensor*–a unit is placed on the liquor storage rack that signals the bartender (by a flashing key on the keyboard) that a particular ingredient is finished and must be replenished.

The third support option involves the use of an interface. Interfacing can be achieved either within the beverage system (by linking different dispensing systems) or with extraneous system considerations (to a restaurant or hotel system). Two interface options for connecting to a remote processing unit are:

1. *Electronic Store and Forward (ESF)*–the liquor-dispensing system collects all of its own transactional data which it sends, at a later time, to a remote central processing unit; also called batch transmission; requires only a minimal amount of component alteration to work.
2. *On-Line Transmission*–the liquor-dispensing system is directly connected to a remote central processing unit and sends each transaction forward as it occurs. Also called live transaction transmission, it may require a two-way communication between the sending and receiving units.

The development of add-ons and assorted peripheral device options for a beverage control system enables an operator to achieve a total information system. This system eventually may be able to perform all functions with the exception of serving the drink and collecting money for it.

SYSTEM CONFIGURATIONS

Because of the detailed descriptions of many of the component parts of a beverage system, only a few selected system configurations are presented here. The critical decision variables in configuring a system involve the type, number, and location of 1) delivery and dispensing networks, 2) temperature and pressure control units, and 3) recording and accounting information devices. Such delivery and dispensing considerations as calibration, drink recipe, and solenoid valves must be dealt with early in the system design and planning stages.

FIGURE 10-12 Wine Gun Dispensing System

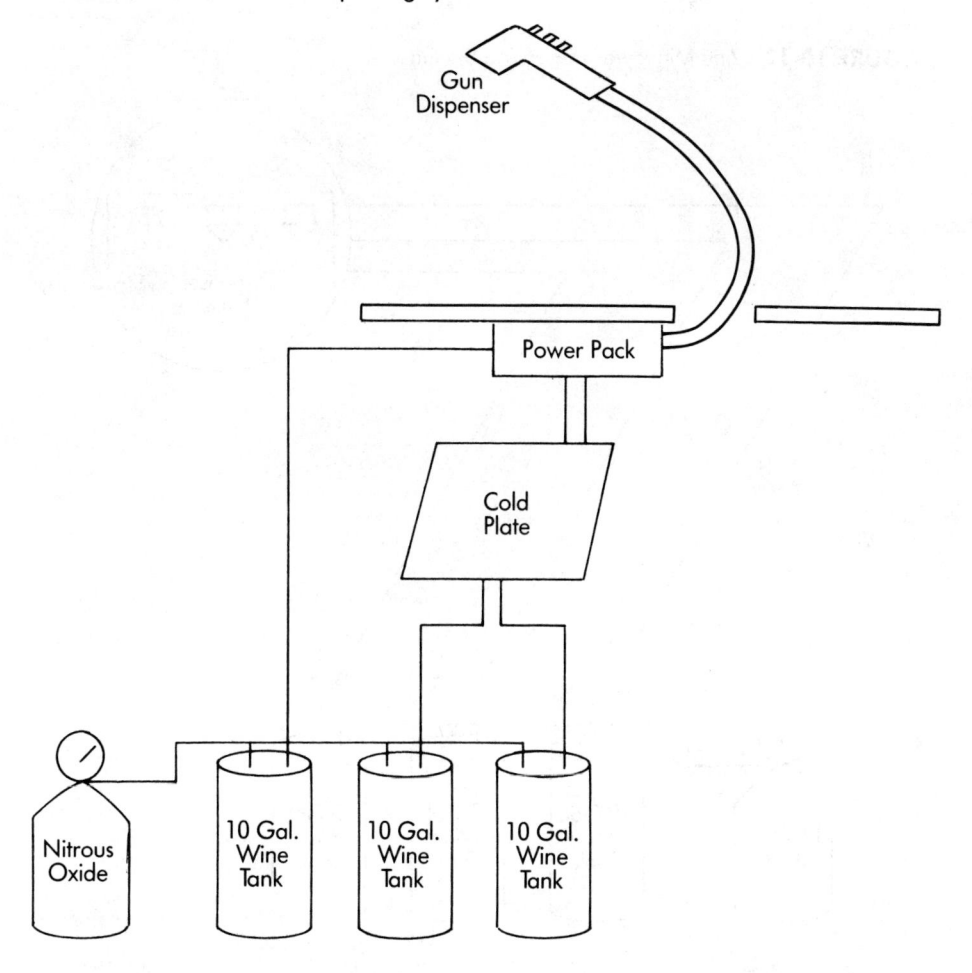

Source: Based Upon Bar-O-Matic Systems

234 BEVERAGE CONTROL SYSTEMS

Figures 10-12 and 10-13 illustrate the use of alternative dispensing units in a wine-dispensing system configuration. The importance of temperature and pressure control units cannot be overstated. Without an efficient refrigeration system, product quality and service could not be maintained; and without a reliable pressure system, there would be sporadic product movement and a loss of control over calibration and timing. Figure 10-14 presents an abbreviated sketch of a total beverage system displaying the use of various temperature and pressure control units. Note the location of the nitrogen, CO_2, and compressed air containers in this illustration.

Recording and accounting information equipment is essential to achieving control and reporting capabilities within a beverage system. Figure 10-15

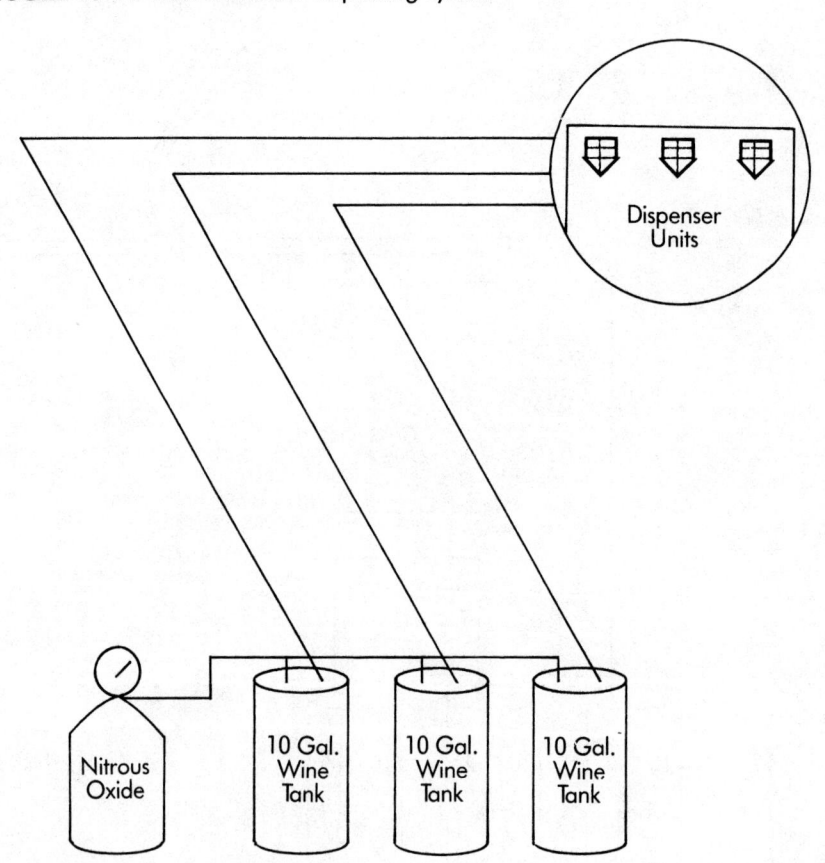

FIGURE 10-13 Wine Minitower Dispensing System

Source: Based Upon Easy Bar Systems

FIGURE 10-14 Total Beverage System Configuration

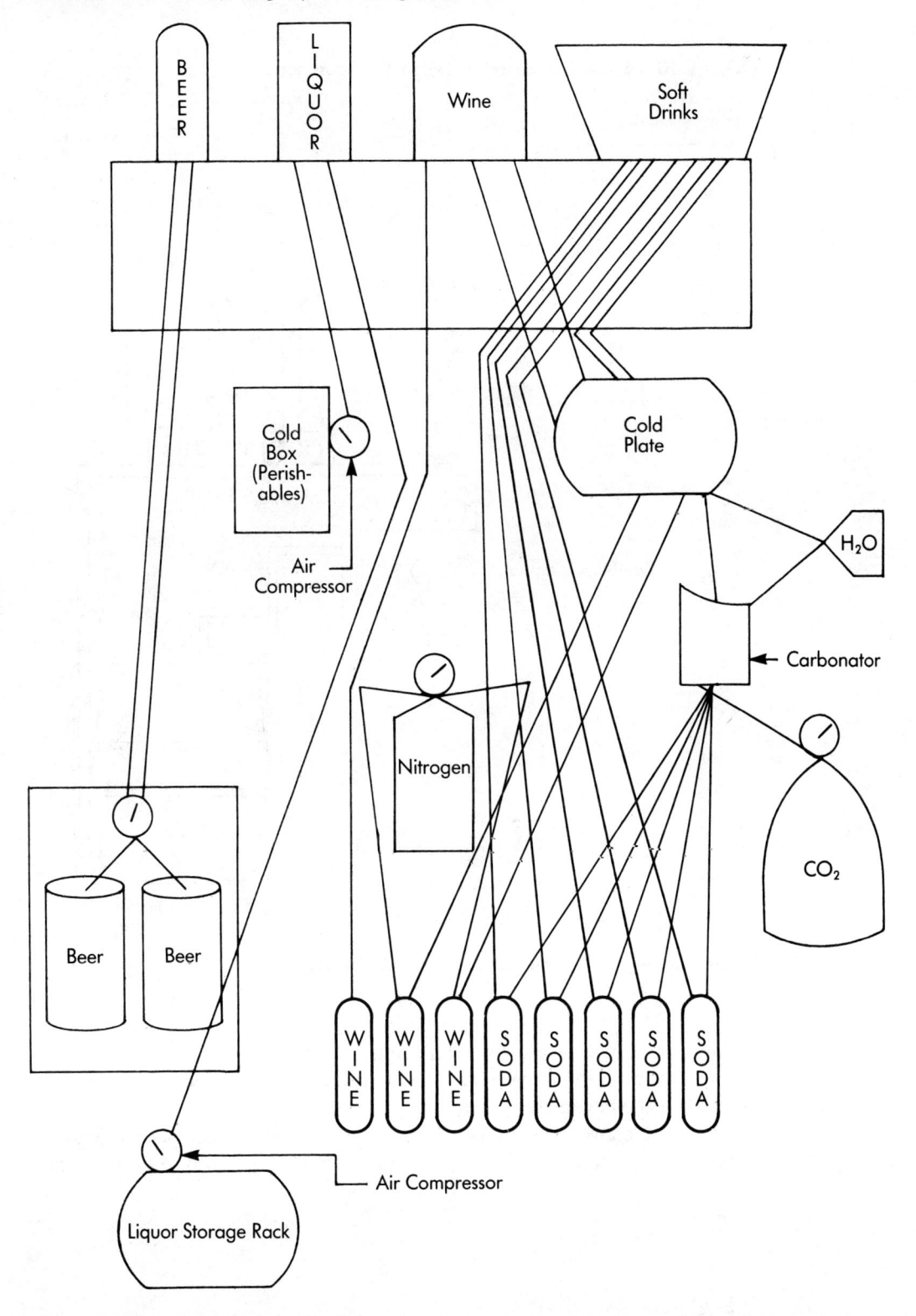

236 BEVERAGE CONTROL SYSTEMS

FIGURE 10-15 Alternate Beverage System Configuration

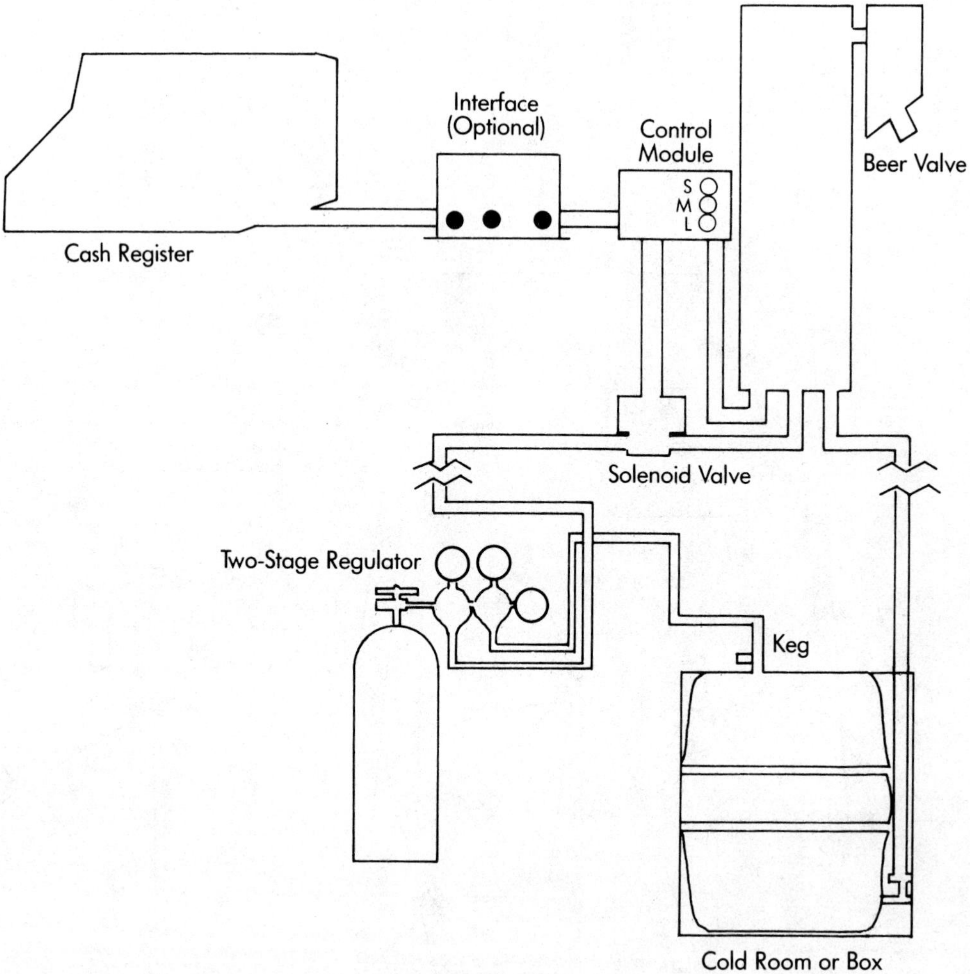

Source: Courtesy of Gamble National, Inc.; dba/EASYBAR®

outlines an actual system configuration and illustrates the role of transaction initiation and control. The use of recording equipment is an essential element of the beverage system data processing cycle.

A beverage control system is a complex configuration composed of various storage areas (dry and cold), pressure systems (CO_2, compressed air, and nitrogen), dispensing temperatures (room temperature, refrigerated, and cold plate), calibrations (wine, beer, soft drinks, liquor, and perishables), order entry devices (keyboard, dispenser, and combination), and dispensing valves (gun, tower, and touchbar faucet).

ADVANTAGES OF BEVERAGE SYSTEMS

The major advantages of a beverage control system are:

1. *Consistency*-quality and quantity of drink ingredients are reliably repeated with 1/1,000th-of-an-ounce accuracy.
2. *Control*-significant internal controls are gained in server, bartender, and cashier accountability areas.
3. *Training*-bartenders are more easily trained because the system contains drink recipes and dispenses the necessary ingredients. Spillage, overpouring, and pricing errors are reduced or eliminated.
4. *Flexibility*-drink prices and recipes can easily be altered to special time periods or functions.
5. *Security*-enhanced security over system resources (inventory, cash, and records) is achieved through key locks, modes, and access codes.
6. *Profitability*-contribution margin increases because of consistent unit pricing, portion and inventory control, improved labor productivity, and better information.
7. *Information*-information storage and retrieval are largely enhanced through order entry devices and optional printing formats.

POTENTIAL PROBLEM AREAS

The following factors have been cited as potential problem areas experienced with beverage control systems:

1. *Sanitation*-refers to failure to maintain clean delivery network and dispensing unit lines; more of a concern with perishables, wine, and postmix systems. Dirty lines inhibit fluid movement.
2. *Intermixing*-not as important a concern as it once was since most systems do not use shared lines or common dispensing heads.
3. *Malfunctions*-typical malfunction areas are insufficient pressure regulation, incorrect valve calibration, and leakage in storage or delivery equipment. Overpouring or underpouring may be the result of improper pressure regulation.
4. *Psychology*-the operator, bartender, and customer may perceive an inferior product because of an automated production process.

5. *Cost Benefit*-not all beverage application areas or operations can cost justify a system purchase.
6. *Reliability*-although beverage systems contain few moving parts, the lack of a back-up system could lead to losses of information and operation.
7. *Production*-most systems allow operators to enter multiple drink orders and then dispense them in the order they were entered into the terminal. The bartender's ability to recall the correct drink sequence and to make the appropriate glassware selection may be impaired.

SUMMARY

Vendors believe that with the implementation of a beverage control system, operators do not have to increase drink traffic in order to increase profits. The increased control and improved production capabilities gained from system use usually lead to a larger contribution margin. This may or may not be the case. Beverage systems are designed to 1) enhance production and service capabilities, 2) monitor and expand accounting information, 3) provide tight controls over inventories and cash, 4) enable effective maintenance and cleanliness, and 5) insure that liquids are transported and dispensed in controlled portion sizes. The amount of fluid that flows is a function of timing, pressure, and valve calibrations. Adjustments in portion size, drink recipes, and price modes can be made by an order entry terminal or a system control box.

A liquor control system translates a drink request into signals that can be communicated to the delivery network dispensing units and recording devices (see Figure 10-16). A beverage system transaction can be activated in two ways: 1) over an order entry terminal, and 2) with a selection button located on a dispensing unit. Either method triggers the delivery network. The delivery network transports the ingredients from their storage locations to the dispensing units. Five types of dispensers are available to the operator: gun, touchbar faucet, console faucet, minitower, and tower dispensing units. While a drink is being dispensed, its sale is simultaneously recorded within the system's hardware. Menu mix, server and cashier analyses, and a host of assorted reports are constructed from the system's data base.

Vendors estimate that beverage outlets should experience an 18 percent improvement in their gross revenues and a 4 to 6 percent decrease in product cost shortly after system implementation. They further estimate a 20 to 40 percent of labor cost savings and an 18- to 24-month system payback period. These and other claims are summarized in Figure 10-17.

BEVERAGE CONTROL SYSTEMS 239

FIGURE 10-16 Computerized Liquor-Dispensing Systems

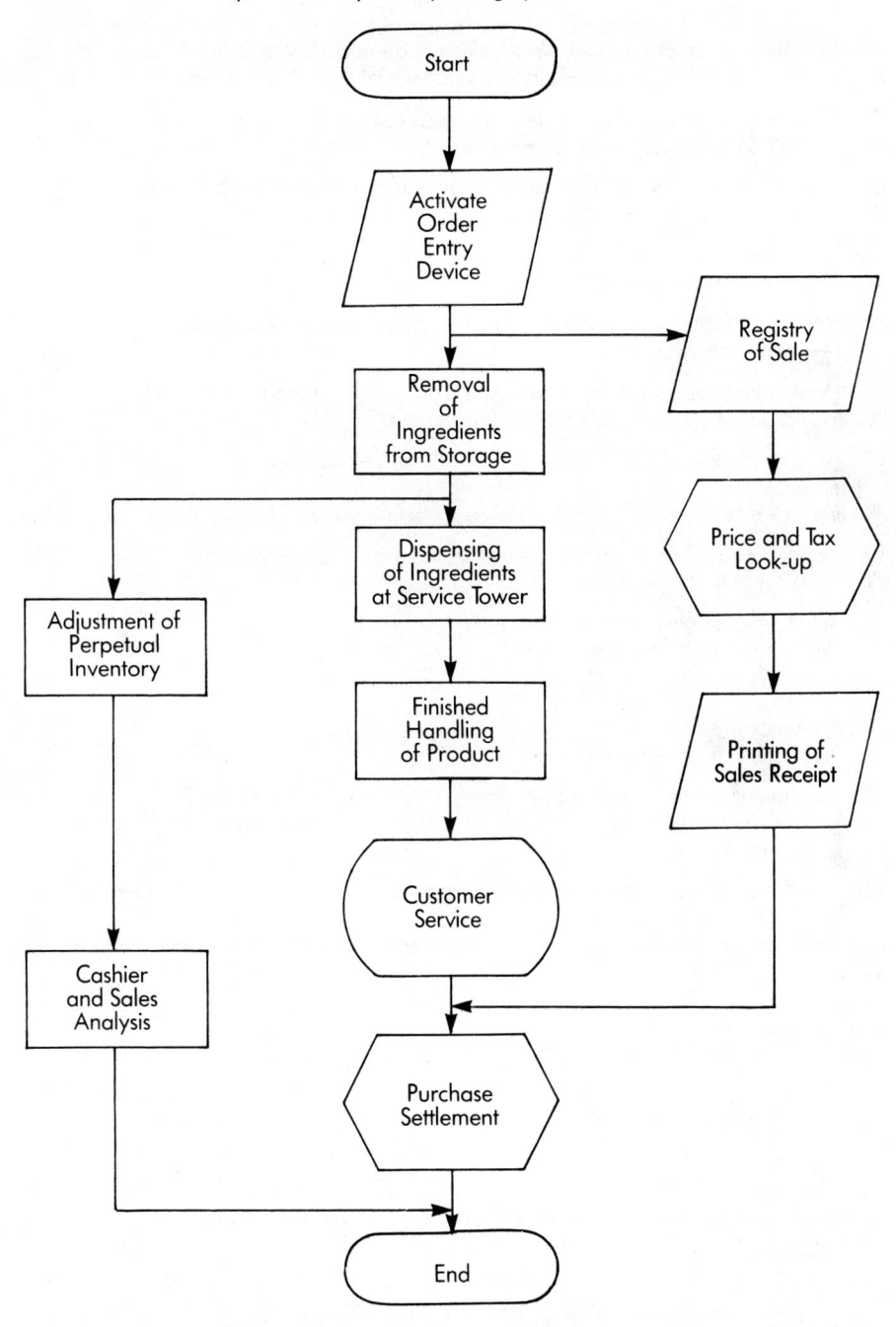

FIGURE 10-17 The Claims

Q. How fast can an automated bar produce and price a drink?
A. Approximately 1½–3 seconds (hence approximately 1 oz. per second).

Q. How accurately does a computer bar measure and serve liquor?
A. To 1/1000th of an ounce repeated accuracy.

Q. How much can a bar owner benefit by buying half gallon versus fifths or quarts?
A. Between 4–6 percent product cost.

Q. How many price level modes are available to bar operators?
A. Three different price modes.

Q. How much labor cost savings can be anticipated with a computer bar?
A. Twenty to forty percent.

Q. How much should gross revenues increase due to improved operations?
A. Expect about 18 percent.

Q. How many different service stations (bars) can be controlled by one liquor storage rack?
A. Up to 4 stations.

Q. How far can liquor storage racks be located from dispensing stations?
A. No greater than 300 feet.

Q. What types of gases are employed in a total system?
A. Liquor → (gravity) compressed air
Wine → nitrous oxide (nitrogen)
Beer → compressed air
Postmixes → CO_2
Perishables → compressed air

Q. How many customers can a bartender service with a computer bar?
A. Each bartender should be able to handle 150 customers in a lounge setting and 250 diners in a restaurant.

Q. How long will it take a system to pay for itself?
A. Normally 18–24 months.

KEY CONCEPTS

The following concepts were introduced in this chapter. Their meanings should be completely understood.

1. *Automatic Keg Switching*-a beverage system component that controls and directs the continuous flow of beer from among several storage units (kegs).
2. *Beverage Control System*-a network designed to regulate the inventory, transportation, and dispensing of liquid products.

BEVERAGE CONTROL SYSTEMS 241

3. *Bundled Tower Unit*–a sophisticated dispensing unit connected to a liquor storage rack, capable of dispensing a large assortment of products, each through its own line.
4. *Calibration*–the determination of specific measurement settings to regulate the flow of liquids.
5. *Closed System*–describes a system in which no outside chemicals or fluids can interact with the temperature and pressure of circulating liquids.
6. *Console Faucet*–a dispensing unit offering a limited selection of product size and variety.
7. *Control Unit*–the major governing influence having control over all system resources; basically, the name given to a central processing unit in a beverage network.
8. *Head Control Adjustment*–the component part of the dispensing unit responsible for the timing and accuracy of a poured drink (head).
9. *Hose and Gun*–a dispensing unit option that has a limited number of selection buttons; initiation of a transaction takes place at the gun unit.
10. *Journal Printer*–a device that logs a perpetual listing of transactions occurring within a system.
11. *Keyboard Mask*–a preprinted keyboard display that depicts preset drinks (and often glassware) and assorted register function keys.
12. *Keyboard Unit*–an array of beverage items available as preset and price look-up keys; associated with keyboard masks.
13. *Minitower Pedestal Unit*–a dispensing unit that is a compromise between a bundled tower (affording a large liquor selection) and a console faucet (with push-button activation) unit.
14. *Postmix Drinks*–carbonated soft drinks prepared from syrup and water at the time of dispensing.
15. *Register Devices*–mechanical or electrical monitoring units that track the movement of menu items.
16. *Reporting System*–the output phase of an information system; communicates hard copy results to the user.
17. *Sensing Devices*–automatic, built-in system functions that prompt operator assistance and/or corrective action.
18. *Syrup Flow Regulators*–the elements responsible for controlling the precise flow of syrup in a postmix unit.
19. *Timing*–refers to the regulation of product mix within a beverage control system.
20. *Touchbar Faucet*–a dispensing unit that requires activation from the lip of a glass to begin the pouring of a premeasured amount of product.

Glossary

Account a means of classifying and summarizing money transactions within an accounting system.

Account Payable Transactions a financial procedure in which goods and services are received before the payment for them is made (amounts of money owed to creditors for previous purchases).

Account Receivable Load the proportion of total sales that are charged to accounts for future collection. Related to credit-card volume.

Account Receivable Summary a listing of charged sales within the restaurant. Normally a summary entry in a comprehensive report of operations.

Account Receivable Transaction a financial procedure in which goods and services are provided on the premise that payment will be received in the future (money owed to the business by its customers).

Account Settlement the payment by cash or credit card of outstanding balances on a house account or city account. Related to Zeroing Out.

Accountability the delegation of responsibility for financial transactions (holding specific individuals accountable for cash and/or charge transactions).

Accounting a system for recording, analyzing, and summarizing the financial transactions of the firm.

Accounting Cycle the period of time from when a financial transaction occurs until it is reconciled and appears on the financial report of the restaurant. This cycle is concerned with the proper recording and analysis of all transactions.

Acoustic Coupler a modem device (a modulator-demodulator unit) that converts digital signals of a terminal or computer to analog signals that can be transmitted over a common carrier network (e.g., a telephone line). Related to Telecommunications.

Algorithm a prescribed set of well-defined, unambiguous rules or procedures leading to the solution of a mathematical problem in a finite number of steps. A term given to solutions for computer problems.

Analytical Flowchart a graphic representation of interdepartmental information and documentation flows; covers several departments or the entire firm.

Arranging a data processing function whereby data elements are sorted, or ordered, in a predetermined sequence. Similar to the filing routine.

Asset an item of monetary value and/or economic resource. May also be a service or utility that can be expressed in monetary terms (they constitute the resources of the business).

Audit the review, test, and verification of financial transactions in an account system.

Audit Trail the logical order or processes involved in a proper recording of an accounting transaction (a reverse tracing of cross-reference documents to substantiate a transaction).

Back-of-the house *see* Back Office.
Back Office that part of the foodservice facility which with the guest does not come directly in contact. Also referred to as the heart-of-the-house.
Batch Processing a system technique in which data are first collected and coded into groups (batches) before being entered into a computer system for processing.
Beverage Control System a dispensing network capable of monitoring inventory, transporting product, and recording transactions related to beverages.
Break Unit the first pack derived from a purchase unit (e.g., a case breaks to cans).
Budget a document of expected expenditures constructed from anticipated revenues and available financial resources.
Budgeting the process of preparing a budget.
Byte a binary element string operated as a unit and usually shorter than a computer word (a collection of bits, or 8 bits).

Calculating a data processing function in which an arithmetic and/or logical manipulation of data occurs.
Capital Budget a budget document prepared for the capital account of a business organization
Capturing a data processing function that involves the recording of data from an event for the purpose of system input. Related to Source Documentation.

Cash-Dispensing Terminals an electronic bank terminal designed to dispense cash or travelers checks on validation and authorization of a commercial asset card.
Cash Drawer the component part of a cash register that contains currency.
Cash Flow the period of time from when a good or service is sold until the actual collection of cash from the sale.
Cash Operating Cycle that period of time associated with cash flow of a business. More specifically, it refers to the time interval between a guest charge and the eatery's receipt of cash payments.
Cash Register a mechanical device used to record and maintain cash balances; may be mechanical, electromechanical, electronic, or automated in design.
Cash Transaction an exchange of goods and/or services for cash.
Cashier Reconciliation the audit of a cash register and cashier to establish accurate transactional balances and procedures.
Cathode Ray Tube (CRT) a combination video display screen and typewriter keyboard that serves as an input/output device in a computer system.
Central Processing Unit (CPU) the nucleus of a computer system responsible for a) controlling all processes, b) completing all arithmetic and logical operations, and c) interfacing with all other system components.
Chart of Accounts a complete listing of the names and account numbers of all accounts in a ledger.
Chip a piece of silicon containing many electronic circuits for computer system construction. May also be referred to as a silicon chip.

GLOSSARY

Classifying a data processing function whereby data are placed into specific categories that provide meaning for the user.

Coding the transformation of data into established symbols for the purposes of simplifying systematic procedures and comprehension.

Combined Network an information system in which both distributed and integrated subsystems or processes exist.

Computer an electronic machine capable of performing data processing and problem-solving functions.

Computer Based describes a foodservice information system that uses an electronic computing machine as its base of operations.

Computer Dependent a business that bases a significantly large portion of its information and operational procedures on the functioning of a computer system (unable to operate without computer assistance).

Computer Generations the segmentation of computer development according to the substantial advances in: a) hardware, b) software, c) systems application, and d) impact on the surrounding environment.

Computer Operator a person who uses a computer system and is responsible for overall business operations and system continuity.

Computer Oriented a business that uses a computer system as a support tool in handling its information and operational procedures.

Computer Service Bureau an off-the-premises concern providing computer expertise and capabilities for a fee.

Computer System an electronic system composed of I/O (input/output) devices, a memory unit, and a CPU. This system can be applied to either problem solving and/or data processing functions.

Computeritis the belief that all aspects and operations of a firm can be computerized without regard to cost justification or practicality.

Configuration describes the design and relative arrangement of component parts in a computer system.

Contract Programming basically, computer programming for a fee. Programs that are custom designed for a specific purpose and that are very expensive to the user. Also referred to as "customized programming."

Contribution Margin (CM) the difference between the selling price (sales) and the direct variable expenses (total variable costs) of any given item (or group of items).

Contribution to Profitability that portion of revenues left after the subtraction of variable and fixed expenses. Can be simply stated as the contribution margin minus fixed expenses.

Conversational Programming a technique enabling the user to communicate directly with the computer system, thereby enhancing response time and operating procedures. Also referred to as "interactive programming."

Cost Benefit financial analysis aimed at determining whether or not the benefits of a system outweigh its costs.

Cost Effective a system in which the benefits far outweigh the costs. Also referred to as Cost Justified.

Cost Justified *see* Cost Effective.

CPU *see* Central Processing Unit.

CPU Options refers to those variations of CPU devices available in the market

GLOSSARY

(e.g., minicomputer, macrocomputer, and microcomputer).

CPU Time a measure of system usage, by the user, based on the total amount of computer processing time used.

Credit see Credit Entry.

Credit Card Volume that proportion of total sales charged to credit cards. May be a significant indicator of the cash flow position of a firm.

Credit Entry the recording of financial transactions on the right-hand side of a "T" account. Credits increase liabilities and revenue accounts while decreasing asset and expense accounts.

Customer Display a cash register component part showing the customer what is being entered through the register keyboard and the corresponding transaction total.

Daily Report of Operations a managerial report that is developed following the daily audit; it includes such information as operating statistics, bank activity, revenue activity, and transaction activity.

Data raw, unevaluated facts that alone have little or no meaning, but that as a group allow for more meaningul relationships and conclusions to be drawn.

Data Base 1) the entire collection of information available to a computer system, 2) a structured collection of information as an entry or collection of related files treated as an entry.

Data Capture the collection and storage of large amounts of data for analysis either through an alternate computer device or at a later time.

Data Cartridge a device for storing data. May be of a cassette tape or disk-like nature. May also be referred to as a diskette.

Data Processing a three-phase (input--process-output) operation on data to achieve desired results.

Data Processing Cycle refers to the time and procedures involved in the handling of data in a data processing operation (input-process-output phases).

Data Recorder that person in a computer environment who is responsible for compiling and preparing data for system input.

Debit see Debit Entry

Debit Entry the recording of financial transactions on the left-hand side of a "T" account. Debits increase asset and expense accounts while decreasing liability and revenue accounts.

Debt a financial condition in which a person or business organization owes its creditors more money that it can pay at a given time.

Degree of Verification the level of investigation that is followed during an auditing procedure. Primarily a function of the frequency and/or magnitude of previous errors.

Disk Drive (DD) a computer system component responsible for controlling the memory unit function.

Disk Pack Unit (DPU) a storage medium into which information is placed for storage in a computer system.

Disk Storage a method of high-speed memory using a rotating circular plate coated with a magnetic material. Addressable portions can be accessed at random. Also referred to as magnetic disk storage.

Diskette: see Data Cartridge.

Dispensing Unit component part of a beverage control system responsible for releasing transported fluids from the system.

Display Terminal a CRT or VDT unit that presents a soft copy of information on a video screen. *See* Cathode Ray Tube.

Dissemination the distribution of information along some predetermined lines of communication.

Distributed Intelligence an intelligence-based network of remote terminals and central system components, each having memory capability.

Distributed Processing a network where computer power is not centralized but is distributed to the user.

Distributed Series Network a system of linked stand-alone terminals that permit multiple users to access a common CPU concurrently, or to communicate with one another.

Documentation a set of written procedures detailing or authenticating the specific requirements and/or results of a system or its components.

Dump a computer term referring to a back-up copy of the system data base stored on a less expensive storage medium than the primary base.

Dunning Letters a series of collection statements dispensed at various time intervals to former guests with delinquent accounts.

Electronic Cash Register (ECR) a cash control device whose moving parts are electronic as opposed to mechanical or manual.

Electronic Data Processing (EDP) an automated method for reducing the number of times data are handled in a data processing system; equipment that processes data by electronic means (e.g., digital computers).

Electronic Fund Transfer (EFT) the method of payment for goods and services involving the transfer of actual cash balance between two accounts, performed electronically, at a point-of-sale.

Electronic Store and Forward (ESF) the concept of capturing data at the point-of-sale and later transporting that data to another computer component or system (e.g., in-register data cassettes).

End User person who employs a computer system to accomplish some task.

Environment everything outside a system that either affects the operation of the system or is affected by the system's operation.

Event Driven a system that remains inactive until a predetermined condition is achieved (initiation of a system's capabilities depends on the occurrence of an event).

Feedback information concerning the status of a specific situation is returned to the input, by some portion of the output, for corrective action.

Field Developed Program (FDP) a software package developed by a user, at the user's site, not by a manufacturer. Resale of an FDP by a vendor usually returns a royalty or fee to the innovative user.

File a collection of logically arranged records.

Financial Reports a group of documents depicting the profitability and solvency of a firm. Related to Financial Statements.

Financial Statements a set of commonly constructed forms that collectively detail the profitability and solvency of the firm.

Financial Transactions the exchange of goods and services for cash or deferred cash payments.

Flexible System a computer system in which the user can perform some software additions and/or modifications (can be user programmed).

Floppy Disk a diskette used to store application software and data. *See* Data Cartridge.

Flowchart a schematic diagram highlighting the flow of information and documentation between various persons, factors, or departments.

Foodservice Information System (FIS) an orderly arrangment of foodservice-related data procedures and decision-making criteria designed to increase managerial effectiveness through the proper handling and flow of information.

Front-End Loaded term used to describe an information system whose volume of input processes far exceeds its output functions.

Front-of-the-house that portion of a foodservice facility with which the guest comes directly in contact. Also referred to as "service areas."

Function Keys a keyboard element that enables multiple program executions to be activated within a computerized system.

Graphic Terminal a computer system peripheral device capable of displaying output in a graphic format.

Hard Copy a printed version of information generated by or stored in a computer system.

Hardware the physical components that make up a computer system.

Hardware System the configuration of central system devices and peripherals that compose the overall computer network. Normally used with reference to system cabling and design and layout.

High-Level Language any computer language that uses symbols and command statements an operator can intelligently read. (Examples: BASIC, COBOL, and FORTRAN languages.) Essentially, language closely associated with the spoken language.

Host Computer a powerful, intelligent device capable of controlling several remote computers and/or peripheral devices.

Human Engineering the automation of routine tasks thereby freeing personnel to apply their human capabilities more productively elsewhere.

Implementation the application of a tool, device, or system to achieve a desired end; also refers to putting into use or carrying out.

Imprinting the recording of a credit card account number by pressing the card against a blank credit card voucher.

In-House refers specifically to on-the-premises information systems; all components of a network are located within the restaurant.

In-House System a computer system that wholly operates within one facility.

Income Statement a report on the profitability of the firm, as determined by revenue and expense items in an account period. Also referred to as an earnings statement.

Inflexible describes a computer system in which the user cannot do any programming.

Inflexible System a preprogrammed computer system that does not allow the user to alter and/or add to the software (cannot be user programmed).

Information that which adds to what is known or alleged. Information serves three basic purposes: 1) communicates knowledge, 2) provides feedback, and 3) reduces uncertainty.

Information Dissemination   the flow of communications and documents throughout a department or unit.

Information Flow   the path that communication and/or documentation follows. The sequence of activities that result as a consequence of a business transaction.

Ingredient   a raw product used as a component in a foodservice recipe.

Input   the initial phase of a data processing or computer system operation.

Input Data   raw, unevaluated facts entered into a data system for processing. Related to Data.

Input Formats   the various options available to users of data processing and/or computer systems (e.g., punch card, CRT key pad, optical character recognition).

Input/Output (I/O) Devices   the components of a computer system through which instructions and data enter or reports exit the computer system.

Input Unit   that component of a computer system through which instructions and data are entered.

Integrated Circuit (IC)   a solid state electronic component of a computer system's construction design. See Chip.

Integrated Network   a system configuration in which a centralized, shared data base and intricate communication links among all users are found.

Integrated System   a system configuration in which a centralized data base is intricately linked and available to all operating departments.

Intelligent Terminal   a computer hardware input/output device that contains local memory capabilities.

Interchangeable Keyboard(s)   a cash register component part that can be removed and replaced to depict various meal-period menus. Price modes are also altered to reflect menu changes.

Interface   the formation of a shared boundary (common line) between system components.

Internal Control   the verification of proper handling and documentation of financial transactions.

Interregister Communications (IRC)   the technology that enables registers to send and receive information from one another.

Inventory   a collection of stock on hand.

Inventory Unit   package, size, or container ingredient by which inventory is monitored. Related to Issue Unit.

Issue Unit   package, size, or container by which an ingredient is requisitioned from the storeroom (e.g., #10 can, bottle, pound).

Keyboard   input component part of a cash register or computer terminal device.

Kitchen Printer   a remote printer that is interfaced to a precheck terminal.

Knowledge   familiarity and/or education gained through experience.

Lead-Through Programming   a computer programming format in which the operator is forced to follow a specified routine of inquiries requiring responses before advancing in the software. Also called drop-through programming or interactive programming.

Ledger   a complete collection of all the accounts of an entity (a summarized posting of account debits and credits). Also referred to as a general ledger.

Liabilities   debts or financial obligations by the firm to a creditor.

Line of Authority   the traditional hierarchy of increasing administrative responsibilities; usually depicted in an organizational chart.

GLOSSARY

Line Printing Terminal (LPT) a computer system component capable of producing hard copy output.

Low Level Language a computer programming language used by machines, not people.

Machine-Assisted refers to a foodservice information system that incorporates machines in its mode of operation.

Mainframe a large central processing unit that controls all computer system components and resources. Also referred to as a macrocomputer.

Management Information System (MIS) a systematic approach to the enhancement of managerial effectiveness achieved through improved handling of the firm's most important resource, information.

Managerial Reports a series of documents providing management with targeted feedback on the financial status, productive efficiency, and overall effectiveness of business operations.

Manually Oriented describes a foodservice information system that is completely manual in operation.

Master-Slave Configuration an ECR system in which a host terminal containing a CPU, memory unit, and I/O capability is interfaced to nonintelligent POS devices. Note: host is similar to a stand-alone unit.

Memory Unit the component of a computer system that is composed of addressable storage locations and that serves as an intermediate buffer between input/output devices and the CPU.

Menu list of products offered for service at a foodservice establishment.

Menu Engineering an analytical approach to evaluate menu design, pricing, and marketing success.

Menu Item a food or beverage product included on a menu.

Menu Mix a popularity index or sales mix of menu transactions. Also referred to as a Menu Score.

Menu Score: *see* Menu Mix.

Microcomputer a computer classification in which a stand-alone unit has all major CPU functions self-contained on a single printed circuit board. Related to Distributed Intelligence.

Micromotion Keyboard an input pad requiring very slight physical contact to operate.

Microprocessor a single high-density, integrated circuit that is capable of performing complex CPU functions. Related to the Chip.

Minicomputer also called a stand-alone device; describes a computer system component that contains all the required parts of a computer system in one compartment.

Modifier Key *see* Function Key.

Modular the implementation of computer assistance in modules (by functional subsystems).

Module 1) a program that is discrete and identifiable, 2) a packaged functional hardware unit designed for use with other components.

Monolithic a total or completely integrated system. *See* Integrated System.

Multitasking a computer system capable of satisfying many user requests at the same time (i.e., capable of executing several jobs simultaneously).

Network a structured connection of computer systems or peripheral devices, or both, each remote from the other, capable of exchanging data or information as needed.

Nonautomated (DP) a data processing system in which all operations and procedures are carried out manually.

Off-line the operating mode of a computer peripheral device that is not interacting directly with the central processing unit in the system.

Off-the-Premises computing that is done off the property.

Omission Error the deletion of an important transaction by mistake.

On-Line the operating mode of a computer peripheral device that is directly interfacing or connected to the central processing unit of the system (direct communications with the computer).

Operating Budget *see* Budget.

Operating System a structured set of software routines whose function is to control the execution sequence of programs, supervise input/output operations, and to support the entire system resources. A critical system feature.

Optical Character Recognition (OCR) an input option for a computer system.

Order Entry System a system in which the user automatically sends messages (e.g., purchase orders to a purveyor via telecommunications).

Order Entry Terminal a computer peripheral used as a specialized input device (e.g., beverage control system initialization).

Other Equipment Manufacturer (OEM) a vendor that constructs a customized system for a user, or specialized group of users, from various manufacturers' components.

Output the end result of a data processing or problem-solving operation; data that has been processed and transferred from internal storage.

Output Formats the various options available to a computer system user (e.g., magnetic tape, printed page, and punch cards).

Output Information the transformation of raw data into aggregated, intelligible pieces of information of knowledge.

Output Unit a system device for displaying or printing processed and/or stored information.

Paperless Environment A computer-aided business complex in which documents and communications are maintained in soft copy, except where required by law.

Parameter Driven System a computer system configuration in which the requirements of the system's hardware and software are designed to satisfy specific user needs.

Peripheral Device computer system components that are located away from, but controlled by, a central processor unit. Also referred to as a Satellite Device.

Point-of-Purchase related to the point-of-sale; the time and location of a consumer's purchase. The point-of-purchase is basically the same as the point-of-sale, except that it is from the consumer's perspective, not management's.

Point-of-Sale (POS) the time and physical location of the sale of a good or service; provides a communication link between a remote sales location and central accounting system. *See* Point-of-Purchase.

Point-of-Sale (POS) Terminal a peripheral system device employed to communicate transactions at scattered, remote locations to a centralized processor and/or data base.

Polling the ability of one computer device to retrieve information from another remote computer device(s). Related to Telecommunications.

Precheck a foodservice technique in which all items must be entered and charted before their removal from a production area.

Precheck Terminal a computer-based component used as an input device in a precheck system.

Precost A foodservice technique in which all items are costed out, according to a menu mix forecast, before their actual service.

Preprogrammed a computer programming technique in which software is purchased as part of the system. Preprogrammed peripherals may be of a flexible or inflexible nature.

Preset Key a keyboard element that is dedicated to one menu item. Preset designations can be changed by the user.

Pressure System used to regulate and control the flow of beverages in a dispensing system.

Price Look-Up (PLU) Key enables the expansion of preset key capabilities to a large number of memory locations accessed via predesignated menu item numbers.

Process a particular way of accomplishing something.

Processor-Based Configuration an ECR system in which nonintelligent POS devices are interfaced to a singular CPU and memory unit.

Program Flowchart a graphic representation of the steps involved in an information system process; usually is limited to one or two tasks per flowchart.

Programmable see Flexible System.

Programmer the person in a computer system environment who converts data and instructions into a computer comprehensible language.

Programming the means by which the programmer communicates to the computer what instructions are to be used in data processing and/or problem solving.

Programming Language the vehicle used to communicate instructions to the computer.

Purchase Unit package, size, or container an ingredient is purchased in (e.g., case, drum, gallon).

Random-Access Memory (RAM) a computer memory designed so that the time to access any data item in storage is the same as for any other item. See Disk Storage.

Random Entry a computer input that can occur at any time and with unpredictable impact on the system.

Real Time a method of processing data so fast that practically no time elapses between input and output.

Receipt Printer a peripheral device used to produce a hard-copy recipt of purchase.

Recipe a standardized set of procedures and ingredient quantities that result in the production of a menu item.

Recipe Unit package, size, or container describing how an ingredient is used in a recipe (e.g., pound, ounce, each, slice).

Reconciliation of Account the reduction in balance of a ledger account to zero because of payments received or via transfer to another ledger.

Record a systems term connoting a set of logically related fields within a computer memory unit.

Recording a data processing function wherein measurements, observations, and/or activities are documented for manipulation and storage.

Reliability the high level of dependability and trust normally expected in an automated system environment; a measure of an electronic system's failure rate.

Remote Data Entry the inputting of data from a terminal located away from the central processing unit.

GLOSSARY

Remote Printer a peripheral device, interfaced to a precheck terminal, capable of producing hard-copy instructions at remote sites (e.g., hot and/or cold food production stations).

Reorder Point an inventory technique requiring the designation of predetermined stock levels to initiate replenishment orders.

Request for Proposal (RFP) Survey of vendor-suggested configurations for a system application (both hardware and software).

Request for Quotation (RFQ) survey of vendor prices for a specific application or piece of equipment selected by the user, not the vendor.

Retrieving a data processing function in which data are selected and brought from a computer memory for further processing and/or display.

Sales Journal a permanent, summarized record of current business.

Satellite Device a system component located outside the CPU. Also referred to as a Peripheral Device.

Sector adressable storage locations on a disk pack unit.

Semiautomated a data processing system in which mechanical and electromechanical machines are used to perform operations and procedures.

Sequential Memory the sorting and rank order storage of documents by alpha, numeric, or chronological identification.

Slip Printer a peripheral device used to produce hard copy documentation of data entry. Related to Receipt Printer.

Soft Copy a display of information (can be either input or output) on a CRT video screen.

Software the collection of data, programs, and instructions used to extend the capabilities of a computer system.

Software Broker the agent between a program developer and an end user.

Software System a priority arrangement of instructions and routines that command the computer system resources.

Sorting a data processing function in which data are categorized and classified based on some critical quality or characteristic.

Source Document any original recording of a transaction. Basically, all those items that contribute to the eventual recording of all financial transactions (e.g., guest check, registration card, and voucher).

Specialty Vendor a computer system vendor that develops a series of programs on a selected manufacturer's product, for sale to a specialty group of end users.

Stand-Alone Configuration a complete, independent ECR system capable of processing all data and producing all required information in a system application; contains its own CPU, memory, and I/O unit.

Standard Recipe a well-established set of procedures and ingredient quantities that result in a standardized (portion and quality) menu item.

Storage a data processing function in which data are placed in a select area of the system for future access and retrieval.

Subroutine a term describing the performance of a precisely defined operation within a computer program.

Subsystem a minor arrangement of interdependent parts in one branch of a larger network or assemblage.

Synergy a combined action or operation wherein the aggregate production of the component parts by far exceeds the contribution of the individual factors composing the whole.

System an orderly arrangement of components in an interrelated series.

System Analyst The person in a computer system environment responsible for the overall design of the system.

System Concept *see* System.

System Flowchart an illustration of the information and documentation of a transaction within one or more departments.

System Life Cycle a four-phase process ranging from problem situation and environmental analysis, through design and implementation, to refinement.

Telecommunications compter interfaces accomplished via telephone lines. Related to Acoustic Coupler and Polling.

Teletype Terminal (TTY) a computer system component that employs a keyboard and roll or paper to produce hard-copy output.

Text Editing the alteration of input data to remove errors or omissions before processing.

Throughput a measure of system efficiency; the rate at which work can be handled by a system.

Time Sharing use of a computer to process multiple requests by users.

Transactional Accounting an accounting system based on a proper chronological sequencing of transactions, postings, and financial statements.

Transformation Error describes the incorrect handling of a data procedure because of misconception or misunderstanding.

Transposition Error the erroneous arrangement of digits in quantitative analysis.

Turnaround Time a measurement of the time from when data are entered into a system until they are available as output information.

Turnkey a preprogrammed system designed to perform specific unalterable functions; requires no computer staff.

Uniform System of Accounts a standardized technique for the recording and reporting of financial transactions and for the specification of terminology.

User *see* End User.

User's Manual a document that describes the specific operations and maintenance requirements of all system components.

Vanilla System a one-vendor system; all components in a system are produced by one manufacturer.

Vendor-Designed System a computer application designed for a specific user (or group of users); normally provides for some customization but does not requie an EDP staff.

Verification the confirmation or establishment of accuracy within an information system (the validation of data to insure correctness).

Video Display Terminal (VDT) *see* CRT.

Voice Synthesizer a verbal system response generated by a computer from a limited syntax (voice output from a restricted vocabulary).

Zeroing Out to bring an account balance to zero by having debits and credits offset one another. Also referred to as account settlement.

Index

Accounting, general ledger, 197-199
Accumulator windows, 61, 67
Achievement rate, 151
Acoustic coupler, 44
Algorithm, 48, 206
American Business Computers Company, 213
Analog computer, 31-32
Analytical flowchart, 48
APL, 50
Application software, 10-12, 50-51
Arithmetic and logical unit (ALU), 43
Assembly language, 50
Autoanswer modem, 204
Autodial modem, 204
Automated form number reader (AFNR), 93
Automated precheck application, 109-110. *See also* Prechecking systems
Automatic change dispensers, 90-91
Automatic keg switching, 225-226
Automatic slip feeding (ASF), 93
Average contribution margin, 153

Back office systems, 191
   financial statements in, 202-203
   general ledger accounting in, 197-199
   inventory control in, 191-194
   order entry systems in, 203-207
   payroll in, 194-197
   sales and revenue analysis in, 199-201
   summary of, 207-208
Backward integration, 62
BASIC, 12, 50
Batch processing, 51-52, 53
Beverage control systems, 213-214
   advantages of, 237
   configurations in, 233-237
   delivery network in, 218-228
   dispensing units in, 228-229
   order entry devices in, 215-218
   potential problem areas in, 237-238
   summary of, 238-240
   support equipment options in, 232
   tracking devices in, 229-231
Bruner, Richard, 180

Bubble units, 47
Budgets, dynamic, 197
Buffered memory, 104
Bundled tower unit (BTU), 229
Burden of margin, 179
By-product, 181

Calibration, 220
Cash drawer, 61, 66
Cash-handling equipment, 85, 90-91
Cashier reconciliation, 8
Cash registers, 61. *See also* Electronic cash registers
   advanced electronic, 68
   with advanced keyboards, 68-70
   basic component parts of, 62-67
   historical overview of, 61-62
   summary of, 70-72
Cassettes and cartridges, digital, 47
Cassette tapes, 43
Cathode ray tube (CRT), 9, 45
Central processing unit (CPU), 8-9, 43-44;
   options, 46
Change plate, 61, 66
Check
   digit verification, 91, 112
   preparation, 101, 107
   printer, 102
   settlement, 101, 107-108
   tracking, 101, 107
Closed refrigeration system, 226
Closed system, 218
COBOL, 12, 50
Compiler, 49, 50
Computer(s)
   analog, 31-32
   analysis of menu engineering, 169-179
   -based precost systems, 121-145
   defined, 31
   digital, 31, 32
   in foodservice, 8-12
   functions, basic, 43-44
   generations, 37-43
   operator, 54

255

INDEX

processing modes, 51–53
  summary of, 55–56
  system options, 53–54
  systems, personnel in, 54
Configuration, 8, 12
  combined, 12, 15–16
  distributed, 12, 13–15
  integrated, 12, 13
  master-slave, 78–80, 83
  processor-based, 80–83
  stand-alone, 75–77, 83
Console faucet unit (CFU), 228
Contribution margin (CM), 151, 153, 155
  average, 153
Control unit, 229–230
Cost justification, 17
Cost-multiplier, 152, 155
CPU, see Central processing unit
Customer display, 61

Data, 23
  collector, 77
  recorders, 54
Data base, 13, 23
  system, 80
Data processing, 23
  electronic (EDP), 32
  FIS and, 30–31
  and general system life cycle, 25–28
  and information, 23–25
  objectives of, 30
  and source documents, 28–30
  summary of, 32
  and systems concept, 23, 25
Decision matrix, 151
Delivery network, 218–228
Demand generators, 179
Digital computer, 31, 32
Disk drives, 8
Diskettes, 43
Disk packs, 8, 48
  hard and floppy, 45
Disks, 43
  flexible and floppy, 47
  hard and fixed head, 47
Dispensing units, 228–229
Disposable recipe sheets, 133
Distributed configuration, 12, 13–15
  combined with integrated configuration, 15–16
Distributed intelligence, 23, 76
Distributed processing, 79
Dogs, 167, 171, 180
Downstreaming, 203–204
Dynamic budgets, 197

Electronic cash register(s) (ECR), 61, 63, 68, 75
  configurations, selection of, 84–85
  keyboard, 65
  master-slave configuration, 78–80, 83
  peripheral equipment options in, 85–93
  processor-based configuration, 80–83
  stand-alone configuration, 75–77, 83
  summary of, 95–96
  telecommunications in, 93–95
Electronic data processing (EDP), 32
Electronic fund transfer (EFT), 95
Electronic store and forward (ESF), 72, 77, 232
Empty bottle sensor, 232
Environment, 24
Expediter, 87

Feedback, 23, 24
Financial statements, 202–203
Firmware, 9, 10, 49
Flowchart, 48
Food item data file (FIDF), 122
Foodservice
  characteristics of, 3–5
  computers in, 8–12
  hardware, 8–9
  software, 8, 9–12
  telecommunications and, 93–95
Foodservice information system (FIS)
  characteristics of, 6
  concept of, 6–8
  configurations, 12–16
  and data processing, 30–31
  definition of, 18
  objectives of, 31
  performance evaluation, 17–18
  summary of, 18–19
  and task criteria, 7–8
Forecast module, 204–205
FORTRAN, 12, 50
Forward integration, 62
Front-end loaded, 46

General ledger, 142, 145
  accounting, 197–199
General system life cycle, 25–26
  machines in systems, 28
  system analysis, 26–27
  system design, 27
  system implementation, 27
  system refinement, 27–28
Glass sensor, 232
Graphics output, 47
Graphic terminals, 45

INDEX 257

Gross profit, *see* Contribution margin
Group cost summaries, 142
Guest-check
  considerations, 110–112
  numbering, 85, 91
  sensor, 232

Hard copy, 9, 47–48
Hardware
  components, 44
  components of prechecking systems, 102–106
  concepts, 44–48
  CPU options, 46
  foodservice, 8–9
  input formats, 45–46
  memory units, 47
  output formats, 47–48
Head control adjustment, 223
Hose and gun unit (HGU), 228
Human engineering, 6, 23
Hurst, Michael, 151
Hurst menu score, 171

Impact printer, 48
Indicator panel, 64, 66
Inflationary impact, 152
Information, 23
  knowledge, uncertainty, and feedback of, 23, 24
  pressures for, 24
  value of, 25
Ingredient
  code number, 124–125, 131
  description, 125–126
  file, 122–127
  module, 206
  yields, 132–133
In-house systems, 53, 54
Input, 23;
  formats, 45–46
  and output (I/O) devices, 8, 9, 52
  and output (I/O) units, 43–44
Integrated configuration, 12, 13
  combined with distributed configuration, 15–16
Integration
  backward, 62
  forward, 62
Intelligence, 76
  distributed, 23, 76
Interfacing, 232
Interpreter, 49
Interregister communications (IRC), 63, 72, 76

Inventory
  control, 191–194
  extension, 193
  file, 142, 145
  module, 206
  perpetual, 5, 191–192
  physical, 5, 192
Issue unit, 192–193, 194

Journal printer, 90, 104, 232

Kasavana, Michael, 151, 169, 185
Keyboard(s)
  cash register, 61, 63–64, 65
  cash registers with advanced, 68–70
  masks, 215
  units, 215
Key pad terminals, 45
Kitchen printers, 102–104
Knowledge, 23, 24

Languages, computer, 12, 48–49
  high-level, 12, 49, 50
  low-level (or machine), 12, 49, 50
Laser-beam printing, 48
Light-emitting diodes (LED), 68
Liquid crystal display (LCD), 64, 68

Macrocomputers, 8, 46
Magnetic ink, 45
Magnetic tape, 43, 45, 47
Mainframes, 8, 46
Marginal profit, 176
Market basket analysis, 169
Mark-sense cards, 45
Master-slave configuration, 78–80, 83
Meal cost summary, 140–142
Meal cycle summary, 138–140
Memory units, 8, 43, 47
MENENG, 185
Menu
  explosion, 8
  graph, 179
  mix (MM), 153–155
  plan, 119
Menu engineering, 151
  computerized analysis of, 169–179
  concept of, 151–155
  decision making in, 179–184
  example of, 158–160
  manual analysis of, 161–169
  steps to, 155–158
  summary of, 184–186
Menu item
  classification, 179–180

INDEX

development, new, 181–182
file, 134–137
master file (MIMF), 134
Microcomputers, 8, 46
Microfilm and microfiche, 48
Microprocessor, 46
Minicomputers, 8, 46
Minitower pedestal unit (MPU), 229
Minority veto syndrome, 180
Modem, 93–95
Modular systems, 8, 12
Multiple portion product, 181
Multitasking, 46

Net weight, 126
Network controller, 87, 104
Nonimpact printer, 48
Nonvolatile, 47
Number of portions, 130–131
Nutrient file, 142

Off-line systems, 52
On-line systems, 38, 52
On-line transmission, 232
Open checking, 101, 107
Operating system, 43, 49–50
Operator displays, 68
Optical character recognition (OCR), 45
Order entry
devices, 215–218
systems, 203–207
Output, 23
device, 8, 9, 52
formats, 47–48
unit, 43–44

Paper tape, 45, 47
Par level, 191
Par stock, 5
Payroll, 142, 145, 194–197
Peripheral device, 9, 43
Peripheral equipment options, 85–93
Perpetual inventory, 5, 191–192
Physical inventory, 5, 192
Plowhorses, 167, 171, 179–180
Point-of-sale (POS) station, 5
Point-of-sale (POS) terminal, 9, 63, 78
Polling, 93
Portion cost summary, 140–142
Postmix drinks, 219
Precheck, 76
register, 101, 102
terminal, 102
Prechecking systems, 8, 101–102
hardware components of, 102–106

software components of, 107–112
summary of, 115
Precost
file, 138–142
module, 207
Precost systems, 119–120
additional files, 142–145
computerized, 121–145
ingredient file, 122–127
menu item file, 134–137
precost file, 138–142
recipe file, 127–133
steps involved in manual, 120–121
summary of, 145
Preset, 7
Price changes, making, 182–184
Price look-up, 7
Printed page, 47
Problem solving, 51
Process, 28
Processor-based configuration, 80–83
Production procedures, 133
Program flowchart, 48
Programmer, 54
Programming, 48–49
statements, 49
Punch(ed) card, 45, 47
Purchase order, 191
module, 207
Purchase unit, 126, 192–193, 194
price of, 127
weight of, 126
Puzzles, 167, 171, 180

Random access, 43
Real time, 51, 52, 53
Receipt printer, 61, 67, 104
Recipe
code number, 127–130
description, 130
file, 127–133
ingredient information, 131–133
module, 205–206
portion size, 131
unit, 192–193, 194
Redundant memory, 75
Register devices, 229, 230
Remote job entry (RJE), 78
Remote (kitchen) printers, 85–90, 102–104
Reorder points, 5, 191
Reporting system, 229, 230–231
Request for proposal (RFP), 84

Sales and revenue analysis, 199–201
Schuler, Win, 151

Sectors, 9
Sensing devices, 232
Sequential access, 43
Server banking, 5
Service bureau systems, 53
Shared systems, 53–54
Signature items, 179
Silicon chips, 47
Slip printers, 104
Smith, Don, 151, 169, 185
Soft copy, 9, 47–48
Software
  algorithmic design, 48
  application, 10–12, 50–51
  components of prechecking systems, 107–112
  concepts, 48–51
  foodservice, 8, 9–12
  problem solving, 51
  programming, 48–49
  system, 9, 10, 50, 51
Source documents, 28–30
Stand-alone configuration, 75–77, 83
Standard recipe, 119
Stars, 167, 171, 179
Subassembly recipes, 135
Support equipment options, 232
Symbolic logic, 6
Syrup flow regulators, 226

System(s). *See also* General system life cycle
  analyst, 54
  concept, 23, 25
  flowchart, 48
  software, 9, 10, 50, 51

Target-pricing schemes, *see* Cost-multiplier
Telecommunications, 93–95, 203
Terminal display, 47
Throughput, 30
Time in attendance, 197
Time sharing, 38, 51, 52–53
Timing, 219
Touchbar faucet unit (TFU), 228
Touch-tone telephone (TTP), 45
Tracking devices, 229–231
Turnaround time, 30, 52

Uncertainty, 23, 24
Uniform System of Accounts, 199
User, 44
User-friendly, 84
User's manual, 54

Verbal recognition (VR), 45
Video display terminal (VDT), 45
Voice synthesizer, 48
Volatile, 47

Withington, Frederic G., 37, 42